GOD'S AWESOME GRACE

Bennett Broadway

ISBN 9781520272399

See also the author's 30 page evangelistic booklet entitled "What's It Take To Get Into Heaven?" and now offered in Spanish as well from Amazon.com and a different, one page, two sides, 15 ½ x 7 ¼, glossy, evangelistic tract entitled "Can God Accept You? from Crown & Covenant Publications, 7408 Penn Ave., Pittsburgh, PA 15208-2531

ACKNOWLEDGEMENTS

I want to thank God for the courage to start and finish this special task. It was done for Christ's Crown and Covenant. May He be glorified on earth as He is in heaven. May the earth be filled with "the knowledge of the Lord, as the waters cover the sea" (Isa. 11:9 NKJV).

My love goes to my wife Judy and to my children, Beth, Rebecca, Sarah, and Anna. I want to thank them for their patience and for the precious time I took away from them while writing this book.

I am indebted to God, John Girardeau, Arthur W. Pink, the Reformers, and the Puritans for the use of their writings in this book.

My sincere gratitude goes to Professor Wayne Spear, Dr. James D. Carson and Professor J.I. Packer for their unquestionable kindness to me.

Bennett Broadway

CONTENTS

PREFACE

The author is a ruling elder in the San Diego Reformed Presbyterian Church. He has a deep longing to help others in their Christian lives and walks and to escape the erroneous beliefs current in the world and in evangelical Christianity. He has covered a broad range of Christian doctrine, although not in great depth, for the purpose of giving the reader in a relatively few pages an overview of the answer to the questions: What does the Bible teach about who saves us and how we are saved?

The Christian church will be the richer for gaining a clear understanding of the truth that we are saved, not by the goodness of our lives, but solely by the grace of the Lord Jesus Christ. This truth, which lay in shadows for a time, was brought to light in the days of the Reformation but is today in danger of being relegated to the shadows again. May God be gracious to bring these precious truths to our generation in great power and clarity.

Dr. James D. Carson
Dean of Students
Westminster Theological Seminary West Escondido, California

God's Awesome Grace contains a clear presentation of what the Bible teaches about human sinfulness, God's sovereignty and covenant dealings with the human race, the saving work of Christ, and the work of the Holy Spirit in bringing God's chosen ones to new life in Christ.

Three sorts of readers will find help in this book: those who are not yet converted, Christians who have been taught and have embraced an Arminian understanding of salvation and therefore, need to rethink their position in the light of Scripture, and finally, Christians who embrace the Reformed and Covenantal understanding of salvation, but who need help in articulating it. *God's Awesome Grace* may be used for individual study, small group discussions for inquirers, or for growing Christians.

Professor Wayne Spear, Ph.D.
Reformed Presbyterian Theological Seminary
Pittsburgh, Pennsylvania

Bennett Broadway gives us a full and exact survey of the saving sovereignty of God as conservative Calvinists have affirmed and argued it against Arminianism over the past four centuries.

Professor J.I. Packer
Regent College (Canada)
D. Phil., The University of Oxford

INTRODUCTION

Who saves us from our sins and their punishment—death and hell? Does God save us, or do we save ourselves? To put it another way, who initiates man's salvation? Is God the first cause of man's salvation, or is man? Who is really the determining agent of man's salvation? This has always been an issue at the heart of Christianity.

Some falsely teach or assume that God decided to permit men to save themselves without His assistance. So, He left them in their unregenerate state to determine whether or not they would comply with the condition of salvation (saving faith). And since they must save themselves by exercising a saving faith in Jesus Christ which comes only from God as a gift and is not given to everyone, they will find they cannot hope to inituate their own salvation. So much then for man being the First cause of his salvation. These people think that Jesus only died to make salvation possible for all and not actual for some, and it is by their act of their faith that determines whether a possible salvation shall become an actual salvation.

They say salvation does not directly depend on any decree or act of God but wholly on man's independent activity in believing. *This false teaching causes us to think that, ultimately, we really save ourselves.* Therefore, they believe that they are the First cause of their salvation. They think they had to choose to accept Christ into their hearts first before God could choose to accept them. But, according the Bible, God chose us first and chose us in Christ Jesus *before time began*. Ephesians 1:4 tells us that God chose us in Christ *before the foundation of the world*. 2 Timothy1:8-9 says this, . . . "God who has saved us and called us with a holy calling, not according to our works, but according to His own purpose and grace which was granted us in Christ Jesus *from all eternity,*"

"Even the love we have for God was first caused by His love for us. 1 John 4:19 says, "We love Him [God] because He loved us first."

Those who believe the Biblical views of the Protestant Reformation believe that God's grace is sovereign which means our salvation is determined for us by the Lord alone. This makes Him the first cause of our salvation. It is God who makes the first move to save us actually and experientially. We first experience His saving grace when He regenerates us or infuses spiritual life into our spiritually dead hearts[1] by the regenerating power of the Holy Spirit.[2] We experience regeneration when He grants us the gifts of faith and repentance. The Holy Spirit's unmerited, powerful, regenerating, infusion of grace and life into our hearts causes or enables us to respond positively to His gospel message by our acts of faith and repentance. Those gifts give us the desire and power to to receive Jesus. [3]

Our previous lack of desire to be saved and inability to make a decision to receive Jesus was caused by the bondage of our unregenerate wills to sin. Thankfully, God has determined to deliver His elect sinners' unregenerate wills from the bondage of sin by renewing their wills through regeneration. God's regenerating power and His gift of faith enable the sinner's will to freely act to receive Jesus into his heart as his Savior and Lord. So, what do we Christians have that we did not receive first from God as a gift? (Eph. 2: 8-9; Acts 13:48; 2 Thess. 2:13) So, if God chose us first and if regeneration, saving faith and repentance are God's gifts to us, how can we boast that we were the First cause of our salvation?

---

[1] Eph.2:1; 1 Thess. 1:5; Col.2:12-13
[2] 1 Corinthians 2:4-52 Cor, 4:3-7; Eph. 1:17-20; 3:20; 2 Pet. 1:3
[3] Ps. 110:3; Rom. 3:11; Ps. 27:8; Matt. 7:7.

So, then who determines who will be born again and who will receive the gifts saving faith and repentance? It is our Sovereign God. He decides who will be saved. Before the world was created, God decreed to elect or choose certain individual sinners from all nations to receive an actual (not a possible) salvation secured eternally for them through Jesus' perfect obedience and atoning sacrifice for their sins. False teaching says that it is only *after* we make the decision to accept Jesus, that God chooses us to be His elect children. False teaching boastfully declares that, "We owe our election to our faith" instead of correctly teaching, "We owe our faith to God's election."[4]

Therefore, which of these teachings is correct? Are we saved by an act of God's will and decree which would make God the First cause of our salvation, or are we saved by the act of our own will as the First cause of our salvation? Does God's decision to grant certain sinners His grace determine their salvation, or do sinners determine their own salvation by deciding to be saved? Do sinners choose God first, or did God choose sinners first? And, if God chose certain sinners (called the Elect) from among all the sinners *before time began*, was His choice of them based on some foreseen good in them (such as their faith, their decision to accept Jesus, their repentance, or some other act of their obedience), or was it based on God's grace alone? And finally, who then gets the glory for man's salvation? Does God get the glory for man's salvation, or does man get the glory because he believes that he ultimately determined his own salvation by his decision to be saved?

If we Christians do not understand how we are saved, how can we have a clear understanding about who saves us? What does the

---

[4] Packer, J.I., Introductory Essay to *The Death of Death* by John Owen, The Banner of Truth Trust (1802) , Edinburgh, Reprint, 1963, Vol. ii, pp. 9–10.

Bible teach about how a person is saved and who saves them? These are the questions we will answer in this book.

CHAPTER 1

MAN'S DILEMMA: HIS FALL INTO SIN

Shortly after the one and only true, living God created Adam, God sovereignly and graciously established a covenant with him. We call this covenant God made with Adam "the covenant of works".[5]

> And the LORD God formed man of the dust of the ground, and breathed into his nostrils the breath of life; and man became a living being....And the LORD God commanded the man, saying, "Of every tree of the garden you may freely eat; but of the tree of the knowledge of good and evil you shall not eat, for in the day that you eat of it you shall surely die." (Genesis 2:7, 16–17 NKJV)

This covenant was a legal arrangement of promises to be performed by God when Adam met His requirement. God clearly explained the covenant terms to Adam in order that their covenant relationship would be meaningful and maintained. He allowed Adam to eat the fruit of every kind of tree in the Garden of Eden except one—the tree of the knowledge of good and evil. God told Adam that if he ate the fruit from this tree he would surely die. So, God put Adam on trial for a limited time of probation. He promised Adam a permanent state of life in paradise and His close friendship, as long as Adam served Him with a pure, committed love and perfectly obeyed His commandment. Disobedience would amount to high treason against Him. Spiritual death (i.e., being cut off from

---

[5] Hos. 6:7; 1 Cor. 15:22; Rom. 5:12-19

spiritual fellowship with God) and physical death were the consequences for disobedience. God also appointed Adam as the federal head or the legal representative of all mankind. This meant that Adam was more than mankind's parental head. If Adam were merely our parental head, we would not be held accountable for his actions.[6] But as our federal head and legal representative, Adam acted before God on behalf of all mankind.[7] In principle, this meant what Adam does as our legal representative, we ourselves do. Adam acted as our substitute. So, when Adam sinned, we sinned. Adam's sin was imputed or counted as our sin as well. As a result, we were legally declared "condemned sinners"[8]. In addition, from conception our human natures are enslaved by sin because we inherited Adam's fallen, sinful, human nature. For example, as infants, we did not need to be taught how to be cruel, stingy and self-centered. By the time we reached adulthood our sinful actions just became more sophisticated.

Adam's obedience or disobedience determined mankind's spiritual relationship with God. At first, this might seem unfair to us. Why should Adam make a decision that has such dire consequences for us? Actually, if you think about it, this is a common thing in our world. In America, we have what is known as a Federal or a representative government. Our President, for example, as Commander in Chief of our Armed Forces may decide to send troops into war which has dire consequences for them and our nation. Then, there are also our Congressman, our Senators, and our Supreme Court Justices who make decisions that have dire consequences for us. In our everyday world, we also rely on decisions made by people with authority over us. We rely on our

---

[6] Deut. 24:16.
[7] Rom. 5:12, 19.
[8] Psa. 51:5; John 3:18; Rom. 5:16, 18

13

parents, police, judges, teachers, union bosses, employers, etc., who make decisions that affect our lives. Furthermore, we often allow people who have expertise in certain areas to make important decisions for us. We trust our stock market brokers, our doctors, our lawyers, our ministers, our bus drivers, etc., to make the right decisions for us every day. Their wrong decisions can have dire consequences for us. We are born under someone's authority or representative leadership and whether we like their decisions or not, their decisions affect us.

God created Adam with a free-will. Adam's human nature (mind, affections, and will) was created with a sinless, holy, and righteous disposition. It had no defects. However, Adam's human nature was put to the test when Satan tempted him to doubt God's word. Satan questioned God's authority by questioning the reasoning behind God's command to abstain from eating the fruit of the tree of the knowledge of good and evil. As John Calvin commented,

> Very dangerous is the temptation, when it is suggested to us, that God is not to be obeyed, except so far as the reason of his command is apparent. The true rule of obedience is, that we being content with a bare command, should persuade ourselves that whatever he enjoins is just and right. But whosoever desires to be wise beyond measure, him will Satan, seeing he has cast off all reverence for God, immediately precipitate into open rebellion.[9]

Then Satan implied that God was jealously withholding something good from Adam by denying him the knowledge of good and evil. Next, Satan implied to Adam that God lied about the death penalty

---

[9] John Calvin, *Calvin's Commentaries: Genesis*, vol. 1 (Grand Rapids: Eerdmans, 1948), pp. 147–148.

for disobedience. By slandering God in this way, Satan tempted Adam to question God's authority, wisdom, and goodness. Satan had carefully laid his trap to get Adam to violate God's commandment. He succeeded in getting Adam to rebel against God. Despite God's goodness to Adam, Adam believed Satan's false characterization of God and Adam was convinced that he had justification for his rebellious actions against God. Also, Satan tempted Adam with the same selfish ambition that Satan himself had. Satan's ambition was to become divine like God.[10] He tried to deceive Adam just as he had deceived Eve by saying they as mere creatures could become divine like God. All that Adam must do was to eat this forbidden fruit. The devil was really tempting Adam with the idea of becoming equal with God and therefore, becoming autonomous or independent of God's authority. In his pride, Adam must have thought he could make himself be his own god and a law unto himself. Then he would have the right to decide what was good and what was evil for himself. He would not have to answer to God for his behavior. Adam then usurped God's authority by standing in judgment of God and His commandments and by choosing to make himself the highest authority for his conduct. The subtle idea of an autonomous self - became Adam's idol. Adam had already tasted the forbidden fruit with his heart before he ever tasted it with his mouth. Sadly, when Adam chose to disobey God, he refused God's truth, rules, help, love, and friendship. He turned his back and left God.

And since Adam acted on our behalf, his act of disobedience (sin) caused God to transfer Adam's sin to us all. God legally declared Adam and all mankind to be covenant-breakers or sinners. As the Westminster Shorter Catechism says: "The covenant being made with Adam, not only for himself, but for posterity; all mankind, descending from him by ordinary generation, sinned in

---

[10] Isa. 14:12–14.

him, and fell with him, in his first transgression.". [11]The apostle
Paul wrote,

> Therefore, just as sin entered the world through one man,
> and death through sin, and in this way, death came to all
> men, because all sinned. ... Consequently, just as the result
> of one trespass was condemnation for all men through the
> disobedience of the one man the many were made sinners.
> (Rom. 5:12, 18–19 NIV; see also 1 Cor. 15:22)

How did Adam's disobedience affect mankind spiritually? It
caused all of us to be born spiritually dead or born without a
spiritual relationship with God. Adam's disobedience also caused
us to be alienated from God by inherited our sinful, fallen human
nature. We were born totally depraved. Being born totally depraved
does not mean that we are as bad as we could be. Rather, it means
that every part of our human nature has been corrupted by sin.
When sinners see the term "total depravity" used to described their
true condition in Adam, they usually try to deny it because they do
not like to think of themselves that way. Instead, they would like to
think of themselves as respectable, religious, or at least not as bad
as some people are. They quickly compare themselves to others
who have what they think is greater sins than theirs. But this will
not work because eventually they will find out that God will not
compare them with others on Judgment Day. God will compare
them with Himself. God said, "Be holy for I am holy."[12] David
described human birth in this general way: "The wicked are
estranged [from God] from the womb; they go astray as soon as
they be born, speaking lies".[13] He described his own birth like this:

---

[11] Westminster Shorter Catechism Answer to Question #16
[12] Lev. 11:44(NKJV); 1 Pet. 1:16; Matt.5:48
[13] Psalm 58:3

"Behold, I was shapen in iniquity; and in sin did my mother conceive me". [14] Was David describing conception itself as sinful? No, God commanded Adam and Eve to multiply. Well, then, was David an illegitimate child? No, he was not born out of wedlock. His description of his own birth was a humbling, truthful admission to his personal sins and their Adamic origin. We were born into the world as sinners. The apostle Paul describes mankind as "by nature the children of wrath."[15] If babies were born innocent, they could not possibly die at birth. Death can only come as the result of sin.[16] Babies can experience physical death because Adam's sin was imputed, or reckoned or accounted to them.

During Adam's time of innocence his mind, affections, and will were still free to serve and obey God. However, Adam's human nature was different from God's divine nature. Adam's nature could change. When he willfully chose to disobey God, it was a sure indication that his former innocent human nature had drastically changed. His disposition now lacked the ambition and temperament to love and serve God. Instead, another ambition and temperament filled the vacuum. His disposition was now inclined to love self and to serve sin.

As unsaved sinners we are often brought up short by our guilty conscience when we know we have done something wrong. So how do we deal with our sins and the guilt feelings that come with them when God convicts us of transgressing His commandments? We usually try to pacify our consciences by believing in blind fate, false religions or philosophers who tell us we can blame the mythological Greek or Roman gods for our sins. Or we may choose to believe the scientific experts who tell us we can blame our wickedness on our bodies, our genetic make-ups, our society, our

---

[14] Psalm 51:5
[15] Eph. 2:3; see also Gen. 8:21; Job 14:4; 15:14–16.
[16] Rom. 6;23.

parents, our friends, our living environments, or life's circumstances. Philosophers and experts have tried to give us victim mentalities and with them excuses so we can shift the responsibility for our personal sins from ourselves to someone or something else. But when we excuse our own wickedness, we become more insensitive to our consciences and consequently, more wicked.

The source of an unsaved person's wickedness is not outside of him; it lies within his fallen human nature. It is sin. Sin is the principle that motivates his life. The unsaved man is not concerned about his sin. He is comfortable with his alliance with it. Thus, he does not hate sin in himself; he delights in it. He is so easily enticed by sin that he makes a practice of it when he is tempted. Sinning is as natural to him as drinking water because God is not included in his day-to-day thoughts, decisions, or in his world and life views. The unsaved man does not look at everything in the light of God's Word because he does not choose to have this holy God rule over him. When the unsaved man is confronted with the idea that his main purpose in life is to glorify the God of the Bible and to enjoy Him forever, he cannot tolerate it. He will privately and publicly oppose and suppress that idea. [17] He will not have this Jesus to rule over him.

Unsaved man serves sin and Satan by habitually sinning regardless of the consequences.[18] Is there anyone who can help the unsaved man with his dilemma? Where does he get help? Can he turn to the Bible for help? Yes, God's written Word reveals the solution to his dilemma, but he may get discouraged at first when he reads it because it exposes his sins, and the idea of seeking a holy and just God, who punishes man for his sins, is terrifying. So, he

---

[17] Rom. 1:18–23.
[18] John 8:37–47; Acts 26:18; 2 Tim. 2:26.

purposely avoids reading the Bible altogether and keeps his mind occupied with other things less important.

Man's basic problem is his sinful heart. Being descendants of Adam, we inherited his sinful (worldly, proud, independent, lustful, greedy, hateful) human disposition and we voluntarily became slaves to it.[19] Jesus said, "Truly, truly, I say to you, whoever practices sin is a slave to sin."[20] For this reason, when we, as unbelievers, are faced with choosing between consciously obeying God's commandments or obeying our own sinful desires, we usually choose to cling affectionately to our sinful inclinations.[21] Do you see our dilemma? As God's creatures we still owe a debt of perfect obedience to God, but now, we owe Him the right to punish us for our disobedience. This punishment insures that God will sentence us to eternal separation from Him and torment in hell. Is there any solution to our double debt dilemma?

---

[19] Rom 7:14; 6:16–22.

[20] John 8:34 NIV.

[21] Rom. 6:17–18; Gen. 6:5; 8:21.

CHAPTER 2

GOD'S SOLUTION TO MAN'S DILEMMA

What is God's solution for man's bondage to sin? It is the good news about Jesus. It is through this good news that God reveals His grace or unmerited favor towards us and calls us to Himself. What is the good news about Jesus? Before the world was created, God the Father made a Covenant of Redemption with God the Son.[22] By this covenant God the Son agreed to redeem many people from their bondage to sin. In return the Father promised His Son these redeemed people as His inheritance and He also promised Him a kingdom to rule over.[23] But in order to fulfill this covenant the Son would have to become a man and be sent to earth to represent man. This is because God knew the Covenant of Works that He would make with the man, Adam, as man's representative would be transgressed and therefore broken. So, centuries later after Adam's fall into sin God sent His Son from heaven to be born on earth with a sinless human nature. and a human body of flesh.[24] God the Son became man (the man, Jesus Christ) so that He could fulfill for sinners the essential requirement of the Covenant of Works (which is perfect obedience to God's commandments). Christ Jesus was born to keep God's commandments for us and to pay the death

---

[22] Isa. 42:6; 49:8; 53:11; 54:10; 55:3; 59:21; Jer. 31:31-34; Psa. 2:8; 25:14; 89:3, 27-34; Zec. 6:12-13; 2 Sam.7:12-13; Acts 2:29-36; Gal. 3:15-19; Heb 7:2; 8:6; 13:20; Titus 1:2
[23] Gen. 49:10; Psa. 2:8-9; 110:1-3; Heb. 1:8, 2:12
[24] 1 Cor. 15:47; Gal. 4:4-5; John 1:14; Lk. 1:26-35; Isa. 7:14; Matt. 1:23; Phil. 2:5-8; Heb2:14-16; 10:5, 7; 1John 4:2-3

penalty for our failure to keep them.[25] Jesus was born to live, to die, and to be resurrected from grave for all that will place their trust in Him for their salvation from God's just wrath for their sins. Thus, the Covenant of Redemption comes into play and it forms the basis for a Covenant of Grace with sinners whereby God can promise grace and salvation to sinners and to their children.[26]

J.G. Vos commenting on these covenants and quoting from The Reformed Presbyterian Testimony said,

> " '. . . there are not besides the Covenant of Works, two distinct covenants - one a Covenant of Redemption made with Christ and the other, a Covenant of Grace made with us, DISTINCT from the Covenant of Redemption.'[27] It will be observed that the force of the above quotation turns on the word DISTINCT covenants, one made with Christ, and the other made with the elect. Section 4, Chapter IX says,' . . . the same establishment, which is to them a Covenant of free Grace, is to Him a Covenant of Redemption.' It is correct to say that the one covenant has TWO ASPECTS, an eternal aspect and historical aspect. The eternal aspect may properly be called the 'The Covenant of Redemption', and the historical aspect the 'Covenant of Grace', so long as we bear in mind that these are only two aspects or phrases of one and the same covenant, not two distinct covenants made by God with different parties."[28] "From the beginning

---

[25] Gen. 3:15; Zec. 13:7; Rev. 13:8.

[26] Gen. 9:9; 17:7, 9-14; Col. 2:8-11; Acts 2:38-39; 16:15, 33-34; Heb. 8:10; Gal. 3:16; 2 Cor. 1:19-20.

[27] The Reformed Presbyterian Testimony, IX. 4 and error 3.

[28] *The Covenant of Grace,* by J. G. Vos, Blue Banner Faith and Life, Reprinted by The Reformed Presbyterian Church of North

to end biblical theology is founded upon the promise of the covenant. This is the overall [unified] pattern that gives substance and meaning to the biblical concept of grace. . . The whole concept of election [from eternity past] derives from the principle of a covenant relationship between man and God [in history]."[29]

He has sent redemption to His elect people; He has commanded His covenant forever: Holy and awesome is His name (Psalm 111:9).

In Isaiah 42 we hear the Father saying to the Son:
"I the Lord have called thee in righteousness, and will hold thine hand, and will keep thee, and give thee *for a covenant* of the people, for a light of the Gentiles."

"The first germinal publication of the everlasting covenant is found in Genesis 3:15: 'I will put enmity between thee and the woman, between thy seed and her seed; it shall bruise thy head, and thou shalt bruise his heel." [30] [It is also the first glimpse of the Covenant of Grace because it is a prophecy about Jesus, our kinsman redeemer (goel), defeating Satan according to the determinate counsel of God to make due satisfaction, payment or ransom for our sins by shedding His blood on a Roman cross for His elect people (The word "redeemer" is found throughout

---

America Board of Education and Publication, Pittsburgh, PA 15208
[29] Jocz, Jacob, *The Covenant A Theology of Human Destiny*, William B. Eerdmans Publishing Co., Grand Rapids, Michigan, 1968, pp.9, 13.
[30] Pink, Arthur W., *The Divine Covenants*, Baker Book House, 1973, p.16

chapters 40-66 of Isaiah; Job 9:25; Ex. 13:13-15; Lev. 25:25-27,
47-54, cf. Ruth 4:1-12; Mark 10:45; Eph. 1:7; cf. 1 Pet. 1:18-19;
Acts 3:18; 4:25-28). "As [covenant] revelations they exhibited in
ever augmented degrees of fullness and clearness the plan of
salvation through the mediation and sacrifice of the Son of God; for
each of those covenants consisted of gracious promises *ratified by
[blood] sacrifice* (Gen. 8:20 and 9:9; 15:9-11 and 18)"[31]. God
displayed the covenant of grace to Adam and Eve when He showed
them how they could receive the forgiveness of their sin. They
understood the direct connection between their sin and the necessity
of shedding the blood of an innocent animal used as a vicarious,
atoning sacrifice to cover their sin (Gen. 3:21). They understood
that the sacrificial animal took the penalty of their sin in their place.
And by this sacrificial offering they were taught to trust that God
would send someone who would Himself die in their place for the
punishment of their sins. Abel by faith looked forward into the
future for this person who would be his Substitute; a person who
would take his place as his sin offering and shed His blood for him.

We have a conversation in heaven (recorded in the Bible for the
benefit of our understanding since it had already had been decided
from eternity past) between Jesus and His Father about replacing
the animal blood sacrifices and offerings with the blood sacrifice of
Jesus. This is what Jesus said:

"Sacrifice and meal offering You have not desired; My
ears You have opened; Burnt offering and sin offering
You have not required. Then I said, 'Behold I come; In
the scroll of the book it is written of me. I delight to do
Your will, O my God; "Your law is written within my
Heart.' (Psalm 40:6-8);

---

[31] Ibid., p.16

"For it not possible for the blood of bulls and goats to take away sins. That is why when Christ came into the world he said to God, 'You did not want animal sacrifices or sin offerings. But you have given me a body to offer. You were not pleased with burnt offerings or other offerings for sin. Then I said, 'Look, I have come to do your will, O God – as it is written about me in the Scriptures. First, Christ said 'You did not want animal sacrifices or sin offerings or burnt offerings or other offerings for sin, nor were pleased with them' (though they are required by the law of Moses). The he said, 'Look I have come to do your will'. He cancels the first covenant in order to put the second into effect. For God's will was for us to be made holy by the sacrifice of the body of Jesus Christ, once for all time. Under the old covenant, the priest stands and ministers before the altar day after day, offering the same sacrifices again and again, which can never take away sins. But our High Priest offered himself to God as a single sacrifice for sins, good for all time. Then he sat down in the place of honor at God's right hand" (Hebrews 10:4-12, NLT)

When Jesus begins His ministry John the Baptist announces Jesus as "the Lamb of God who takes away the sin of the world." Then when Jesus speaks at the Passover/Communion meal about the shedding of His blood at the crucifixion, He says, "*this is my blood of the covenant*, which is poured out for many for forgiveness of sins."

"knowing that you were not redeemed with corruptible things, like silver or gold, . . . but with the precious blood of Christ, as the lamb without blemish and without spot. He indeed was foreordained before the foundation of the world, but was manifest in these last times for you." (1 Peter 1:18-20) NKJV

In Revelation 13:8 Christ Jesus was called the "Lamb of God slain from the foundation of the world."

"Now the God of peace, that brought again from the dead our Lord Jesus, that great Shepherd of the sheep, through the blood of *the eternal [eternity past] covenant* . . . (Hebrews 13:20, See also Isa. 55:3

Cain, Abel's brother, on the other hand refused God's method of salvation by the sacrificial blood offering and Cain offered a bloodless sacrifice instead. He offered the work of his own hands to God and God refused him and his offering (Gen. 4:3-14). Nevertheless, ever since Cain many have hoped to please God some other way than a blood sacrifice. For example, some think that before God will accept them they must make themselves a better person or make promises to do better. So, they try to stop their sinful habits. The result is they usually trade their old sinful habits for new sinful habits. They fool themselves by thinking God will accept them because they have made an effort to reform themselves. Instead, the very thing they trusted that would bring them God's acceptance actually prevents them from receiving it. This is because they have devised their own way to make themselves right with God. Others imagine God will accept them if their good deeds outweigh their bad deeds. Still others foolishly think they must add their imperfect deeds to Jesus' perfect deeds for

God to accept them. Wrong! God forgives and accepts sinners solely on the basis of the person and work of Jesus. [32]

---

[32] Isa. 9:6; 7:14; Zech. 13:7; John 1:1; 10:30, 38; 20:28; Acts 20:28; Rom. 1:2-4; 9:5; Phil. 2:6; Titus 2:13; Heb. 1:8; 1 John 5:20

Chapter 3

God's Righteous and Atoning Grace

Do not try to cover the nakedness of your sins with your good deeds so that God will accept you as His own. Your best deeds and behavior will never be good enough. As an unbeliever, all the deeds you perform become dirty and rotten because, as Gardiner Spring says, "The moral quality of actions lies in the disposition of heart with which they are performed."[33] The Bible says: "Can the Ethiopian change his skin or the leopard its spots? Then may you also do good who are accustomed to do evil" (Jer. 13:23 NKJV). "No good tree bears bad fruit, nor does a bad tree bear good fruit" (Luke 6:43 NIV). "A haughty look, a proud heart, and the plowing of the wicked are sin" (Prov. 21:4 NKJV). Your good deeds are not done with a pure heart to promote God's glory. Instead, they are defiled either with a desire for your own praise, your profit here on earth, or with the desire to earn your way to heaven to escape hell hereafter.

William G. T. Shedd, in *A History of Christian Doctrine*, pointed out,

In the fifth book of the *De Civitate Dei*, Augustine shows that God rewarded the natural virtues of the early Romans with temporal prosperity; yet that their frugality, contempt of riches, moderation, and courage, were merely the effect of the love of glory that curbed those particular vices which are antagonistic to national renown, without ceasing to be a vice itself. He concedes the praise of external rectitude

---

[33] Gardiner Spring, *The Distinguishing Traits of Christian Character* (Phillipsburg, N.J.: Presbyterian and Reformed Publishing, 1976), p. 9.

(justitia civilis) to many actions of the heathen, yet he maintains that when these are viewed in the motive or principle from which they sprung they are sins; for whatsoever is not of faith is sin (Rom. 14:23). "It is sin, then," objects Julian, "when a heathen clothes the naked, binds up the wounds of the infirm, or endures torture rather than give false testimony?" Augustine replies that the act in itself, or the matter of the act, is not sin; but as it does not proceed from faith, and a purpose to honor God, the form of the act, which contains the morality of it, is sin.[34]

L. Berkhof, in his *Systematic Theology*, explained,

When the Pelagians pointed to the virtues of the heathen, who "merely through the power of innate freedom" were often merciful, discreet, chaste, and temperate, he [Augustine] answered that these so-called virtues were sins, because they did not spring from faith. He admits that the heathen can perform certain acts which are in themselves good and from a lower point of view even praiseworthy, but yet considers these deeds, as the deeds of unregenerate persons, to be sin, because they do not spring from the motive of love to God or of faith, and do not answer to the right purpose, the glory of God. He denies that such deeds are the fruit of any natural goodness in man.[35]

So, offering your good deeds to God to be accepted by Him is no better than offering the cloth of a menstruating woman to Him.

---

[34] William G. T. Shedd, *History of Christian Doctrine*, vol. 2 (New York: Charles Scribner's Sons, 1863), pp. 75-76.
[35] L. Berkhof, *Systematic Theology* (Grand Rapids: Eerdmans, 1939), p. 433.

The Bible says, "All of us have become like one who is unclean, and all our righteous acts are like filthy rags" (Isa. 64:6 NIV). The apostle Paul wanted above all "to gain Christ and be actually in union with Him, not having a supposed right standing with God which depends on my doing what the law commands, but one that comes through faith in Christ, the real right standing with God which originates from Him and rests on faith" (Phil. 3:8–9 WILLIAMS). The Bible says there are people who are:

> Ignorant of the righteousness that comes from God, and trying to set up their own righteousness, they have not submitted to the righteousness of God. For Christ brought the Law to completion so that everyone who believes in Him may be justified [have right standing with God]. (Rom. 10:3–4 NEW BERKELEY)

> For it is by His [God's grace or] unmerited favor through faith that you have been saved; it is not by anything that you have done, it is the gift of God. It is not the result of what anyone can do, so that no one can boast of it. For He has made us what we are, because He has created us through our union with Christ Jesus for doing good deeds which He beforehand planned for us to do. (Eph. 2:8–10 WILLIAMS)

In short, Christians do not obey God's commandments or do good deeds to be saved; they do them as a result of being saved. It is an evidence of their salvation. Their love for God and their thankful gratitude to God for being saved are the motivating drives behind their obedience and good deeds.[36]

Wonderfully, one act of righteousness done by Jesus provided justification and life to all men. It was through the obedience of the

---

[36] John 14:15; Matt. 11:30; 1 John 5:3

one man, Jesus, that many will be made righteous. [37] God said concerning Jesus, "This is my beloved Son, in whom I am well pleased; hear ye Him."[38] Paul said, "He [God the Father] has made us accepted in the Beloved [Jesus]". [39] The objective, historical deeds done by Jesus for us 2000 years ago are what make us acceptable to God. After all, what are your deeds worth compared to Jesus' perfect obedience? He obeyed and honored God's law. He satisfied His Father's requirement of perfect obedience to all the commandments.

Jesus can now secure your release from the necessity of perfectly obeying the law as a condition of right standing with God. How? By placing your trust in Jesus' righteous obedience, God will impute or legally transfer Jesus' alien righteousness [a righteousness which is separate from and outside of you and not yours] to your account and He will declare you "righteous". God will count or legally reckon Jesus' perfect obedience to you as if you had performed it. It is as if you were as obedient as Jesus. Stated another way, Robert L. Dabney in his *Lectures in Systematic Theology* explains imputation this way: "In the imputation of Christ's righteousness . . . [it is that] which is the exact counterpart of guilt - the title to acquittal."[40] Thus, <u>for the believer's justification</u>, or right standing before God he receives the legal benefits of Christ's righteousness, not an infused inherent righteousness standing by itself all on its own.

Long ago, God foretold that the Lord Jesus Christ would be our righteousness by faith.

---

[37] Rom. 5:18-19
[38] Matt. 17:5
[39] Eph. 1:6
[40] Robert L. Dabney, Lectures in Systematic Theology (Grand Rapids: Zondervan, 1975), p.641.

See, the days are coming, says the Lord, when I will raise up to David a righteous Branch, and . . . this is His name whereby He shall be called: **The Lord Our Righteousness."** (Jer. 23:5-6 New Berkley version)

But from Him you have your existence in Christ Jesus, who became for us divine wisdom and **righteousness** and holiness and redemption. (1 Cor. 1:30 New Berkley version)

For all of you who were baptized into Christ have clothed yourselves with Christ. (Gal. 3:27 NIV)

I will greatly rejoice in the Lord, my soul shall be joyful in my God; for He has clothed me the garments of salvation, He has covered me with the **robe of righteousness,** as a bridegroom decks himself with ornaments, and as a bride adorns herself with her jewels. (Isa. 61:10)

God sees you differently when He looks at you through Jesus. He sees you as covered with the dazzling, radiant, pure, white robe of Jesus' righteousness. "When a ewe's newborn lamb dies, the shepherd often brings an orphan lamb to her to mother it. The ewe may reject the orphan because he does not have the "family scent". In this case, the shepherd skins the ewe's dead lamb and ties its skin to the orphan lamb's back. The ewe now recognizes the familiar scent of her dead newborn lamb and she will accept the orphan lamb as if it were her own.[41] Likewise, Jesus, the sacrificial Lamb of God

---

[41] Ephesians 5:2; 2 Corinthians 2:15

can cover you with His righteousness and assure your adoption into God's family."[42]

"You see at just the right time, when we were still powerless, Christ died for the ungodly. Very rarely will anyone die for a righteous man, though for a good man someone might possibly dare to die. But God demonstrates his own love for us in this: While we were yet sinners, Christ died for us. Since we have been justified by his blood, how much more shall we be saved from God's wrath through him [Christ Jesus]! For if, when we were God's enemies, we were reconciled to him through the death of his Son, how much more, having been reconciled, shall we be saved through his life"! [43]

Jesus is the only ladder to heaven. Therefore, sinners must look to Him as the only way to God. Salvation is not offered through anyone else; for there is no other name under heaven given among men by which we must be saved.[44] Jesus said, "I am the way, the truth, and the life: no man cometh unto the Father, but by me."[45] He also said, "Come to Me all you who labor and are heavily burdened, and I will give you rest. Take My yoke upon you and learn of Me, for I am gentle and humble of heart, and you shall find rest for your souls".[46] If you come to Jesus by faith, your soul can rest from its

---

[42] Bennett Broadway, Can God Accept You? (Pittsburgh, PA: Crown and
  Covenant Publishing, 1989) an evangelistic tract. See also John 1:12; 1
  Peter. 1:18-19; Matthew. 22:11-13.
[43] Rom. 5:6-10
[44] Acts 4:10, 12.
[45] John 14:6.
[46] Matt. 11:28-29

weary laboring to earn salvation because you have trusted that His works or His labor has already earned your salvation for you. Jesus, the Messiah, had to die but certainly not for any sin of His own. He died as a substitutionary sacrifice for our sins. Why? Long ago covenants were ratified by shedding the blood of an innocent animal in a substitutionary sacrificial ceremony before God.[47] The parties of the covenant would then walk together between the pieces of the dead animal sacrifice, indicating that if either party should fail to keep the covenant made between them, he should be killed and cut in half and their blood spilled like the animal sacrifice.[48]

In Abram's vision in Genesis 15, God passed between the slain animal sacrifices. Abram perceived the Lord's presence in the visible signs of a smoking oven and a burning torch. God ratified or confirmed a covenant made between God and Abram as Abram lay helpless in a deep sleep a short distance from the sacrifices. This ceremony was unusual because Abram did not walk between the sacrifices with God. By his non-participation, or better yet, by his non-cooperation in this sacrificial ceremony, Abram may have understood that God would perform Abram's part of the covenant conditions for him so Abram would be guaranteed the promised benefits of the covenant.[49] This is a picture of God's covenant of grace. Just as God did for Abram what Abram could not do for himself, likewise, Christ Jesus did for us what we cannot do for ourselves.[50]

---

[47] Ps. 50:5; Isa. 53:4–12; Gen. 4:3–5; Heb. 11:4; 9:22; John 1:29; 1 Pet. 1:18–19; Eph. 5:2; Matt. 26:26–28; Gal. 3:26.
[48] Gen. 15:9–12; Jer. 34:18–20; Zech. 13:7; Matt. 27:51; Heb. 10:19–20.
[49] Gal. 3:16–18; 2 Cor. 1:19–20; see also Heb. 7:22 and Rom. 15:8.
[50] Gen. 17:1–2; Matt. 5:48; Heb. 7:22; John 8: 51–58.

Christ Jesus was qualified by being both God and man to repair His Father's damaged honor by perfectly obeying His commandments. He also satisfied His Father's wrath by paying the death penalty for His people who disobeyed those commandments. Thus, the Covenant of Grace required the moral necessity for Jesus' death.[51] Ernest F. Kevan, in his book *The Grace of Law,* wrote, "The law of God is the permanent, unchanging expression of God's eternal and unchangeable holiness and justice. God could not change this law, or set it aside, in His dealings with men, without denying Himself. When man sins, therefore, it is not God's nature to save him at the law's expense. Instead, He saves sinners by satisfying the law on their behalf." [52] Therefore, the necessity of Jesus' death arose from God's holiness which required that God's justice be carried out against those who broke the Covenant of Works. In Adam, we broke the Covenant of Works and we are under its curse of death. We are the ones who deserve to die as covenant breakers. We are the ones who deserve to be cut in half. Instead God made Jesus our Sacrificial Lamb and offered Him up in our place. Jesus gladly volunteered to substitute Himself for sinners. He suffered for us and was executed in our place on the cross to satisfy God's wrath against our sins. Jesus took our death penalty upon Himself. When he hung on the cross and spilled His blood, He took the curse of the Covenant of Works upon Himself for all of us who put our trust in Him. The prophet Isaiah who foretold of Messiah's suffering and death wrote:

He was despised and rejected by men, a man of sorrows, and familiar with suffering. Like one from whom hide men hide their faces he was despised, and we esteemed him not. Surely,

---

[51] Luke 24:25-27, 44-47.
[52] Ernest F. Kevan, *The Grace of Law: A Study of Puritan Theology* (Grand Rapids: Baker, 1976), pp. 67–68.

he took up our infirmities and carried our sorrows, yet we considered him stricken by God, smitten by him, and afflicted. But he was pierced for our transgressions, he was crushed for our iniquities; the punishment that brought us peace was upon him, and by his wounds we are healed. We all, like sheep, have gone astray, each of us has turned to his own way, and the Lord has laid on him the iniquity of us all. (Isaiah 53:3-6)

For God so loved the world, that he gave [as a sacrifice for our sins] his only begotten Son, that whosoever believes in him should not parish, but have everlasting life.
(John 3:16; see also Acts 2:22-23; 4:27-28)

God presented him [Jesus] as a sacrifice of atonement, through faith in his blood. He did this to demonstrate his justice ... at the present time, so as to be just and the one who justifies those who have faith in Jesus.
(Rom. 3:25; 5:9)

So, how is it possible for God to be just and Justifier at the same time? How can a holy God be just and merciful at the same time? Will a holy God show us mercy at the expense of His justice? He cannot and will not compromise His character to save us. He will not bend His commandments for us nor will He lower His standard of perfect obedience to His commandments. He will not turn His head the other way when we sin so our sin can slip by His notice. He not only sees our sins, but He must punish them. But by imputing or transferring the sinner's sins to Jesus, God can show His mercy in a way that is consistent with His justice. God will count the sinner who places his trust in Christ's atoning blood to be justly punished because Jesus took that sinner's punishment on the cross for him. On the cross, "Mercy and truth are met together; righteousness and peace have kissed each other."[53]

This is how God the Father can forgive you and acquit you of your past, present and future sins without compromising His holiness or His justice. Only God, in His infinite wisdom and sacrificial love, could have conceived a way like this to save a people for Himself. By punishing His Son for their sins, God could save sinners and still remain true to Himself.

When our sins are thus removed, God removes the legal guilt of sins from us and delivers us from our guilt feelings as well. In Adam, we are all under the curse of breaking God's commandments or law as a Covenant of Works. Sin is the transgression of God's law. And the strength of sin is found by condemning power of God's holy law. However, the condemning power of the law is removed when we believe that Jesus by His life and death fulfilled our legal obligations to the law as a Covenant of Works. [54] With the knowledge of this removal of legal guilt of our transgressions comes the removal of our guilt feelings also. When we believe God has, through Jesus, removed the guilt of our transgressions which separated us from Him, we can draw near to God with a sincere heart with in full assurance of faith, having our hearts sprinkled to cleanse us from a guilty conscience and having our bodies washed with pure water we may serve the living God and spur one another on toward love and good deeds.[55]

Jesus died a shameful death and rose again from the grave. Jesus' resurrection is proof of our justification. It is proof that Jesus actually made things right between God the Father and us and consequently, we have been forgiven and reconciled to God. Jesus

---

[53] Psa. 85:10
[54] Rom. 7:4-5; 8:1, 31-34
[55] Heb. 9:14; 10:22, 24; 1John 1:9

was put to death on account of our misdeeds and was raised on account of our justification (our right standing with God).[56]

The apostle Peter explained the significance of that resurrection morning as the prophetic fulfillment of God's promise to King David.

Ye men of Israel, hear these words; Jesus of Nazareth, a man approved of God among you by miracles and wonders and signs, which God did by him in the midst of you, as ye yourselves also know: him, being delivered by the determinate counsel and foreknowledge of God, ye have taken, and by wicked hands have crucified and slain: whom God hath raised up, having loosed the pains of death: because it was not possible that he should be holden of it. For David speaketh concerning him, I foresaw the LORD always before my face, for he is on my right hand, that I should not be moved: therefore did my heart rejoice, and my tongue was glad; moreover also my flesh shall rest in hope: because thou wilt not leave my soul in hell, neither wilt thou suffer thine Holy One to see corruption....Men and brethren, let me freely speak unto you of the patriarch David, that he is both dead and buried, and his sepulcher is with us unto this day. Therefore being a prophet, and knowing that God had sworn with an oath to him, that of the fruit of his loins, according to the flesh, he would raise up Christ to sit on his throne; he seeing this before spake of the resurrection of Christ, that his soul was not left in hell, neither his flesh did see corruption. This Jesus hath God raised up, whereof we all are witnesses.... For David is not ascended into the heavens: but he saith himself, The LORD said unto my LORD, Sit thou on my right hand, until I make

---

[56] Rom. 4:25

thy foes thy footstool. Therefore, let all the house of Israel know assuredly, that God hath made that same Jesus, whom ye have crucified, both LORD and Christ.[57]

By raising Jesus from the dead, God the Father vindicated Jesus' claims to be God the Son[58], to have come from heaven[59], to be the Messiah[60], to be sinless[61], to be able to forgive sins[62], and to have existed before Abraham or David[63] contrary to the Pharisee's false charges of blasphemy.

---

[57] Acts 2:22–27, 29–32, 34–36
[58] John 10:30,33
[59] John 3:13; 17:5
[60] John 4:26; Matt. 26:63-65
[61] John 8:46
[62] Matt. 9:2
[63] John 8:56-59; Matt. 22:41-46

CHAPTER 4

GOD'S REGENERATING GRACE

In John 3 Jesus pointed out to the Pharisee, Nicodemus, the necessity of God's regenerating grace. Jesus was pointing Nicodemus to the only remedy for being spiritually dead was to be spiritually reborn. Nicodemus asked, "How can a man be born when he is old? Can he enter a second time into his mother's womb, and be born?" Jesus answered, "Marvel not that I said unto you, you must be born from above."[64] Nicodemus' reaction to Jesus' announcement was an expression of astonishment and a confession of his utter helplessness. Nicodemus recognized the impossible task of a second physical birth. But Nicodemus missed Jesus' point about the need for and the source of a spiritual rebirth (e.g., Ezekiel 36:26–27; 37:1–14). But had he thought about it, he would have realized that it would have been just as impossible for him to make a decision to be born spiritually as it would have been to have made the decision to be born physically. This was not a decision he could or would have made on his own. Because Nicodemus was spiritually dead, his natural, unregenerate, will was helpless. It could not determine its own rebirth. Nicodemus could not just decide to be reborn. Jesus told Nicodemus he would have to be born spiritually (regenerated) from above. So, it was God's will that determined that Nicodemus would be reborn. It was necessary for God to regenerate Nicodemus' mind, affections and will before Nicodemus could make a decision to receive Jesus.

The Bible says,

---

[64] John 3:3–8.

> "But as many as received him [Jesus], to them gave he power to become the sons of God, even to them that believe on his name: which were *born,* not of blood, nor of the will of the flesh, NOR OF THE WILL OF MAN, but of God [GOD'S WILL]. [65]

Therefore, it is God's decision, made from eternity past, who will and who will not receive Christ by the regenerating power of the Holy Spirit, not the unsaved sinner's decision. It is God who has determined who will experience rebirth. [66] The Lord said to Job, "Hast thou an arm like God? or canst thou thunder with a voice like Him? Then will I also confess unto thee that thine own right hand can save thee".[67] Nicodemus could not regenerate himself.

Before his regeneration, Nicodemus was incapable of any spiritual activity that would please God since he was spiritually dead. He was dead in his trespasses and sins. The Holy Spirit's powerful, mysterious, work of regenerating grace was necessary to change this. The Holy Spirit had to quicken or breathe spiritual life into Nicodemus' heart.[68] To do this the Holy Spirit had to reveal Nicodemus' sins to him. Then He had to convince Nicodemus of the truthfulness of God's saving Gospel promises to forgive his sins. It was then that the Holy Spirit captivated Nicodemus' personal affections when he understood the worth of God's love for him given through Christ Jesus. The Holy Spirit then energized Nicodemus' will with life to act to serve God's will instead of continuing to serve his old self-will and ultimately Satan's will. So,

---

[65] John 1:12-13

[66] Ps. 119:50; John 3:8; Rom. 8:8–9; 1 Cor. 4:15; Mark 4:3, 14, 20.

[67] Job 40:9, 14; see also Isa. 53:1–12

[68] John 3:6,8; 1 Peter 1:23; 1 John 3:9; 1 John 5:11-13

when the Gospel was shared with Nicodemus the Holy Spirit's regenerating power caused him to be "born again".

It has been said by some that after Adam's fall, man's spiritual condition was not as bad as it has just been described. They deny that man was left without any spiritual strength to save himself. They believe he has enough spiritual strength to tread water on the surface and when he is given the opportunity to save himself, he is able to do it. However, this is not a true picture of the sinner's situation. In Adam the sinner has already gone down for the third time, drowned, and died. God must take the initiative to save the sinner. God must dive into the ocean and swim to the bottom to retrieve the spiritually dead sinner to the surface. God must bring him to his senses by infusing grace or spiritual life into him to regenerate his heart. Until then the sinner neither has the desire nor sees the need to be saved or reborn because the field of his heart has not been plowed or prepared by the Holy Spirit's regenerating power for the planting of the seed of God's Word. Until that happens the unsaved sinner is without strength and is spiritually helpless.[69] The unsaved sinner is spiritually blind. He does not see his spiritual bankruptcy. He does not see his need to be born again. Therefore, he will not be inclined to seek the Kingdom of God. .[70]

Jesus taught Nicodemus that rebirth or regeneration is something only God could do for him and in him. **It is not a "do it yourself" project**. Only God has the ability to give the spiritually dead sinner spiritual life.[71] Once this is done, the sinner's regenerated will is irresistibly drawn to seek God and His kingdom.[72] As the apostle Paul said,

---

[69] Rom. 5:6

[70] 1 Cor. 2:6-14; Heb. 11:10,16; 12:22; 13:14; Rev. 3:12

[71] John 3:6; 6:63; Eph. 4:24; 2 Cor. 5:17; Eph. 2:1–5; Col. 2:13.

[72] Psalm 110:3

He saved us, not for upright deeds that we had done, but in accordance with His mercy, through **the bath of regeneration and renewal of the Holy Spirit**, which He abundantly poured out upon us through Jesus Christ our Saviour, so that we might come into right standing with God through His unmerited favor and become heirs of eternal life in accordance with our hope. (Titus 3:5–7 WILLIAMS)

Of his own will he [the Father] brought us forth [gave us new birth] by the word of truth that we should be a kind of firstfruits of his creatures. (James 1:18 ASV)

Sinners are "born again," not of perishable seed, but of imperishable seed, through the living and enduring Word of God (1 Peter 1:23).

The miracle of rebirth sets the unsaved sinner's will free from the reign of sin and Satan. It gives him freedom from the sin's reign over his will so that he now has the ability to receive Jesus as his Savior when Jesus is offered to him. Jesus said, "The Spirit of the Lord is on me, because he has anointed me to preach good news…to proclaim freedom for the prisoners…to release the oppressed".[73] "If the Son therefore shall make you free, ye shall be free indeed"[74]. Jesus also said, "You shall know the truth and the truth will set you free"[75].

"In Reformed orthodox divinity, God's action in regenerating was held to follow a definite order. The individual is transformed instantaneously, but several different things, regarded as causally related, were held to occur in the crucial moment. Analyzed into its components, regeneration encompasses, in order: (1) calling, in

---

[73] Luke 4:18 NIV; see also Isa. 61:1
[74] John 8:36
[75] John 8:32

which a supernatural principle of action is infused into the soul; (2) an act of faith arising from this new principle, accepting the offer of Christ's righteousness presented in the gospel; (3) repentance, the effective turning of the person away from evil and toward true good; (4) justification, in which God, in virtue of Christ's righteousness believed in, absolves the person from the guilt of sin and from his debt of [perfect] obedience to the moral law [as a Covenant of Works]; (5) adoption, in which the person acquires the status of a "son" of God, with all the perquisites thereof; (6) sanctification, one of the perquisites, in which, by infusion [or a better term, I believe, is "imparting"] of gracious habits, the person [progressively] becomes himself actually holy; and (7) glorification, also one of the perquisites, in which the person experiences a foretaste of the joy and peace of heaven and hopes for fulfillment of both. At point (3), a person is said properly to be "converted," to have entered the covenant of grace, and to be in "union" with Christ, though strictly speaking "conversion" and "regeneration" begin in "calling"; at points (5) through (7) a person is said to enjoy communion with Christ." [76]

---

[76] Wm. K. B. Stover, *A Faire and Easie Way to Heaven* 1978, p.123

CHAPTER 5

IS GOD'S GRACE BASED ON THE SINNER'S FAITH AND REPENTANCE?

The Christian cannot boast that his faith and sincere repentance caused God to choose him.[77] He cannot boast at all because he did not always have saving faith. In 2 Thessalonians 3:1–2, Paul asked the saved brethren to pray for his deliverance from the unsaved who persecuted him. He gave the reason for this persecution when he said, "For all men do not have faith." Saving Faith in Jesus is the gift of God.

The sinner is not born with the gift of saving faith. Therefore, he cannot draw upon it at a moment's notice. Faith does not originate in the unsaved sinner. He is not its author and he does not cause it. [78] Faith is wrought in him by regeneration and it becomes his possession. Saving faith is a gift from God, and because it is a gift, it cannot be thought of as the sinner's meritorious work.[79] On the contrary, God chose certain sinners before time began and sometime in their lifetime, Christ Jesus gives them the gift of faith before they believe so they can believe. It is as the writer of the Book of Hebrews has said: "Looking unto Jesus the author and finisher of our faith".[80]

Acts 18:27 talks about the faith of converted sinners in Achaia "which had believed through grace." Also, look closely at the words in this verse: "And as the Gentiles heard this, they were glad,

---

[77] 1 Cor. 4:7.
[78] Heb. 12:2.
[79] 2 Thess. 3:2; Eph. 2:8–9; Phil. 1:29; Heb. 12:2.
[80] Heb. 12:2

and glorified the word of God: and as many as were ordained [chosen] to eternal life believed".[81]

Here are several other verses that show that faith is not the meritorious work of sinners: "Buried with him [Jesus] in baptism, wherein also ye are risen with him *through the faith of the operation of God*"[82], that is, the faith which God's operation in the human heart produces. How about "For unto you *it is given* in the behalf of Christ, not only *to believe on him*, but also to suffer for his sake".[83] Faith is the gift of God. The Bible says, "For by grace are ye saved through faith; and that not of yourselves: *it is the gift of God*".[84] By God's grace you are given the means or instrument of faith to save you.

So, while it is true that God requires the condition of faith from you, it is also true that He graciously provides the faith that He requires from you at the time of your conversion. The Holy Spirit's work of regeneration causes the elect sinner's heart to passively receive the faith he needs so he can actively exercise it when he hears God's word.

Some interpret the phrase "Justification by Faith" incorrectly. For them, justification by faith seems to take on a new meaning. They think of their faith as having a meritorious virtue all of its own. They understand "the righteousness of God, which is by faith of Jesus Christ" to mean the righteousness of their faith, not the righteousness that comes by faith. For them, faith takes on a value or virtue that becomes their righteousness before God. They think of their faith, not as a gift, but originating solely from them and therefore, they think it must merit their salvation. So, by their act of exercising faith it would make God indebted to them. For them,

---

[81] Acts 13:48 ASV
[82] Col. 2:12
[83] Phil. 1:29
[84] Eph. 2:8

their faith would merit both God's election and salvation. However, the gift and exercise of faith owes its value entirely to God's appointed purpose. Faith is merely God's instrument, or the means God uses to unite the elect sinner with the object of his faith, Jesus Christ. They have forgotten that it is the virtue of Christ's righteousness imputed to them that is their ground of justification or acceptance with God. It is Christ believed in, rather the human act of believing, that is the efficient cause of justification.

The Westminster Shorter Catechism says: "Justification is an act of God's free grace, wherein he pardoneth all our sins, and accepteth us as righteous in His sight, only for the righteousness of Christ imputed to us, and received by faith alone." The Westminster Larger Catechism states:

Justification is an act of God's free grace unto sinners, in which he pardoneth all their sin, accepteth and accounteth their persons righteous in His sight; *not for anything wrought in them, or done by them*, but only for the perfect obedience and full satisfaction of Christ, by God imputing it to them, and received by faith alone.

What is justifying faith? Justifying faith is a saving grace, wrought in the heart of a sinner, by the Spirit and word of God; whereby he, being convinced of his sin and misery, and of the disability in himself and all other creatures to recover him out of his lost condition, not only assenteth to the truth of the promise of the gospel, but receiveth and resteth upon Christ and His righteousness therein held forth, for pardon of sin, and for the accepting and accounting of his person righteous in the sight of God for salvation.

William Stoever cites John Norton's book *Orthodox Evangelist* to explain in detail justification by faith:

The phrase "we are justified by faith," Norton observed, is a metonymy, "whereby that which belongs to the principal cause [i.e., Christ's righteousness], is attributed to [faith] the instrumental cause or secondary cause of justification. Faith in the matter of our justification, is the instrument apprehending, and applying that which doth justify." Faith justifies neither for its own worth, nor as an act of ours, but for the worth of and in virtue of the object that it apprehends, namely Christ's obedience; nor is it faith apprehending that justifies, but Christ's obedience apprehended.[85]

The Scriptures never say we are justified *on account* of our faith but always *by* or *through* faith. So, just for the sake of clarity here, it might be clearer to say "we are justified by the object of our faith, Christ Jesus" rather than to say "we are justified by the virtue of faith itself".[86]

Notice what the Westminster Confession of Faith says about the difference between the evangelical obedience of faith and Christ's obedience and righteousness:

Those whom God effectually calleth, he also freely justifieth; not by infusing righteousness into them, but by pardoning their sins, and by accounting and accepting their persons as righteous: not for anything wrought in them, or done by them, but for Christ's sake alone: not by imputing faith itself, the act of believing, or any other evangelical

---

[85] William K. B. Stoever, *A Faire and Easie Way to Heaven* (Middletown, Conn.: Wesleyan University Press, 1978),

p. 66. *Orthodox Evangelist* by Norton, pp. 301-8 (cf. 319-22).

[86] Rom. 3:27-28; 5:1; Gal.2;16-17; Titus 3:7

obedience to them, as their righteousness; but by imputing the obedience and satisfaction of Christ unto them, they receiving and resting on Him and His righteousness by faith; which faith they have not of themselves, it is the gift of God. Chap. XI, - Of Justification Article I.

When John Wesley spoke on "imputation" from Romans 4:22–24, he contradicted the Biblical or Reformed view of imputation. How does this passage read starting from verse 18:

In hope he believed against hope, that he should become the father of many nations, as he had been told [by God], "So, shall your offspring be." He did not weaken in faith when he considered his own body, which was as good as dead (since he was about a hundred years old), or when he considered the barrenness of Sarah's womb. No distrust made him waver concerning the promise of God, but he grew strong in his faith as he gave the glory to God, fully convinced that God was able to do what he had promised. That is why his faith was counted to him as righteousness. But the words "it was counted to him" were not written for his sake alone but for ours also. It will be counted to us "who believe in him who raised from the dead Jesus our Lord, who was delivered up for our trespasses and raised for our justification."

John Wesley stated, "Now it was not written for his [Abraham's] sake alone, that it was imputed to him; but for us also, to whom it shall be imputed, **faith shall stand instead of perfect obedience, in order to our acceptance with God.**"[87] At first this sounds good

---

[87] John Wesley, *Sermon on the Righteousness of Faith* (Harrisonburg, Va.: Sprinkle Publications, 1890), p. 524.

but please tell us what would be the essential difference between the requirement of perfect obedience to the law and the requirement of evangelical Arminianism which is the law of perfect obedience of faith? Both of them would require us to do them and we would take the credit for doing them. In theological circles grace is customarily defined (as in this case, God) doing someone, (in this case, the sinner), a favor he does not deserve."

It was not wrong for the O. T. saints to pursue *the law of righteousness* (the 10 commandments) by the obedience of faith, to bring forth by grace works of faith, as a means of their Sanctification and for God's glory (Eph. 2:10; Matthew 5:14-16). But God warned them that it would be wrong for them to trust in *their attempt to keep the righteousness of the law perfectly* for their Justification instead of trusting in Christ who by his perfect obedience to the law fulfilled the righteousness of the law for them as the means of their Justification (Romans 9:30-33).

Actually, the lesson taught from Romans 4 is that when we display the outward evidence of faith in God's righteousness He imputes His righteousness to us. However, we believe Wesley understands this passage differently. Wesley substitutes the value of a man's faith for the value of the object of that man's faith (which is the perfect obedience of Christ to the Law on our behalf). Wesley is saying that faith now becomes one's righteousness, rather than the object of one's faith being his righteousness. Furthermore, Wesley's emphasis on faith makes you think that God credits your faith as your own *inherent* righteousness, that merits your justification. No, faith is something wrought in them by God as His gift to save them. So, to claim that God's gift of faith is really an inherit righteousness that merits your justification rather than simply the means God uses to justify you is a subtle form of evangelical "Legalism". Wesley says your exercise of faith is your inherit righteous work of perfect obedience to the Covenant of Works. You cannot confound or blend the Covenant of Works with the Covenant of Grace by claiming your obedience of faith was a work that merited your justification.

"It is one thing to be justified *by* faith, merely as an instrument by which, a man receives the righteousness of Christ; and another, to be justified *for* faith, as an act or work of the law [as Wesley claims it can be done]. If a sinner, then, rely on his actings of faith, or works of obedience to any of the commands of the law, for a title to eternal life; he seeks to be justified by the works of the law, as really as if his works were perfect. If he depend, either in whole or in part, on his faith and repentance, for a right to any promised blessing: he thereby, so annexes that promise to believe and repent, as to form them for himself, into a covenant of works. Building his confidence before God, upon his faith, repentance, and other acts of obedience to the law, he places them in Christ's stead, and his grounds of right to promise; and so he demonstrates himself to be of the works of the law, and to be under the curse."[88]

The lesson we gain from the Romans 4 passage is that God imputes His righteousness to Abraham. But on what basis? Was Abraham's faith the source of his righteousness? No, Abraham did not place his trust in the existence or obedience of his faith as the source of his righteousness. So, what are we speaking about here? Simply this, God's righteousness was imputed or credited to Abraham when he placed his faith in *the righteousness of the object of his faith* – which is God's righteousness. When Abraham placed his faith in God's righteous character to carry out or back up His promises to Abraham, God's righteousness was imputed to Abraham. Abraham trusted in the promises of God's forgiveness, a new country (Genesis 15: 7, 18-21) and a son through whom God

---

[88] Colquhoun, John, A treatise on the Law and the Gospel, Wiley and Long Publisher, New York, 1835, p, 3

would bless the whole world (Genesis 15:4-5; 17:16, 21; 22:16-18). Even after Isaac was born Abraham continued to believe in God's righteousness to carry out His promises to Abraham. Abraham believed that whatever God did or commanded was righteous. Abraham did not question God's righteousness even when God commanded him to sacrifice his only son, Isaac.[89] Abraham believed so much in God's righteousness, that he believed that God would raise Isaac immediately from his sacrificial death, if necessary, to fulfill God's righteous promise to bless Abraham with a promised seed of posterity through Isaac. And more importantly, through Isaac's seed, Abraham saw the promise of the coming day of the "the promised seed", Jesus Christ, "in whom all the nations of the earth would be blessed" and Abraham was glad to see it.[90] Because Abraham believed in the object and source of his faith – the righteousness of God - it was accounted unto him for righteousness. So, no one should ever boast in their faith as if it is the source of their righteousness.

Martin Chemnitz had this to say about imputed righteousness and the part faith plays in the imputation of that righteousness,

"Imputation is made on the basis of Christ's righteousness. And indeed that basis is not in us, for righteousness is imputed without [our] works according to Rom. 4. Thus, faith is imputed for righteousness not because of its worthiness as a virtue but because it apprehends the merit of Christ and the mercy of God in the promise of the Gospel, in which is found both the basis and the conferring of the imputation of righteousness for blessedness."[91]

---

[89] Gen. 22:2
[90] Gen. 12:1-3; 22:1-18; Gal. 3:16
[91] Martin Chemnitz, *Examination of the Council of Trent* (St. Louis: Concordia, 1971), p. 533.

John L. Girardeau raised the question: Does this mean that if Christ is not our righteousness, He is our faith? No, Christ will always remain the object of our faith. So we must "understand *faith* here to include its object, i.e., the righteousness of Christ; so that it is not faith considered as an act which is imputed, but faith considered as including the merit which it apprehends and appropriates."[92] Wesley was incorrectly saying that the imputed righteousness of Christ (His perfect obedience) has been replaced by the so-called imputed righteousness of our imperfect, evangelical obedience of faith.

Charles Hodge wrote,

Arminians...understand the apostle to say, "Faith was imputed for righteousness," as teaching that faith was regarded or counted as complete obedience to the law. As men are unable to render that perfect obedience which the law given to Adam required, they believe God, under the gospel, according to this [Wesley's] view, is pleased to accept faith...instead of the righteousness which the law demands. Faith is thus made, not simply the instrument, but the ground of justification. It is imputed for righteousness in the sense of being regarded and treated as though it were complete obedience to the law. This is totally incorrect. Instead, the phrase "faith is imputed for righteousness" ... must express the idea that Abraham came to be treated as righteous, and not that his faith was taken in lieu of perfect obedience. Faith must either be the ground of our acceptance, or the means or instrument of our becoming

---

[92] Charles Hodge, *A Commentary of Romans* (Carlisle, Pa.: Banner of Truth Trust, 1835), p. 108.

interested in the true meritorious ground, viz., the righteousness of Christ. It cannot stand in both relations to our justification.[93]

Finally, the Puritan John Colquhoun (1748-1827) said, "Is it by the doctrine and the grace of faith, that we establish the law? Then it is plain, that they who transform the gospel or doctrine of faith, into *a new law,* requiring faith, repentance, and sincere obedience, as the proper conditions of salvation, [in the place of Christ's keeping the Law perfectly for us] do thereby *make void the law.* By substituting sincere faith, and sincere obedience, in the room of perfect obedience; as grounds of title to justification, they make void the law as a covenant; and, by inventing what they call gospel-precepts, requiring sincerity only, in the place of those old and immutable precepts, which require of believers, perfect obedience, they invalidate the authority of the law as a rule. By asserting that, Christ having satisfied for the breach of the old law of works of works, both procured and given a new, a remedial law or a law of milder terms than the old, suited to our fallen state, and accepting of sincere obedience, instead of that perfect obedience of the old law required ;" that, "Christ hath by his death obtained, that our sincere obedience to this remedial law, should be accepted for a gospel righteousness, and that we are truly justified before God, by gospel works;" "The act of faith as a principle all sincere obedience, is our righteousness, which entitles us to justification and eternal life;" and that, "The act of faith, is our justifying righteousness, *not* as it receives the righteousness of Jesus Christ, but as it is our obedience to that new law:" by these assertions, I say, they set aside

---

[93] Ibid., pp. 108–110.

the obligation of the moral law, and so make it void. Though such men have usually been called Legalists; yet, perhaps, they may, with more propriety, be termed Antinomians, or, enemies to the authority and honor of the Divine law [that Christ Jesus gave it with his perfect obedience and sacrificial atonement by his death]. They undermine, as was already hinted, the whole authority and honor of it, both as a covenant of works, and as a rule of life [for believers today]. Reader, the moment you rely on your faith and obedience, for a title to justification before God, you thereby rob the law as a covenant [of works], both of its commanding and condemning power; and . . . you invalidate the high obligation of the law as a rule of duty [for believers today]."[94] " . . . "God sent forth his Son, made of a woman, made under the law, to redeem them that were under the law" (Gal. 4:2:-5). From this passage it is plain, that Christ was made under the law, in that form in which, they whom he came to redeem were under it. Now, as they were under it as a covenant of works, it was requisite, that he also should be made under it as a covenant of works; in order to answer for them, all its demands in that form, and so to redeem them from the bondage of it. Were any man to suppose or affirm, that Christ was made under the law, not as a covenant, but merely as a *rule* ; according to such a supposition the meaning of the passage cited above, would be this: - "God sent forth his Son, made under the law as a law, to redeem them who were under the law as a rule, from the authority and obligation of it, and consequently from all

---

[94] Colquhoun, John, A Treatise on the Law and the Gospel, Wiley and Long, New York, 1835, pp, 210-211.

obedience to it." - Now would not this be the very soul of Antinomianism?"[95]

Here then there are two different kinds of imputed righteousness proposed. The first kind of imputed righteousness is extrinsic, an outside-of-us righteousness. This righteousness was done outside of us for us. It is Christ's righteousness imputed to our souls so that we could be treated *as righteous* through faith. This makes Christ's perfect righteousness the ground of our justification. On the basis of Jesus' righteousness, God *declares* us legally righteous and legally acquitted of the guilt of our sins. Therefore, the imputation of Christ's righteousness changes the legal standing of the sinner.

According to Charles Hodge,

It [imputation] produces no change in the individual to whom the imputation [of Christ's righteousness] is made; it simply alters his relation to the law. All those objections, therefore, to the doctrine expressed by this term [imputation], which are founded on the assumption that imputation alters the moral character of men; that it implies an *infusion* of either sin or holiness, rests on the misconception of its [imputation's] nature....The Protestant doctrine [of imputation] does not suppose that God regards any person or thing as being other than he or it really is. When he pronounces the unjust to be just, the word is taken in different senses. He does not pronounce the unholy to be holy; he simply declares that the demands of justice have been satisfied in behalf of those who have no righteousness of their own. In sin there are the two elements of guilt and

---

[95] Ibid, p.220

pollution—the one expressing its relation to the justice, the other its relation to the holiness of God; or, what amounts to the same thing, the one expressing its relation to the penalty, and the other its relation to the precept of the law. These two elements are separable. The moral character or inward state of a man who has suffered the penalty of a crime, and thus expiated his offence, may remain unchanged. His guilt, in the eye of human law, is removed, but his pollution remains. It would be unjust to inflict any further punishment on him for that offence. Justice is satisfied, but the man is unchanged. There may therefore be guilt where there is no moral pollution, as in the case of our blessed Lord, who bore our sins; and there may be freedom from guilt, where moral pollution remains, as in the case of every justified sinner. When, therefore, God justifies the ungodly, he does not regard him as being other than he really is. He only declares that justice is satisfied, and in that sense the man is just; he has a righteousness [Christ's righteousness imputed] which satisfies the demands of the law. His moral character is not the ground of that declaration and is not affected by it [he is not instantaneously made incapable of sinning by it]. [Whereas, Roman Catholicism teaches that God pronounces a man just only when he is just; the divine verdict is only a statement of what is true in the man himself.] Hence, [true] justification consists of three parts: 1. The imputation of the merit of Christ. 2. The remission of punishment. 3. The restoration of the favor and the blessedness forfeited by sin.[96]

---

[96] Ibid., pp. 106, 108, 112.
[205] Num. 21:8; John 3:14–15.

The second kind of imputed righteousness proposed by Mr. Wesley is an inherent or intrinsic righteousness. This is an inside-of-us kind of righteousness. It is a righteousness that comes from making the *instrumental cause* of justification (our faith) the *principle cause* of our justification. This happens when a person makes his act of faith the ground of his justification which is at the expense of the true ground of justification which is Jesus Christ's righteous obedience. Somehow, it is mistakenly thought that everyone is born with faith and that the sinner's act of believing in Jesus is something that makes God indebted to justify him. Consequently, the sinner by his own act of faith justifies himself. Here it seems the phrase "Justification by faith" takes on a new meaning. The sinner's act of faith now becomes the meritorious work that justifies him. On the contrary, faith is just the means or instrument by which the Holy Spirit applies the meritorious work of Christ to the sinner. Faith directs the sinner to look outside of himself to Christ alone as his Savior. [97] Thus, the sinner relinquishes all self-righteous confidence in anything he has done or can do by casting himself entirely on the free grace of God found in the finished work of Jesus. The sinner should not place his faith in his faith. But, if we were to take Wesley's kind of self-righteousness as the ground upon justification rests, we would be making this fatal error.

The Roman Catholic teaching of Justification says that we are justified by the Holy Spirit's work in us. They call it "Infused Righteousness". The Protestant Reformers understood the difference between "imputed righteousness" and "infused righteousness". They rejected the idea that "infused righteousness" is the basis of the sinner's justification. They said that God did a work of grace for us in Christ Jesus (Christ's doing and dying alone). This work of grace was done outside of us, but it was imputed to us.

> Those whom God effectually calleth, he also freely justifieth; not by infusing righteousness into them, but by pardoning their sins, and by accounting and accepting their persons as righteous: ***not for anything wrought in them,*** or done by them, but for Christ's sake alone: not by imputing faith itself, the act of believing, or any other evangelical obedience to them, as their righteousness; but by imputing the obedience and satisfaction of Christ unto them, they receiving and resting on Him and His righteousness by faith; which faith they have not of themselves, it is the gift of God. Westminster Confession of Faith Chap. XI, - Of Justification Article I.

God imputes Christ's righteousness to us when we trust in Christ's righteousness and not in our own righteousness. It is at this point in time, God justifies us. This is called *justification by faith.*

The Protestant Reformers, however, acknowledged that God does do a work inside us. It is called *sanctification.* Through sanctification, God infuses grace into us to impart a righteousness which causes us to change inwardly and to gradually or progressively be made more like Jesus (Eph. 4:24). "*Progressively,* this inward righteousness is *developed* as we grow in grace and in the knowledge of our Lord and Saviour Jesus Christ," Which is through our using the appointed *means* and by learning to draw our strength from the Lord. *Perfectly* [meaning perfect or complete] inward righteousness will only be consummated at our

glorification, when we shall be filled with all the fullness of God.'
[98]

But we are never solely justified on the basis of God's renewing work of sanctification in us as Roman Catholicism teaches because our sanctification never reaches perfection on this earth. Sanctification is a work done within us by the Holy Spirit but done in conjunction with our cooperation (Romans 8:4). R. D. Brinsmead explains the justification/sanctification relationship this way,

The justification/sanctification relationship finds its parallel in the relationship of the divine and human natures in the Person of Christ. Since Chalcedon, orthodoxy has maintained the distinct identity of the divine and human natures in the one Person of Jesus Christ. While there is union of the two natures, there is no fusion. Protestantism maintains that the principle of *union* without *fusion* holds good for the soteriology as well as Christology. That is to say, justification and sanctification must always be kept together, but not confused. Says Spurgeon in his sermon on "Rightly Dividing the Word of Truth": "Let the knife penetrate between the joints of the work of Christ for us, and the work of the Holy Spirit in us." And says James Buchanan: "There is, perhaps, no more subtle or plausible error, on the subject of Justification, than that which makes it rest on the indwelling presence, and the gracious work of the Holy Spirit in the heart."

Arthur Pink tells us:

[98] Pink, Arthur W., An Exposition Of The Sermon On The Mount, Baker Book House, Grand Rapids, Michigan, 1969, p.64.

"It is true that the sinner's title to heaven can consist only of the perfect righteousness of Christ being imputed to him upon his believing, yet there must be an experimental meetness for the inheritance of the saints in light as well as a legal right, and this we obtain through our regeneration and sanctification. . . . Surely [Christ's] righteousness alone secures for us a [right] standing before God, but evangelical righteousness is a certain proof, thereof and as the tree is known by its fruits so imputed righteousness can be recognized in no other way than by inward righteousness with its effects in the life. . . Thus, we read of the inward as well as the outward apparel of the Church: 'The King's daughter is all glorious *within;* her *clothing* is of wrought gold' (Psa.45:13). Two kinds of righteousness belong to the queen: her imputed righteousness is her outward robe, the 'clothing of wrought gold'; but imparted righteousness is her inward adorning, which makes her 'all glorious within.' This inward glory is the new man in the heart, with all his gifts and graces." [99]

Pink is speaking here about the fruits of sanctification or imparted righteousness given to Christians by the Holy Spirit to change their lives. Among other things it is primarily given to them in the form of the new godly habits produced by their new spiritual natures which are used to combat the old habits of their old fleshly natures (Romans chapters 6-8; 13: 12-14; Eph. 6:10-18; Col. 3:3-17). If imparted righteousness is consistently practiced in the professing Christian's life by his holy living or behavior, it

---

[99] Pink, Arthur W., An Exposition Of The Sermon On The Mount, Baker
Book House, Grand Rapids, Michigan, 1969, pp.62-63.

can be assumed as proof of Christ's righteousness imputed to their lives. But because sanctification is progressive, it has its ups and downs. Believers do experience failure in their sanctification. In times like these the believer must quickly repent and cling to the promises of God's forgiveness. There again though, if they fail to repent and do not hate and turn from their sin, they have good reason to doubt their salvation.

So, a believer can judge his sanctification introspectively. It is legitimate and important for Christians to look for some progress in their sanctification. But if they want to see progress and if they want to make their calling and election sure, they must desire to improve their walk with the Lord and by God's grace the Holy Spirit provides the help that is necessary for them to do this (Phil. 2: 12-13; 2 Peter 1:3-11; 3:18). However, if there is no change or fruit in their lives because they are constantly falling back into sin, they have good reason to doubt their salvation. If they have taken the message of the Spirit of grace of God too lightly and they constantly sin willingly after they have received the knowledge of the truth, they have counted the blood of the covenant wherewith thy were sanctified an unholy thing and they show it by forgetting they have been cleansed by it from their old sins (Heb. 10:26-31).

This is not to say that Christians will not sin or do not sin but, if they profess to be Christians, they must make an effort with the help of the Holy Spirit to work out their salvation with fear and trembling by striving for perfection in holiness (2 Cor. 7: 1; Phil. 2:12-13). They must persevere in their fight against their sin.

The Apostle Paul expressed his struggle in his sanctification in various ways. His expressions varied from, "Wretched man that I am! Who will set me free from the body of this death?' to "I am more than a conqueror through Jesus Christ who strengthens me.". His struggle in his sanctification amounted to mortifying or putting his sin nature to death. This consisted of both putting off his old sin nature or his old self with its sinful habits and putting on his new nature or his new self with its godly habits (Eph. 4:23-32; Col. 3:5-10). So, as you can see, this is a lifelong process. The believer's sanctification is slow and progressive. It can even seem to be a halting walk at times. It is like taking two steps forward and one step backwards. The believer's efforts to gain total sanctification are imperfect in this life. However, his efforts to strive for sanctification serve as a good indicator to him that he is rightfully attempting to make his calling and election sure. But he must always remember that his efforts to become more subjectively holy cannot serve as the formal cause or ground of his justification. The formal cause or ground of his justification and his acceptance with God will always remain the objective truth of Christ's imputed righteousness.

The justification/sanctification relationship may be expressed in terms of the *for us/in us* relationship. With Rome [Roman Catholicism], justification is essentially a work of God's grace *in us*—a regenerating, renewing act within man. The work of the Holy Spirit in the heart therefore becomes the *formal cause,* or ground, of acceptance with God.

The Roman Catholic Council of Trent (1547 A.D.) (which has never been changed) Chapter 16 Canon 11 decrees:

> "If anyone says that men are justified either by
> the sole imputation of the justice of Christ or

by the sole remission of sins, to the exclusion
of the grace and *charity which is poured forth
in their hearts by the Holy Ghost,* and remains
in them, or also that the grace by which we are
justified is only the good will of God, let him
be anathema."

One extract from many of the Canones of the Council
of Trent used to enunciate the Roman Catholic
soteriology states that "Justification is not the *mere
remission of sins but also the sanctification and
renovation of the inward man* through the voluntary
reception of grace and gifts of grace; whereby an unjust
man becomes just, the enemy a friend, so that he may
be an heir according to the hope of eternal life."

With the Reformers, the sole ground of acceptance with
God is what Christ has already done *for us* in the concrete
historical acts of His life, death and resurrection. This
means that one system [Roman Catholicism] has a
subjective basis of justification while the other [Reformed
Protestants] has an objective basis.[100]

"What then does the biblical term "justification by faith" mean?
The Roman Catholics teach that God justifies us primarily and
ultimately by all the righteous works that God does *in us* and
through us by His Holy Spirit (The Council of Trent). However,
God's work done within us by the subjective spiritual renewal of
the inner man does not make us legally righteous. Instead, the initial
purpose of the Holy Spirit working in us is to impart faith to our

---

[100] R. D. Brinsmead, "Pinpointing the Issues in the Conflict with
Rome," *Present Truth*, vol. 4, no. 5, October 1975, pp. 42–43.

hearts to cause us to trust in Christ's righteous acts done legally **for us** for our justification. Thus, it is God's grace that justifies us when He uses the effective means of His gift of faith to show us that the principle, formal, or ultimate cause of our "Justification" is based on what Jesus accomplished *for us,* and *outside of us* 2000 years ago. [101]

A summary of basic Catholic/Protestant differences on Justification by faith can be summarized as follows:

Protestant	Catholic
1. To justify means to account as righteous.	1. To justify means to make righteous.
2. Justification comes by the imputation of Christ's righteousness.	2. Justification comes by an infusion of grace.
3. The grace of God in Christ makes the believer acceptable and pleasing in God's sight.	3. Sanctifying grace in the believer makes him acceptable to God.
4. Man is justified by an extrinsic righteousness (a righteousness wholly without)	4. Man is justified by an intrinsic righteousness (a righteousness which God puts within man.
5. God justifies the ungodly who believe.	5. God only justifies those who are born again.
6. Justification is God's verdict upon man in the Person of Christ.	6. Justification is God's regenerating act in man.
7. The sinner is justified by by Christ's imputed righteousness alone.	7. The sinner cannot be justified by imputed righteousness alone but by righteousness poured

---

[101] Acts 28:27; Romans 3:24; Titus 3:7

8. Justification enables God to treat the sinner *as if* he were were just.

9. The believer is pronounced righteous because Christ, his substitute, is found righteous before God.

10. Justification is a declaration of the fact that Jesus, who stands in man's place, is righteousness.

11. Justification is so infinite that it cannot be reduced to an intra-human experience

12. Justification is received by by faith alone.

13. Justification enables God to bring regeneration and and sanctification to the to the heart of the believer.

14. Sin still remains in man's man's nature after justification and sanctification.

15. The believer can claim no merit for good works performed by God's enabling grace. Good works are acceptable only through

into his heart.

8. Justification means that the sinner *is really made* just.

9. The believer is pronounced righteous because the Spirit of grace has made him righteous.

10. Justification is a declaration of what is a fact in the man . himself

11. Justification is an act of grace within man.

12 Justification comes by faith which has become active by charity.

13. Regenerating grace enables God to justify the believer.

14. Justification wholly eradicates sin; only concupiscence and weakness remain.

15. Sanctifying grace within the believer makes good works acceptable to God.

the mediation of Christ's imputed
righteousness, which covers all
human deficiencies in the good works
of the believer.

| 16. At all times the believer is accepted only in the Person of Christ, his Substitute. | 16. Sanctifying grace within the believer makes him acceptable to God. |

102

From this it follows, there are two opposite methods of justification, - the Roman Catholic method, which is justification that comes by an infusion of righteousness and the other method - the biblical method, described to us by the Protestant Reformers is justification that comes only by Christ's imputed righteousness. The Roman Catholic method substitutes the personal obedient exercise of faith for the vicarious obedience of Christ, the Redeemer. The Roman Catholics have confused "Justification" with "Sanctification". They have confounded Jesus' work done for us with the Holy Spirit's work done inside us. They have virtually substituted the work of the Spirit in us for the work of Christ for us.

The Roman Catholics teach "that Christ's merit initiates our salvation, but it views 'infused grace', as merit that God puts within a man. In this way, Christ's merit becomes [or shares with] human merit. [And while] Catholic theologians clearly affirm that there is no merit in 'good works' done by the sinner [they at the same time also affirm that] . . . when 'good works' are done by sanctifying grace within a person, they regard such works as truly meritorious. In short, Catholicism affirms the **saving merit of infused righteousness** (it is the gracious work of the Holy Spirit in man that

---

102 "Understanding The Roman Catholic Doctrine of Justification printed in the October 1975 issue of Present Truth magazine.

ultimately saves him)."[103] They teach "that the sinner is justified on the basis of an inherent righteousness [the work of the Holy Spirit in man] that has been infused into his heart, and which, in turn, is the fruit of the co-operation of the human will with prevenient grace. Prevenient grace is a degree of grace conferred upon all mankind. It operates with the will before full regeneration and enables repentance and faith to precede and condition regeneration. This applies to what they call the first justification; in all following justification the good works of man come into consideration as the formal cause or ground of justification. "[104] However, John Girardeau has defined and explained to us how this is a Romanist theological error. He writes this about their prevenient grace:

> [It is only] a degree of grace imparting ability sufficient to enable every man to make a possible salvation actually his own. Now, the argument is short: a degree of grace which does not regenerate would be a degree of grace which would not bestow life upon the spiritually dead sinner. If it did infuse spiritual life it would of course be regenerating grace; but it is denied to be regenerating grace. No other grace would be sufficient for the dead sinner but regenerating or life-giving grace. How could grace enable the dead sinner to perform living functions—to repent, to believe in Christ, to embrace Christ, to embrace salvation—without first giving him life? In a word, sufficient grace [i.e., prevenient grace] which is not regenerating grace is a palpable impossibility. An ability sufficient to enable the dead sinner to discharge living functions but not sufficient to make him live is an impossibility. The Romanist is therefore shut up

---

[103] Ibid., p. 12.
[104] L. Berkhof, *Systematic Theology* (Grand Rapids: Eerdmans, 1939, 1974), p. 523.

to a choice between two alternatives: either he must confess sufficient grace to be regenerating grace, and then he abandons his doctrine; or he must maintain that grace is sufficient for a dead sinner which does not make him live, and then he asserts an impossibility.

If to this the Arminian replies that the functions which sufficient [prevenient] grace enables the sinner to perform are not functions of spiritual life, it follows: first, that he contradicts his own position that grace imparts a degree of spiritual life to every man; and secondly, that he maintains that a spiritually dead man discharges functions which cause him to live, which is infinitely absurd....[105]

The Arminian, John Fletcher, a contemporary of Mr. Wesley and the staunch defender of his views, said, "The righteousness of God [is] the very thing which God imputes to us for righteousness." He says that the righteousness of faith is the righteousness of God: "Our own righteousness of faith...is the righteousness of God." He says that the righteousness of faith is inherent righteousness: The conclusion is undeniable that the righteousness of God imputed is our own inherent righteousness of faith.[106]

We ask the reader, "What is the difference between believing that we are justified by the inherent righteousness of our act of faith or believing we are justified by the inherent righteousness of our act of obedience to the law? There is no difference because both methods are based on our works or deeds and both methods produce

---

[105] Girardeau, *Calvinism and Evangelical Arminianism*, pp. 316–317.
[106] Ibid., p. 530.

the same legalistic, Pharisaic, self-righteousness. What did the apostle Paul, an ex-Pharisee, have to say about seeking justification on the ground of his own righteousness? He said this:

> Though I might also have confidence in the flesh. If any other man thinketh that he hath whereof he might trust in the flesh, I more: Circumcised the eighth day, of the stock of Israel, of the tribe of Benjamin, an Hebrew of the Hebrews; as touching the law, a Pharisee; concerning zeal, persecuting the church; touching the righteousness which is in the law, blameless. But what things were gain to me, those I counted loss for Christ. Yea doubtless, and I count all things but loss for the excellency of the knowledge of Christ Jesus my LORD: for whom I have suffered the loss of all things, and do count them but dung, that I may win Christ. And be found in him, not having mine own righteousness, which is of the law, but that which is through the faith of Christ, the righteousness which is of God by faith. (Phil. 3:4–9)

Paul is disclaiming any inherent righteousness of his own, and he claims instead to have the imputed, alien (outside of him and separate from him) righteousness of Christ which is of God by faith. Christ alone performed Paul's righteousness. Even though this saving righteousness is reckoned to Paul's account, it is safely kept in heaven in the person of Christ for Paul so that he can never lose it. Those who say that their faith is their righteousness contradict Paul because faith cannot be through faith and by faith. Paul, on the other hand, declares the righteousness he has "is through the faith of Christ, the righteousness which is of God by faith."

Those Protestant Arminians who disagree with us may say the righteousness that Paul speaks against in Philippians 3:4–9 is "of the law," and the righteousness they have is "of faith." But there is really no difference between the "righteousness of the law" and the Arminian's "righteousness of faith." The first is a righteousness that comes by one's obedience to the law, and the other one is righteousness that comes by one's evangelical obedience to the commands to believe, to repent, and to persevere in holiness. Furthermore, many Arminians believe that once a person decides to obey God's evangelical commands, God is then required by His promise to reward that person with salvation.

Dr. Miner Raymond, another person from the Wesleyan camp, has said it the clearest. This statement should leave no doubt in the reader's mind about the Arminian view of evangelical obedience. Dr. Raymond said this:

> The exercise of man's God-given powers is with the man himself and is made within limits subject to his own free choice. God no more believes for a man than he breathes and eats, walks and works, for him; faith, as a power to believe, is the gift of God [i.e., God gave all men the inherent power to believe]; believing, the exercise of faith, is the act of man. This act he must put forth or be damned; if he puts it forth he will be saved; he cannot be lost while believing in Christ. If anyone chooses to call that act of faith works, we shall not contend; if they still affirm that, in asserting that this faith is an act of the human will, we teach the doctrine of salvation by works, very well; we care not what name it is called; we abide the affirmative of the doctrine that a man's eternal destiny is dependent upon a somewhat which he himself may do or leave undone, and that somewhat is called in the Bible faith. To those to whom the Gospel is preached, it is a cordial confiding in Jesus Christ as the Son of God and Saviour of men; to those who have not heard the gospel, it is the same faith in the form of

a filial trust in the mercy of God; or, as it has been designated, "the spirit of faith with the purpose of righteousness."[107]

The truth is, however, those who are not ordained to eternal life continue throughout their lives to stubbornly refuse to believe in and follow Jesus. They do not wish to seek salvation through Him or wish to be holy, and God leaves them where they desire to be. So, God's decree of reprobation is not inconsistent with their unregenerate wills. Jesus, the Great Shepherd, said to some of these people at Jerusalem, "Ye believe not, because ye are not of my sheep."[108] Since they were not His sheep, Jesus knew they would never come to believe in Him.

In addition to the gift of faith, God is also the one who gives us the gift of true repentance at our conversion. Repentance is not inherent in any person. Repentance has to be granted from God before a person can repent. Notice these verses:

Turn thou us unto thee, O LORD, and we shall be turned. (Lam. 5:21)

Him [Jesus] hath God exalted with his right hand to be a Prince and a Saviour, for to give repentance to Israel, and forgiveness of sins. (Acts 5:31)

And when they heard these things, they held their peace, and glorified God, saying, Then to the Gentiles also hath God granted repentance unto life. (Acts 11:18 ASV)

---

[107] Ibid., p. 536-537.
[108] John 10:26.

> In meekness instructing those that oppose themselves; if God peradventure will give them repentance to the acknowledging of the truth. (2 Tim. 2:25)

True repentance produces real changes in us for better behavior. It begins with sorrow, shame, and deep humiliation for the indignity shown to a holy, gracious, and merciful God. The changes brought about in us by this sorrow is a conscious, long-lasting renewing of our minds by the Holy Spirit.[109] We determine to turn from and forsake our sins. We become angry at them, take sides with God against them, and feel a hatred and self-loathing for them. We will not spare any of our favorite sins from exposure when we confess them to God. Motivated by love for Him, we desire to turn from sin and to walk with God in all the ways of His commandments. These penitent actions flow from justification and from thankful hearts that have already received God's forgiveness by faith in Jesus' atonement.

The repentant Christian's main purpose in life is to glorify God with his or her life.

> "So whether you eat or drink, or whatever you do, do
> it all for the glory of God."[110]

To glorify God you must give yourself (your mind, affections, will and bodies) as your reasonable service to God.[111] How do you learn how to do this? You learn it by reading God's word daily. When you abide in His word your mind is renewed so that your life can be transformed instead of being shaped or molded by this world's culture, practices and

---

[109] Rom. 12:2; Titus 3:5; 2 Cor. 4:16; Eph. 4:17–32; Col. 3:1–4:1.

[110] 1 Corinthians 10:31

[111] Romans 12:1-2; John 17:17; Psalm 119:9

philosophies.[112] Abide in God's word by reading, meditating and memorizing it. Ask God to apply His word to you personally as you read it so you can imitate Christ. But when the you fail to abide in God's word your love for Christ cools, and you cease to feed and strengthen your new man or your new self. Consequently, you become weak in your faith. You must stir up your affections for Christ and meditate, or fix your mind on heavenly things lest they decay and you lose your first love.[113]

The Christian must also be motivated by his daily schedule of Bible reading and prayer to face and contend with temptation and sin. God's elect person is concerned about glorifying God on earth by battling daily against the Devil's temptations and his own sin nature.[114] Since a Christian is both a natural born sinner and a supernaturally reborn saint, he struggles within himself. [115] The Christian's inner conflict is caused by his old sinful self and its sinful habits competing with his new self and its new godly habits. Paradoxically, the Christian's war cry is "I have met the enemy and the enemy is me" (my old self, my sin nature).[116] The Apostle Paul tells us what the Christian must do about this conflict with himself. He says the Christian must put off the old man or self with its sinful imaginations and affections and put on the new man or self with its desire to better know and honor Christ.[117]

In this battle with sin the Christian must realize that he has been placed into spiritual union with Christ so that he is now

---

[112] John 15:7-8; Ephesians 4:20-23

[113] Revelation 2:4; Colossians 3:1-3; Philippians 4:8

[114] Ephesians 6:10-18

[115] Romans 7:14-25; Galatians 5:17

[116] James 1:14-15; 4:1; Psalm 73:22

[117] Ephesians 4:22-24; Colossians 3: 1-10

made one with Christ.[118] And since he is one with Christ, the Christian must understand that what has happened to Christ has happened to him. The Christian must acknowledge that it is through his spiritual union with Christ and His crucifixion and death on the Cross that he too was crucified and died with Christ. Paul said, "God forbid that I should glory, save in the cross of our Lord Jesus Christ, whereby the world is crucified unto me, and I unto the world." It is because of this historical past event that took place in Christ's life, that the Christian can now put sin to death in his own life. So, the Christian must, once for all, reckon himself crucified with Christ and dead to his sin nature to put end to his loving relationship to it. Then he must remind himself daily thereafter of the truth of his union with Christ when he is faced with temptation.

Furthermore, when Christ was resurrected the Christian was made to take part in that event also by virtue of his spiritual union with Christ, The Christian was raised with Christ and made alive and available to serve God.[119] The Christian can and must call on God to deliver him from temptation and sin with the same resurrection power that was used to raise Christ Jesus from the grave. He must draw from that same life-giving resurrection power that God promises him in order to live a godly life.[120]

The Christian should know that under the Covenant of Grace he has now been given liberty from sin's dominion.[121] The Christian is no longer under any obligation to live according to the flesh (i.e., according to his indwelling sin nature) or to make

---

[118] Ephesians 5:22-33; 1 Corinthians 6:17

[119] Romans 6:4; 1 Peter 1:3-4; Romans 12:1-2

[120] Romans 6:4; 1 Peter 1:3-4; Ephesians 1:19; 2:4-7; Colossians 2:12,20

[121] Galatians 5:13, 16-24

provision for it. He has been freed from the bondage of his sin nature and it is no longer his master.

However, when the Christian is not careful about his walk with God and not mindful of the daily battle he is engaged in with his old nature, he can backslide. The Christian's sin nature will continue to try to regain its mastery over the Christian so it can then exert its full force to bring the Christian down to the worst version of himself. When the Christian neglects his daily duty of putting his sin nature to death by starving it he allows it greater life. He allows it to become even stronger by feeding his mind with the things of the world (the lust of the flesh, the lusts of the eyes and the pride of life). When instead he should be feeding his new nature daily with God's word and he should be calling upon God in prayer for strength for each new day. In doing this he will not fail to gain God's supply of resurrection power to contend with temptation and sin. [122]

The Christian must be sensitive to the strategies of Satan and be ready to face temptation with the full armor of God [123] When the Christian recognizes he is being tempted he must immediately pray and call upon God's resurrection power to deny temptation a place in his mind [124]. He must not stop to contemplate the temptation, that is, he must not take the time to daydream about it and then plot or scheme to make it happen. Instead his only response should a quick and godly response like Joseph's to the temptation presented to him by Potiphar's wife's proposal. [125] The Christian must first flee the temptation presented to his mind and then flee physically, if necessary. It has been suggested that we should make a covenant with our

---

[122] Psalm 119:9 (KJV); 1Corinthians 10:13

[123] Ephesians 6:10-17

[124] Philippians 3:10; 2 Corinthians 13:4; Ephesians 3:20; 6:10-18a; Colossians 1:11; 2 Peter 1:3

[125] Genesis 39:9; James 1:12-15

eyes as Job did with his (Job 31:1). When he looked at someone or something that was sinfully attractive to him, he would quickly turn his eyes away from them.

The Christian must be quick to recognize temptations that lead him to his old past favorite sins; those sins he was unwilling to part with for a time. Since he is already acquainted with past temptations that have led him to his old besetting sins he should not have to be reminded where they eventually lead him, that is, down the same dead-end road of guilt and shame. The Christian must learn to be wise and take up his own cross daily and habitually deny himself of the temporary pleasures of sin when he is tempted.[126]

While the Christian is being tempted to sin he must remind himself of God's grace and the horror, the vileness, the pain, and the sadness of his sins that caused Jesus to be nailed to the cross. If he chooses instead to willfully disregard God's grace or take it for granted while he is being tempted, he shows that he despises Christ and he does not care about grieving the Holy Spirit. He also shows that he has in some way become discontented with God's providence and worse still, he is ungrateful for God's grace. So, when the Christian chooses to sin it is like trading his birthright (spiritual adoption) for a bowl of soup. By taking God's grace for granted and submitting to temptation he will harden his heart towards God and abuse God's grace.[127] How? Along with the Satan's many temptations the Christian may also be tempted to think that he can indulge in his sin and always ask for God's forgiveness later on.[128]

But the Christian should know he cannot commit sin with impunity (Numbers 32:23). And what happens when he lapses

---

[126] Titus 2:11-12

[127] Galatians 5:13, 16-24

[128] Numbers 32:23

in his love and faithfulness to Christ and disobeys God's commandments and he delays his repentance and his confession of disobedience? God will chastise him. So, when the Christian sins, he must quickly repent. He must humble himself before God and confess his specific sins to God. God, in turn, promises to forgive and cleanse him.

> 1 John 1:9 says, "If we confess our sins, he is faithful and just to forgive us our sins, and to cleanse us from all unrighteousness."

> "He knows our frame and knows we are but dust" and "if we are faithless, He remains faithful, for He cannot deny Himself "(2 Tim, 2:13).]

Christian's sins may go undetected for a while. They may continue to amuse themselves with their sinful, secret, fantasies, daydreams, or imaginations and eventually they scheme how to put them into practice. This will harden their hearts towards God. And, if the Christian's refuses to repent and he continues to practice his sin even when it is pointed out to him from God's Word through the convicting power of the Holy Spirit, he can be sure the shame and guilt on his conscience will cause him to feel like a hypocrite. Or he may be fearful that his sins will surely catch up with him and they will be discovered.by someone. Or even if they are not discovered by someone, he may be fearful that God will judge his sin and chastise him for it. Furthermore, if the Christian continues to refuse to repent, he will soon become spiritually weak and neglect to read God's Word, or neglect to attend church worship services and nrglect to fellowship with Christians or shy away from openly witnessing or testifying to others about his faith and the gospel.

Eventually, the Christian will become miserable by his guilty conscience. He will experience the Holy Spirit's conviction for turning his back on God's grace and yielding to the bold madness of his sin nature. But, if he refuses to repent at this point, he will be chastened by God. Yet, it is because God loves the Christian that God also promises to correct him or chastise him when he strays from God's love and fails to walk in a manner worthy of his calling (Heb. 12:1-17; Psalm 89:30-34). The Holy Spirit's conviction of his sin and God's chastisement of him are God's fatherly kindness meant to bring him to repentance and to bring him back into fellowship with God.

> And ye have forgotten the exhortation which speaketh unto you as children, "My son, despise not thou the chastening of the LORD, nor faint when thou art rebuked of him: for whom the LORD loveth he chasteneth, and scourgeth every son whom he receiveth." If ye endure chastening, God dealeth with you as with sons; for what son is he whom the father chasteneth not? But, if ye be without chastisement, whereof all are partakers, then are ye bastards, and not sons. Furthermore we have had fathers of our flesh which corrected us, and we gave them reverence: shall we not much rather be in subjection unto the Father of spirits, and live? For they verily for a few days chastened us after their own pleasure; but he for our profit, that we might be partakers of his holiness. (Heb. 12:5–10; see also Prov. 3:11–12)

Were the beloved prophets of the Old Covenant chastised when they sinned? Did God look the other way when Moses struck the rock? No, God chastened Moses for not obeying His instructions. In his anger at the Israelites, Moses disobeyed God's instructions to speak to the rock and instead Moses struck the rock twice and he was not allowed to enter the Promised Land (Numbers 20:8-12). Did God overlook or disregard King David's sins just because he was a man after God's own heart? Definitely not! God sent the prophet Nathan to get David to acknowledge, confess, and repent of his sins. We have David's confession to God recorded in Psalm 51. God forgave David and spared his life, but he still faced the consequences of his sins. God spared David's life. David lost a good, loyal soldier, Uriah the Hittite and David lost his child that he had out of wedlock with Bathsheba. Then God told him the sword would never depart from his house. David had trouble in his family for the rest of his life. His son Absalom shamed him openly when he took his father's wives. And worst of all, David gave great occasion by his sins to the enemies of God to blaspheme His name.

God can correct us or chastise us by withdrawing His blessings from us, if we continue to ignore His warnings from His Word about sinning against Him.[129] God will correct us as He did the Levite priests in Malachi 2:1–5 for going through the motions of worship, but really not worshipping God from the heart. He can curse us with bad health, unproductiveness, indebtedness, problems with our children, or by allowing our sins to be discovered to our shame. We should not tell ourselves that these curses are meant only for David and the Old Testament priesthood and they have nothing to do with us as New Testament Christians. Think again! New Testament Christians are called to be a holy nation just like the Old Testament believers.[130]

For those that think the God of the New Testament cannot discipline his children as severely as the God of the Old Testament did, think again. God can discipline us for our sins as He did this with Ananias and Sapphira who lied to the Holy Spirit and for the Corinthians' sins who took the Lord's Supper unworthily He sent

---

[129] Deut. 27 and 28.
[130] Exod. 19:3–6; Isa. 61:6; 1 Pet. 2:5, 9; Rev. 1:6; 5:10; 20:6.

them sickness and death. God can allow us to suffer the consequences of our sins in this life, without taking our salvation from us.[131]

Because God has made a covenant with His Son and. because we are united with Christ, those Covenant of Grace promises extend to us, too. All the covenant promises to us are made good forever because they are yea and amen in Christ Jesus, our Surety.[132] The prophet Isaiah wrote,

> In a little wrath I hid my face from thee for a moment; but with everlasting kindness will I have mercy on thee, saith the LORD thy Redeemer....For the mountains shall depart, and the hills be removed; but my kindness shall not depart from thee, neither shall the covenant of my peace be removed, saith the LORD that hath mercy on thee. (Isa. 54:8, 10)

Once the Christian repents he is restored by God's grace and he perseveres in his walk and covenant fellowship with God by continuing to believe God's promises of forgiveness and cleansing. After being humbled by his sin and then receiving God's forgiveness and cleansing and the joy of renewed fellowship with God, the Christian is then encouraged to press on forgetting what lies behind and reaching forward to what lies ahead, that is, the goal for the prize of the upward call of God in Christ Jesus. Thus, by God's grace the Christian is motivated and compelled by his love for Christ to take up his spiritual armor again and contend with Satan and his own indwelling sin once more.[133] This is how a Christian under the Covenant of

---

[131] 1 Cor. 11:30; 3:10–17

[132] 2 Cor. 1:20.

[133] 1 Corinthians 10:13; Ephesians 6:10;2 Corinthians 10:3-5; Hebrews 12:1-3; Psalm 51; Philippians 3:12-14

Grace contends in his spiritual warfare against temptation and sin until he goes to be with the Lord in heaven.

CHAPTER 6

GOD'S AWESOME GRACE IN ACTION

Faith, repentance, and perseverance in holiness are necessary responses to God's redemptive call. However, these necessary responses are gracious gifts God granted only to those sinners He decreed He would choose before the world was created. They are not to be understood as the conditions that sinners must perform so God will choose them. Nevertheless, some believe Christ's atonement only made it possible for God to set up these conditions for election. It is thought that once they perform these conditions, God is obligated to elect them.

Consequently, once sinners believe they have performed these conditions, they have no reason to praise God for electing them, because they determined their own election by performing the conditions themselves. In this case, it is the sinner who elects God, not God who elects the sinner. So, what is the bottom line here? *This distorted view of election proves to be nothing more than a "works salvation" since God would elect sinners who performed the good works of faith, repentance, and perseverance in holiness.*

John Wesley presents this distorted view in his writings. He said:

> The Scripture tells us plainly what predestination is: it is God's fore-appointing obedient believers to salvation, not without, "but according to his foreknowledge" of all their

works "from the foundation of the world."...We may consider this a little further. God, from the foundation of the world, foreknew all men's believing or not believing. And according to this, his foreknowledge, he chose or elected all obedient believers, as such, to salvation.

Predestination according to Mr. Wesley does not actually mean what he thinks it means. The term *Predestination* "holds that from eternity [past] God has foreordained all things which come to pass, including the final salvation or reprobation of man." [134] Wesley's idea of God's predestination is that God only elects people who He foreknows are going to believe. And based on God's foreknowledge of their believing, God elects them to salvation. However, this doctrine is poles apart from scriptural truth. God's predestination is not based on His foreknowledge of whether someone will believe. Rather, predestination is based on God's Decree of Election in which He elected certain individual sinners to be foreordained to salvation before time began and the rest of mankind were passed over. So, God's foreknowledge of a person's election came from His deliberate choice of that person to salvation before time began, not from His foreknowledge that they would believe later after time began. So, why would God base the certainty of His foreknowledge of a person's election on what He foresees will happen later *in time* (i.e., that a person will eventually believe) when He knows that He has already predestinated them *before time* to believe? Is it because Mr. Wesley is unwilling to give away an inch of his teaching of the autonomous "Free Will" of man?

Mr. Wesley went on to say,

---

[134] Baker's Dictionary of Theology, Baker Book House, 1975, p. 415

If the saints are chosen to salvation, through believing the truth…they were not chosen before they believed; much less before they had a being, any more than Christ was slain before he had a being. So plain is it that they were not elected till they believed, although God "calleth things that are not as though they were."…It is plain the act of electing is *in time*, though known of God before; who according to his knowledge, often speaketh of the things "which are not as though they were." And thus is the great stumbling block about election taken away, that men may "make their calling and election sure."[135]

Regretfully, Mr. Wesley conveniently ignores the chronological order of events listed in Romans 8:29-30. Before time began God foreknew those He chose to save through Christ. His kind intention to choose His elect was to predestine their adoption to make them to be like His Son. Ephesians 1:4 says His choice of His elect took place before time began. It reads:

Just as He [God] chose us in Him [Jesus] before the foundation of the world, that we would be holy and blameless before Him. In love He predestined us to adoption as sons through Jesus Christ to Himself, according to the kind intention of His will, to the praise of the glory of His grace which He freely bestowed on us in the Beloved [Jesus].

---

[135] John Wesley, *The Scripture Doctrine concerning Predestination, Election and Reprobation*, from *Works*, vol. 9, in John L. Girardeau, *Calvinism and Evangelical Arminianism* (Harrisonburg, Va.: Sprinkle Publications, 1890, 1984), p. 22.

This, of course, means they became God's elect before they were born which in turn means they became the elect of God before they believed. So, for Wesley to say that " the elect are chosen to salvation through believing the truth" is putting words into God's mouth as though they were from God's mouth. God elected His chosen ones out of the good pleasure of His will.[136] He did not elect them to salvation because He foresaw their faith.[137]

Furthermore, Wesley said, "they [the elect] were not chosen before they believed, much less before they had a being, any more than Christ was slain before He had being." This is not true. The elect were chosen before they had a being just as Christ was slain [sphazo or sphatto] before He as God the Son took to Himself a human nature and a human body and became a human being. Christ was slain in the mind and purpose of God before time began, even before the foundations of the universe were laid and He is looked upon by God as the slain Lamb at present.[138] Likewise, each and every particular person God chose to elect before time began for Himself as His own also existed in the mind and purpose of God before they had their being (Jeremiah 1:4-5; Psalm 139:16).

Mr. Wesley makes both God's purpose to elect and His election conditional. According to Wesley God purposes to elect people only if those people believe. And even though He foresees that some will believe, He will not actually elect them until they believe. So according to Mr. Wesley, one's act of faith is the condition for his election. This, however, could not be farther from the truth. Faith is the means of salvation but not of election.

---

[136] Isa. 46:10

[137] Rom. 9:11

[138] Rev. 13:8; KJV, NIV, Wuest N.T. version, New Testament in Modern Speech by R. F. Weymouth; Rev.5:6; 1 Peter 19-20

Dr. T. N. Ralston, who holds the same views as Mr. Wesley, said, "This election is almost universally spoken of as conditioned upon repentance toward God and faith in our Lord Jesus Christ; and if, in any passages, the condition is not specifically mentioned, it is plainly implied. If, in any sense, this election is eternal, it is so only in the purpose of the Divine Being to elect; and as the election itself is conditioned upon faith, it follows that **the eternal purpose to elect was based upon that foreseen faith**." [139] A person of this persuasion "holds that the election of individuals is conditioned upon the divine foresight of their faith and perseverance in holiness. Election, then, according to him [Ralston], is not really the election of individuals to a certain salvation, but…the election of a condition upon which individuals may attain to salvation."[140]

According to Dr. Ralston,

Men may do despite unto the Spirit of grace by which they have been sanctified. Till probation terminates, final destiny is a contingency. Two opposite eternities are either of them possible, and the question is decided, never by anything external to the man himself, but by his own free choice, aided by the grace of God. [141]

John Girardeau argued that Dr. Ralston "makes regeneration a work, jointly wrought by divine and human agency, and holds that,

---

[139] Ralston, T. O. Summers, ed. *Elements of Divinity*, vol. 2, in John L. Girardeau, *Calvinism and Evangelical Arminianism* (Harrisonburg, Va.: Sprinkle Publications, 1890, 1984), p.28.
[140] John L. Girardeau, *Calvinism and Evangelical Arminianism* (Harrisonburg, Va.: Sprinkle Publications, 1890, 1984), pp. 45–46.
[141] Ibid., p.28 .

in the order of thought, repentance precedes faith and faith precedes regeneration. The question being, What conditions salvation? His answer is—and it deserves special notice as indicative of the development of Protestant Evangelical Arminian theology—'That salvation is conditioned upon man's acceptance, and co-operation by faith, is implied in all the commands, precepts, exhortations, admonitions, entreaties, promises, and persuasions of the Word of God; and such passages as the following [and here Ralston lists some Bible verses which he believes] are equivalent to a direct affirmation that *man determines the question of his salvation*: 'He that believeth shall be saved; he that believeth not shall be damned,' etc."[142] Thus, if we agree with Dr. Ralston, that the sinner's free-will choice to accept Jesus is the determining cause of his salvation, it follows that by making that choice he also meets the condition for "election" when he believes. Consequently, the sinner, not God, is the cause of election.

On the contrary, God's election is unconditional. His choice of sinners is based solely on the good pleasure and gracious purpose of His will. There are no conditions we must meet to be chosen by God.

> In love, having predestinated us unto the adoption of children by Jesus Christ to himself, *according to the good pleasure of his will*, to the praise of the glory of his grace....being predestinated according to the purpose of him *who worketh all things after the counsel of his own will*. (Eph. 1:4–6, 11)

> Who has saved us and called us with a holy calling, not according to our works, *but according to His own purpose*

---

[142] Ibid., pp. 28-29.

and grace, which was given to us in Christ Jesus before time began. (2 Tim. 1:9 (NKJV; see also Rom. 8:28)

The Swiss Form of Agreement states:

Before the foundations of the world were laid, God, in Christ Jesus our Lord, formed an eternal purpose, in which, out of the mere good pleasure of his will, without any foresight of the merit of works or of faith, unto the praise of his glorious grace, he elected a certain and definite number of men, in the same mass of corruption and lying in a common blood, and so corrupt in sin, to be, in time, brought to salvation through Christ the only Sponsor and Mediator, and, through the merit of the same, by the most powerful influence of the Holy Spirit regenerating, to be effectually called, regenerated, and endued with faith and repentance. And in such wise indeed did God determine to illustrate his glory, that he decreed, first to create man in integrity, then to permit his fall, and finally to pity some from among the fallen, and so to elect the same.[143]

God chose His elect people before they were born. His choice of them came before their choice of Him. Sinners cannot boast that God chose them because they decided to choose Him.

You have not chosen Me, but I have chosen you. (John 15:16 NEW BERKELEY)

Even as He [God the Father] chose us in Him [Jesus] before the foundation of the world. (Eph. 1:4)

---

[143] The Swiss Form of Agreement (Formula Consensus Helvetica).

But we are always bound to offer thanks to God for you, brothers, beloved by the LORD as you are, because from the beginning God chose you for salvation by the Spirit's sanctifying [setting you apart for God] work and by faith in the truth. (2 Thess. 2:13 NEW BERKELEY)

Blessed be the God and Father of our LORD Jesus Christ, who has blessed us with every spiritual blessing in the heavenly places in Christ, just as *He chose us in Him* before the foundation of the world, that we should be holy and without blame before Him in love, having predestinated us to adoption as sons by Jesus Christ to Himself, according to the good pleasure of His will, to the praise of the glory of His grace, by which He made us accepted in the Beloved. In Him we have redemption through His blood, the forgiveness of sins, according to the riches of His grace which He made to abound toward us in all wisdom and prudence, having made known to us the mystery of His will, according to His good pleasure which He purposed in Himself, that in the dispensation of the fullness of the times He might gather together in one all things in Christ, both which are in heaven and which are on earth—in Him: In Him also we have obtained an inheritance, being predestinated according to the purpose of Him who works all things according to the counsel of His will, that we who first trusted in Christ should be to the praise of His glory. In Him you also trusted, after you heard the word of truth, the gospel of your salvation; in whom also, having believed, you were sealed with the Holy Spirit of promise, who is the guarantee of our inheritance until the redemption of the purchased possession, to the praise of His glory. (Eph. 1:3–14 NKJV)

> We also have the testimony of His Spirit of adoption
> witnessing with our spirits that we are the children of
> God; which Spirit is the down payment or earnest of our
> inheritance whereby we are sealed to the day of our
> redemption. [144]

God chose particular sinners before time existed. He wrote each of their names in the Lamb's Book of Life before the foundation of the world was laid.[145] God has from eternity past determined by His own choice which sinners will believe His gospel call and which will not. He knows the exact number of His elect people, and that number cannot be increased or decreased. It cannot be decreased because God the Father has promised His Son that Jesus will see those for whom He died safely in heaven with Him as His inheritance.[146]

> For whom he [God the Father] did foreknow, he also did
> predestinate to be conformed to the image of his
> Son....Moreover whom he did predestinate, them he also
> called: and whom he called, them he also justified: and
> whom he justified, them he also glorified. (Rom. 8:29–30)

Notice the order of God's chain of salvific actions in the verses above. Notice, also, that God does not stop short of completing those actions, from beginning to end, for each elect sinner (vv. 28, 33). First, God foreknows particular sinners before time began. Then He effectually calls them in their lifetime. Next, He justifies them, and then He glorifies them. Before time existed, God foreknew (loved and acknowledged as His own) certain sinners,

---

[144] 1John 5: 9-13; 1 Corinthians 1:7-8; Hebrews 6:1-12
[145] Rev.13:8; 17:8; 20:15; 21:27.
[146] Isa. 53:10.

although He perfectly knew their true sinful characters and actions. The prophet Jeremiah said that the Lord knew him before he was formed in his mother's womb: "Now the word of the Lord came to me saying, 'Before I formed you in the womb I knew you, and before you were born I consecrated you" (Jer. 1:4–5 NASV).

Arthur Pink explains the words "know" and "foreknowledge", he writes:

The words "know" and "foreknowledge" when applied to God in the Scriptures, have reference not simply to His prescience (i.e., His *bare knowledge* beforehand), but to His knowledge of *approbation* [as well]. When God said to Israel, "You only have I known of all the families of the earth" (Amos 3:2), it is evident that He meant, "You only had I any favorable regard to." When we read in Rom. 11:2, "God hath not cast away His people (Israel) whom He *foreknew*," it is obvious that what was signified is, "God has not finally rejected that people whom He has chosen as objects of His love"—cf. Deut. 7:7, 8. In the same way (and it is the *only* possible way) are we to understand Matt. 7:23. [Jesus said, "And then will I profess unto them, I never knew you: depart from me, ye that work iniquity."] In the Day of Judgment the Lord will say unto many, "I never knew you." Note, it is more than simply "I knew you not." His solemn declaration will be, "I *never* knew you"—you were never the objects of My approbation. Contrast this with "I...know (love) My sheep, and am known (loved) of Mine" (John 10:14). [God knows His people with approbation and love. "But if any man love God, the same is known of Him" (1 Cor. 8:3).] The "sheep," His elect, the "few," He *does* "know" but the reprobate, the non-elect, the "many". He never knew them.![147] They were never written in the Lamb's Book of Life.

[Christians are the] "elect according to the foreknowledge of God the Father, through sanctification of the Spirit, unto obedience and sprinkling of the blood of Jesus Christ" (1 Peter 1:2).

Here again election according to the foreknowledge of God the Father precedes the work of the Holy Spirit in [them] . . . who are saved; thus taking it entirely off creature ground, and resting it in the sovereign pleasure of the Almighty. The "foreknowledge of God the Father" does not here refer to His prescience of all things, but signifies that the saints were all eternally present in Christ before [in] the mind of God. God did not "foreknow" that certain ones who heard the Gospel would believe it *apart from the fact that He had "ordained" these certain ones to eternal life.* What God's prescience saw in all men was love of sin and hatred of Himself. The "foreknowledge" of God *is based upon His own decrees* as is clear from Acts 2:23—"Him, [Jesus] being delivered by the determinate counsel and foreknowledge of God, ye have taken, and by wicked hands have crucified and slain"—note the order here: first God's "determinate counsel" (His decree), and second His "foreknowledge." So it is again in Romans 8:28–29, "For whom He did foreknow, He also did predestinate to be conformed to the image of His Son," but the first word here, "for," looks back to the preceding verse and the last clause of it reads, "to them who are the called according to his

---

[147] Arthur W. Pink, *The Sovereignty of God* (Grand Rapids: Baker, 1976), p. 86 (emphasis in original).

purpose"—these are the ones whom He did "foreknow and predestinate."[148]

Just think, when God chooses to elect a sinner before he is born, it is not because God foresees faith or something good in him. There is nothing in a sinner that would cause God to choose him. As Paul said: "(For the children being not yet born, neither having done any good or evil, that the purpose of God according to election might stand, not of works, but of him that calleth.) It was said unto her, The elder shall serve the younger. As it is written, Jacob have I loved, but Esau have I hated" (Rom. 9:11–13).

Some might say that God chose Jacob because He foresaw that he would be better than his twin brother Esau. History has shown us that between Jacob and Esau, Jacob had the reputation of being the deceiver and usurper.[149] Yet, even before Jacob was born, God perfectly knew what Jacob's sinful actions and character flaws would be, and He still chose Jacob rather than Esau. Paul tells us that, if we are chosen, it is not because God foresees that we will be holy. Paul says just the opposite in Ephesians 1:4. God chose us that we should be (in order that we might be) holy.

Similarly, he tells us in Ephesians 2:10 how divine election accomplishes holiness. He creates (or renovates by sanctification) us anew, as His workmanship in Christ Jesus to the end that we should do good works.

Because His love for His elect or chosen ones existed before time, God determined or predestinated whatever comes to pass in time for them. He predestinated when, where, and how these particular sinners would become recipients of His grace so they could be adopted into His family and become like His Son.[150]

---

[148] Ibid., p. 57.
[149] Gen. 27:12.
[150] Eph. 1:5; Rom. 8:29.

Hence, God knows exactly who His elect people are before He calls them in time because He predestinated who they would be before time.[151] God's purpose to carry to completion the unbroken chain of actions in Romans 8:29–30 reveals that He will not change His mind about saving His elect people.

When people are told about the power of God's sovereignty used in election they get suspicious or scared. Non-believers are suspicious of God's sovereign election power since they view it as a decree of absolute, arbitrary, fatalistic, blind determinism (a sovereign power used without any plan or purpose). And there are some Christians, who when faced with the sovereign power of God's grace used in their election, find themselves all of the sudden nervous or scared. Why? Because God's election becomes a personal threat to their belief that they determined their own salvation by their decision to accept Jesus. But God's election takes the control of their salvation out of their hands. Until now they may have had preconceived opinions that caused them to incorrectly presume that they already had determined their own instant election when they made their Arminian "free will" (quid pro quo) decision ***to accept Jesus into their hearts***." But now they find that they had no reason to boast about their decision to receive Jesus because it did not determine their election. Their election was always completely out of their control. It was entirely determined by God's grace which means God chose His elect apart from anything found in them or done by them. God saw them in a spiritually dead condition and without strength to lift a finger to get themselves elected. [152] They were chosen in Christ and not apart from Christ. Christians should then heartily acquiesce to the veracity of the Scriptures that verify God's grace in their election. Their election belongs to God's grace and to His grace alone.

---

[151] 1 Pet. 1:2.
[152] Ephesians 2: 3-6; Romans 5:6; Ezekiel 16:1-14

Election is God's decree made by God's sovereign will and for His good pleasure but His love and grace go before His election. This means His election is a loving election not some abstract decree (standing alone by itself) separate from Christ. God's loving election should be considered as the royal privilege of Christ's courtship and spiritual communion bestowed on His Church, the eternal Bride of Christ.[153] Just think, Christ Jesus, the King of the universe, has chosen to marry us. And since we are wedded to Christ, we are His and He is ours forever.

Apart from Christ your election and salvation would seem to be done by an absolute, arbitrary, impersonal power rather than by the real cause of your election which is the Father's love for Christ Jesus and Christ's doing and dying for you. It would make Christ's work of salvation superfluous, so that His mediatorship and his mediatory work become unimportant. You cannot separate Election from Christ. If we were elected outside of Christ, we would be elected apart from Christ and outside of Christ's work of justification and sanctification.

> John Calvin said, ". . . As long as Christ remains outside
> of us, we are separated from him, all that he has suffered
> and done for the salvation of the human race remains
> useless and is of no value to us , , , When we see
> salvation whole - its every single part [including election]
> is found in Christ, we must beware lest we derive the smallest
> drop from somewhere else. [154]

---

[153] Ezekiel 16:1-13; Psalm 45:13-15; Ephesians 5:22-32; Revelation
   21:2,9
[154] The Whole Christ, Sinclair Ferguson, Crossway, Wheaton Illinois, 2016, pp.54-55

The Confession Helvetica of 1562 says, for instance that
God elects us in Christ and because of Christ (Art. 10).

"Only from such a lack of appreciation is it possible to
conclude that the Reformed doctrine of election is
characterized by a preference for an abstract decree of
election, so that in the exegesis of Ephesians 1:4 it comes
close to the Remonstrant view which interprets it as a
decree of the order of salvation, detached from the
election *in Christ*."[155]

"Even before He made the world, **God loved us and
chose us *in Christ*** to be holy and without fault in His
eyes."(Ephesians 1:4)

Please let me assure you, that the power of God's sovereignty in
election is directed by His gracious plan and purpose. God's plan
and purpose were made in eternity past by His eternal, wise
counsel. His plan and purpose were based on His sovereign grace
to choose the elect from the total mass of condemned sinners so
they could be placed into union with Christ, redeemed and
conformed to Christ's holy image and thereby glorify Christ. In this
gracious economy of being elected "in Christ" there is no room for
your human merit, but only redemption through the obedience and
blood of Christ, forgiveness of our sins, and riches of His grace
(Eph. 1:7).

Election should be seen in the context of God's gracious plan of
salvation through Christ and not apart from Christ. "The absolute
significance of Christ's work stands here in the center: from

---

[155] Devine Election, G.C. Berkouwer, Wm. B. Eerdmans
Publishing Co.
Grand Rapids, Michigan, 1960, pp.137-138

eternity, in time, and in the *eschaton,* when all things in Him "are taken together in their total." (G. C. Berkouwer)

The apostle Paul said, " . . .the dispensation of grace which was given to me for you how that by that revelation He made known the mystery to me (as I have briefly written already, by which when you read, you may understand my knowledge in the mystery of Christ), which in other ages was not made known to the sons of men, as it has now been revealed by the Spirit to holy apostles and prophets : that the Gentiles, should be fellow heirs, of the same body, and partakers of *His promise in Christ* through the gospel, of which I became a minister according to the gift of grace of God given to me by the effective working of His power. To me, who am less than the least of all the saints, this grace was given, that I should preach among the Gentiles the unsearchable riches of Christ, and to make all see what is the fellowship of the mystery, which from the beginning of has been hidden in God who created all things through Jesus Christ; to the intent that now the manifold wisdom of God might be made known by the church to the principalities and powers in the heavenly places, according to the eternal purpose which He accomplished in Christ Jesus our Lord . . ." (Ephesians 3:2-11)

"Therefore, remember that you , once Gentiles in the flesh - who are called Uncircumcision by what is called the Circumcision made in the flesh by hands - that at that time you were without Christ, being aliens from the commonwealth of Israel and strangers from the covenants of promise, having no hope and without God in the world. But now *in Christ Jesus* you who once

were far off have been brought near by the blood of
Christ." (Ephesians 2:11-13)

"For it pleased the Father that *in Him* all the fullness
should dwell, and *by Him* to reconcile all things to
Himself, *by Him* whether things on earth or things
in heaven, having made peace through the blood
of His cross." (Colossians 1:19-20

"Now all things are of God, who has reconciled us
to Himself through Jesus Christ, and has given us
the ministry of reconciliation, that is, that God was
in Christ reconciling the world [both Jew and Gentile]
to Himself, not imputing their trespasses to them, and
has committed to us the word of reconciliation."
(2 Corinthians 5:18-19)

"God has now revealed to us his mysterious [gospel] plan
regarding Christ, a plan to fulfill his own good pleasure
And this is the plan. At the right time he will bring
everything together under the authority of Christ
- everything in heaven and on earth."
(Ephesians 1:9-10)

"All praise to God, the Father of our Lord Jesus Christ,
who has blessed us with every spiritual blessing
in the heavenly realms because we are *united with
Christ*." (Ephesians 1:3)

Your election is always related to Christ Jesus. And it is
because God by His grace has chosen you "in Christ" that you can
be assured of your election. An assurance of this type comes from

the orderliness, constancy and immutability of God's covenant election as opposed to a purposeless, random, meaningless election.

But for practical purposes Christians are pointed in two general directions to gain assurance of their calling and election. One direction given is to place their confidence in the promises of God, that is, to place their confidence in the sufficiency of God's power to accomplish His intent of their initial calling, which is, the final completion of those promises at their glorification in heaven (Rom.8:29-30). The other direction given to Christians to gain an assurance is by reflecting on any particular evidence of regeneration or habit of holiness in their lives. This involves searching their souls for the evidences or fruits of sanctification that they might use to ascertain the divine intent of justification toward them personally.

The first direction given then for assurance of their calling and election is not by seeking an extraordinary or an immediate, totally subjective, transcendent, encounter of the Holy Spirit's inward witness to them that they are the elect. Rather, the assurance of their election comes plainly to them by the witness of the Holy Spirit to the truth of the Scripture which furnishes them with the knowledge of an objective evidence of their election. This was accomplished when the Holy Spirit sealed them with His ownership of them and His responsibility for them (Eph. 1:13; 2 Tim. 2:19). Part of His responsibility for them was to apply the knowledge of the gospel promises to the faculties of their minds, affections and wills. By doing this He sealed these gospel promises to their hearts as a witness to their spirits that they are children of God (Eph.4:30). Here is assurance or security for those seeking objective evidence of their election. Here are a few of those promises:

> "And do not bring sorrow to God's Holy Spirit by the way you live. Remember, He has identified you as His own, guaranteeing that you will saved on the day of

redemption." (Eph. 4:30) NLT translation

For whom He (the Father) foreknew, *He also predestinated to be conformed to the image of His Son* . . . Moreover, whom He predestinated, these He also called, whom He called these He also justified; and whom He justified , these also glorified. (Romans 8:29)

What shall we then say to these things? If God be for us, who can be against us? He that spared not his own Son, but delivered him up for us all, how shall he not with him [Christ Jesus] also freely give us all things? Who shall lay anything to the charge of God's elect? It is God that justifieth. Who is he that condemneth? It is Christ that died, yea rather, that is risen again, who is even at the right hand of God, who also maketh intercession for us. Who shall separate us from the love of Christ? shall tribulation, or distress, or persecution, or famine, or nakedness, or peril, or sword?...Nay, in all these things we are more than conquerors through him that loved us. For I am persuaded, that neither death, nor life, nor angels, nor principalities, nor powers, nor things present, nor things to come, nor height, nor depth, nor any other creature, shall be able to separate us from *the love of God, which is in Christ Jesus our Lord*. (Rom. 8:31–35, 37–39)

Think a minute about this. Do you recognize the assurance of salvation offered in this passage of Scripture? Do you see the spiritual obstacles placed in our way (the world, the flesh, and the devil) which cannot separate us from the love of God which is in Christ Jesus our Lord?

Jesus said, "My sheep hear my voice, and I know them, and they follow me: and I give unto them eternal life; and they shall never perish, neither shall any man pluck them out of my hand. My Father, which gave them me, is greater than all; and no man is able to pluck them out of my Father's hand".[156]

However, when I yield to the temptations mentioned above, I feel like a Judas type traitor to Christ. I concluded I was my own worst enemy and the worst version of myself. I began to doubt my standing with God. I began to lose my assurance and I was tempted to believe I could lose my salvation. After reading John 10:27–29, I thought to myself, *"It may be true that no one else can take me out of Jesus' hand, maybe I can take myself out of His hand by sinning"*. But I had forgotten that Christ had not only paid for all my past sins, but that He had also paid for my present and future sins as well.

Then another thought struck me: *This same Christ who will be the Judge of the world on Judgment Day is also Christ, my Savior, who died, rose again, and who now makes intercession for me now in heaven. Therefore, I will never come into judgment because my Judge is also my Advocate. Therefore, Christ will not condemn me with the world because He loves me and has paid for all my sins.*

In addition, someone pointed out to me from Romans 8:38–39 that the pitfalls of "life" (its trials and tribulations) cannot separate me from the love of God. That means that "things present [even my present sins], nor things to come [my future sins]…shall be able to separate me from the love of God, which is *in Christ Jesus* our Lord." God's promise to His elect is to complete the chain of actions (Rom. 8:29) for His people's salvation. This should cause them, out of their thankfulness to God, to persevere in holiness while on earth until God takes them to heaven where He then makes

---

[156] John 10:27–29

them sinless. God has promised his elect to finish the work that He has begun in them (Philippians 1:6; Hebrews 12:2; 2 Timothy 1:12)

Some object to this teaching because they believe that Christians can lose their salvation. Those who believe this have no assurance of their election or salvation; they live in constant fear of losing it. They find no hope in the promise of eternal life. Even though the Bible clearly explains that all who have been saved shall not come into judgment, they refuse to believe it. Jesus said, "Most assuredly, I say unto you, he who hears My word and believes in Him who sent Me has everlasting life, and shall not come into judgment, but has passed from death into life."[157] This verse shows that a believer not only possesses eternal life before he goes to heaven, but he will not come into judgment. Consequently, the believer will not lose the gift of eternal life on Judgment Day. Moreover, the apostle John said, "And this is the testimony: that God has given us eternal life, and this life is in His Son. He who has the Son has life; he who does not have the Son of God does not have life. These things I have written to you who believe in the name of the Son of God, that you may know that you have eternal life, and that you may continue to believe in the name of the Son of God."[158] Other Scripture references that give us assurance of election and salvation are as follows:

When I said, My foot slippeth; thy mercy, O LORD, held me up. (Ps. 94:18)

Can a woman forget her sucking child, that she should not have compassion on the son of her womb? yea, they may forget, yet will I not forget thee. (Isa. 49:15)

---

[157] John 5:24 (NKJV).
[158] 1 John 5:11–13 (NKJV).

Thou wilt perform the truth to Jacob, and the mercy to Abraham, which thou hast sworn unto our fathers from the days of old. (Micah 7:20)

All that the Father giveth me shall come to me; and him that cometh to me I will in no wise cast out. For I came down from heaven, not to do mine own will, but the will of him that sent me. And this is the Father's will which hath sent me, that of **all which he hath given me I should lose nothing, but should raise it up again at the last day.** And this is the will of him that sent me, that every one which seeth the Son, and believeth on him, may have everlasting life: and I will raise him up at the last day....Verily, verily, I say unto you, He that believeth on me hath everlasting life. (John 6:37–40, 44, 47)

For God so loved the world, that he gave his only begotten Son, that whosoever believeth in him should not perish but have everlasting life. (John 3:16)

My sheep hear my voice, and I know them, and they follow me: and I give unto them eternal life; and they shall never perish, neither shall any man pluck them out of my hand. My Father, which gave them me, is greater than all; and no man is able to pluck them out of my Father's hand. I and my Father are one. (John 10:27–30)

Holy Father, keep through thine own name those whom thou hast given me. (John 17:11)

God commendeth his love toward us, in that, while we were yet sinners, Christ died for us. Much more then, being now justified by his blood, we shall be saved from wrath through him. For if when we were enemies, we were reconciled to

God by the death of his Son, much more, being reconciled, we shall be saved by his life. (Rom. 5:8–10)

I thank my God always on your behalf, for the grace of God which is given you by Jesus Christ; who shall also confirm you unto the end, that ye may be blameless in the day of our Lord Jesus Christ. (1 Cor. 1:4, 8)

But God, who is rich in mercy, for his great love wherewith he loved us, even when we were dead in sins, hath quickened us together with Christ, that in the ages to come he might shew the exceeding riches of his grace in his kindness toward us through Christ Jesus. (Eph. 2:4–5, 7)

The LORD will perfect that which concerneth me: thy mercy, O LORD, endureth for ever; forsake not the works of thine own hands. (Ps. 138:8)

Of this I am convinced, that He [God the Father] who has begun a good work in you will bring it to completion in the day of Christ Jesus. (Phil. 1:6 NEW BERKELEY)

In whom ye also trusted, after that ye heard the word of truth, the gospel of your salvation: in whom also after that ye believed, ye were sealed with that holy Spirit of promise....And grieve not the holy Spirit of God, whereby ye are sealed unto the day of redemption. (Eph. 1:13; 4:30)

For the which cause I also suffer these things: nevertheless I am not ashamed: for I know whom I have believed, and am persuaded that he is able to keep that which I have committed unto him against that day. (2 Tim. 1:12)

And the God of peace himself sanctify you wholly; and may your spirit and soul and body be preserved entire, without blame at the coming of our LORD Jesus Christ. Faithful is he that calleth you, who will also do it. (1 Thess. 5:23–24 ASV)

And the LORD shall deliver me from every evil work, and will preserve me unto his heavenly kingdom. (2 Tim. 4:18)

Come, ye blessed of my Father, inherit the kingdom prepared for you from the foundation of the world. (Matt. 25:34)

Fear not, little flock; for it is your Father's good pleasure [purpose] to give you the kingdom. (Luke12:32)

Blessed be the God and Father of our LORD Jesus Christ, which according to his abundant mercy hath begotten us again unto a lively hope by the resurrection of Jesus Christ from the dead, to an inheritance incorruptible, and undefiled, and that fadeth not away, reserved in heaven for you, who are kept by the power of God through faith unto salvation ready to be revealed in the last time. (1 Peter 1:3–5)

Now to Him who is able to keep you from stumbling and to make you stand in His glorious presence faultless and full of triumphant joy, to the only God our Saviour, through Jesus Christ our LORD, be glory, majesty, might, and authority, as it was before all time, both now and forever and ever. Amen. (Jude 24–25. (Williams translation)

But the common objection raised against anyone possessing this assurance of salvation is: "If he had this assurance, he might be tempted to think he could sin all he wanted and still get into heaven". "The gist of it is that the sons of God are distinguished from the reprobate by this mark, that they continue to repent of their sins and persevere by going on to live holy and godly lives. This is the aim of divine election. From this it is clear how wrongly some of these wicked dogs make mockery of God that when they make His free election of them the excuse for every kind of license, as though they had permission to sin with impunity because they believe they are predestined to heaven" (Calvin). Anyone who tries to abuse or extort the blessings or teachings of Election in order to feel free to sin is standing on dangerous ground. He is not looking to please God but rather to please himself with pleasure and ease all the way to heaven without even a twinge of his conscience when he sins. But the biblical teaching of Election should cause the Christian to want to live his life for God, not for himself. He should want to live his life out of gratitude to God. The aim of Election is a holy life.

The other direction already mentioned that was given to Christians to gain an assurance of their calling and election is by a more subjective means. It was by introspection. It is by searching to see if we are bearing the fruits of a holy life. However, Antinomians have said that Christ is our full and complete sanctification and we don't need to look for any inward evidence of our sanctification to seek evidence for our calling and election. They would say we are totally passive in every area of our sanctification. Therefore, according to them this would mean that Christ believes for us, He repents for us, etc., and we are not held responsible to do any of these things. They would not agree that God infuses His grace and gift of faith by the Holy Spirit into the elect's heart so that by using the second causes of his mind, affections and will, he then himself can exercise faith, repentance, etc. So, because they see Christ believing and repenting for us, they say we should not look for assurance of our calling and election from evidences of Sanctification from second causes within us. Therefore, the Antinomians would say that the only assurance that we may have is "a work of Christ's act of sanctification for us and the witness of the Holy Spirit himself, 'speaking peace" directly to the soul, from a divine work" of Sanctification done without our cooperation. They say that this is more direct route to assurance than that offered by "standard" Puritan divines. "Puritan pastors argued that apart from the evidence of biblical word and gracious work, assurance by intuitive "revelations" is only as sure as the intuition or fancy, which will almost certainly wane, to be replaced once again by doubt [especially whenever they intermittently fall into sin]." (Wm. K. B. Stover p.160)

Furthermore, these antinomians say, if we search for the subjective evidence of the fruit of a holy life within us, we are "legalistic" because we are basing our justification on our sanctification (or human works). This is not true because all those of the Reformed faith know that their personal sanctification will never reach perfection while they are on this earth. So why would Christians want to substitute their imperfect works of sanctification for the perfect work of our justification by Christ?

Those in harmony with reformed orthodoxy maintained that we should make our calling and election sure by finding empirical evidence within ourselves. Sanctification, they believed, inheres in the regenerate; for all the relevant data for trying one's estate and falls within the scope of the natural capacity for perception and reflection; and conscience, and instruction by the Spirit in the word, and is therefore, competent to draw the appropriate conclusions, wholly within the moral and ontological orders of creation.

Jesus said that Christians could observe and discern false teachers by the fruits of their lives (Matt, 7:16-18; 12:33). This means we have the capacity to observe and discern the fruits in others and we have the same capacity to see them in ourselves (Matt.5:16). "Being privy to motives, conscience [directed by the moral law] is able to judge the genuineness of acts of faith, repentance, and sanctification; and on this basis the intellect, knowing the order of redemption, is able to reach a true conclusion about the individual's personal estate, and consequently about his election." [159]

John Calvin said, ". . . only righteousness pleases God, and only by the law, in which He has faithfully testified what He approves or disapproves, can we form a right judgment of our works [or fruits]. [160]

So, it should not be too hard to discern the fruit of a life devoid of obedience to God's moral commandments.. [161] Instead of having the true fruit of redemption in them, this life will display the works of their flesh. "Now the works of the flesh are evident, which are: adultery, fornication, uncleanness, lewdness, idolatry, sorcery, hatred, contentions, jealousies, outbursts of wrath, selfish ambitions, dissensions, heresies, envy, murders, drunkenness, revelries, and the like; of which I tell you beforehand, just as I also told you in time past, that those who practice such things will not inherit the kingdom of God." [162] Today we have people who teach that Christians no longer need to keep God's moral commandments. "For there are certain men crept in unawares, who were before of old ordained to this condemnation, ungodly men, turning the grace of our God into lasciviousness, and denying the

---

[159] Stover, Wm. K. B. , A Faire and Easie Way to Heaven,1978, p.128
[160] John Calvin, Calvin's Commentaries on Romans, Wm. B. Eerdmans
Publishing Company, Grand Rapids, Michigan, 1973, p.162
[161] Luke 8:14.
[162] Gal. 5:19–21 (NKJV).

only Lord God, and our Lord Jesus Christ....But these speak evil of those things which they know not: but what they know naturally, as brute beasts, in those things they corrupt themselves. Woe unto them! For they have gone in the way of Cain, and ran greedily after the error of Balaam for reward, and perished in the gainsaying of Core. These are spots in your feasts of charity, when they feast with you, feeding themselves without fear: clouds they are without water, carried about of winds; trees *whose fruit withereth, without fruit*, twice dead, plucked up by the roots; raging waves of the sea, foaming out their own shame; wandering stars, to whom is reserved the blackness of darkness forever" [163]

Paul by the divine inspiration of Holy Spirit says:

"For those who live according to the flesh set their minds on things of the flesh, but those who live according to the Spirit set their minds on the things of the Spirit. Now the mind of the flesh is death, but the mind of the Spirit is life and peace; because the mind of the flesh is hostility to God, for it does not submit to the law of God, nor can it do so. And those in the flesh cannot please God."

On the other hand truly ransomed saints will be spiritually fruitful. For example, in Psalm 92:12–14 (NKJV), we read:

"The righteous shall flourish like a palm tree, he shall grow like a cedar in Lebanon. Those who are planted in the house of the Lord shall flourish in the courts of our God. They shall still bear fruit in old age; they shall be fresh and flourishing."

---

[163] Jude 4, 10–13.

The prophet Jeremiah wrote,

> "Blessed is the man that trusteth in the Lord, and whose hope the Lord is. For he shall be as a tree planted by the waters, and that spreadeth out her roots by the river, and shall not see when heat cometh, but her leaf shall be green; and shall not be careful in the year of drought, neither shall cease from yielding fruit"
> (Jer. 17:7–8).

While Christians insist that they are justified by faith alone in Christ alone and by His righteous works alone, it must be pointed out that their faith in Christ should produce spiritual fruit in their lives (James 2:26). So, their faith is an on-going, living, dynamic, active faith which is evidenced in their lives by the fruit of the Holy Spirit and their good deeds. As Calvin said, "It is therefore faith alone which justifies, and yet the faith which justifies is not alone . . ."[164] The Christian's Justification is demonstrated by his Sanctification and although these two are distinct in essence from each other they cannot be separated but should not be confused with each other. So, you cannot have one without having the other. A person's Justification would be mocked without some proof of his Sanctification. It would tend to nullify his profession of faith. So, without holiness [or sanctification] no man can see the Lord" (Heb. 12:14) , This means those who merely profess to have saving faith without producing any spiritual fruits of holiness in their lives will not ultimately find heaven as their home.

---

[164] Calvin, *Antidote to the Canons and Decrees of the Council of Trent,*
   in Calvin's Selected Works, 3::152

The true saint will produce fruits of holiness or sanctification, They will be zealous to tell others about Jesus and to live out their lives before them for Him. God will bless the saint's teaching and their testimony of Jesus with fruit. Jesus said, "I am the true vine, and My Father is the vinedresser. Every branch in Me that does not bear fruit He takes away; and every branch that bears fruit He prunes, that it may bear more fruit....Abide in Me, and I in you. As the branch cannot bear fruit of itself, unless it abides in the vine, neither can you, unless you abide in Me. I am the vine, you are the branches. He who abides in Me, and I in him, bears much fruit; for without Me you can do nothing....You did not choose Me, but I chose you and appointed you that you should go and bear fruit, and that your fruit should remain" (John 15:1–2, 4–5, 16 NKJV).[165]

Finally, the Christian's life will display the fruit of the Holy Spirit. The fruit of the Spirit is love, joy, peace, patience, kindness, goodness, faithfulness, and gentleness. We are to look for this fruit at least in some measure in our lives so we can make our calling and election sure.

---

[165] Ps. 92:12–14 NKJV; Jer. 17:7–8; Eph. 5:9; Phil. 1:11; Gal. 5:22–23; see also John 15:8, 16; Rom. 7:4; John 15:1–2, 4–5, 16; Matt. 28:18–20; John 1:45–46.

CHAPTER 7

GOD'S GRACE VS. FREE-WILL

But what about man's free-will? Doesn't the unbelieving sinner have a free-will? Doesn't his choice to be saved determine whether or not he will be saved? Theologian J. I. Packer explains this historic controversy about free-will,

> The historic controversy about "free-will"…concerns the question whether fallen man's slavery to sin is so radical and complete as to make him wholly unable to perform spiritual good or to avoid sinning, or to repent and put faith in Christ. Reformed theology follows Augustine in affirming, on the basis of such passages as Rom. 8:5–8; Eph. 2:1–10; John 6:44; 15:4–5, that man's will is not in fact free for obedience and faith till freed from sin's dominion by regenerating grace. Only on this basis, it is claimed, can human merit be excluded and God's sovereignty acknowledged in the matter of salvation, and justice be done to the biblical insistence that we are saved by faith alone (without works, Rom. 3:28), through grace alone (not human effort, Rom. 9:16), and for God's glory alone (not man's, 1 Cor. 1:28–31). Any alternative view, it is said, makes man a decisive contributor to his own salvation, and so in effect his own Saviour.[166]

The Westminster Confession of Faith says,

---

[166] J. I. Packer, "Freedom, Free Will," in *Baker's Dictionary of Theology*, ed. Everett F. Harrison, Geoffrey W. Bromiley, and Carl F. H. Henry (Grand Rapids: Baker, 1960), p. 230.

God hath endued the will of man with that natural liberty, that it is neither forced nor by any absolute necessity of nature determined to good or evil. Man in his state of innocence, had freedom and power to will and to do that which is good and well pleasing to God; but yet mutably, so that he might fall from it. **Man, by his fall into a state of sin, hath wholly lost all ability of will to any spiritual good accompanying salvation**; so as a natural man, being altogether averse from that good, and dead in sin, is not able, by his own strength, to convert himself, or to prepare himself thereunto. When God converts a sinner, and translates him into the state of grace, he freeth him from his natural bondage under sin, and by his grace alone enables him freely to will and to do that which is spiritually good; yet so as that, by reason of his remaining corruption, he doth not perfectly nor only will that which is good, but doth also will that which is evil. The will of man is made perfectly and immutably to do good alone in the state of glory only. (The Westminster Confession of Faith, chap. 9, art. 1–5)

Author William Cunningham, in his book *Historical Theology,* wrote this,

Man by the fall was not changed into a stock or a stone, or into an irrational animal; he retained that rational power of volition which was a part of the general framework of his mental constitution, and in virtue of which he had, and still has, a natural capacity of willing and choosing spontaneously, and of carrying out his volitions into action. Man retained this natural power or capacity, and he was not, in consequence of the fall, subjected in the exercise of it to any external force or compulsion—to any influence outside of himself, and apart from the exercise of his own power of volition, and from his own actual choice, which determined infallibly whether he should do good or evil.[167]

So man's will is not coerced by an external force greater than himself to do something he does not want to do. He is free to do what he wants to do, **within the limits of his ability**. What is the distinction we are making here between the will's liberty and the will's ability? Unsaved man's will has liberty. It is functional, fully operative, and has spontaneity. Unsaved man is not a mechanical robot that works by some external remote control. What he does, he does willingly and not against his will. This is what makes him responsible for his actions. But A. A. Hodge makes an important point here. He wrote: "Liberty [not only] consists in the power of the agent [person] to will as he pleases, [but also] in the fact that **the volition is determined only by the character of the agent willing**."[168]

So, there is a difference between the will's liberty and the will's ability. Hodge continued: "Ability consists in the power of the agent to change his own subjective state,—to make himself prefer what he does not prefer, and to act in a given case in opposition to the coexistent desires and preferences of the agent's own heart."[169] To this point the prophet Jeremiah wrote, "Can the Ethiopian change his skin or the leopard its spots? Then may you also do good who are accustomed to do evil" (Jer. 13:23 NKJV).

So the unsaved person's will has liberty, but it lacks the ability to will to do something spiritually good or acceptable to God. Why? **His character limits his will's ability. His will is free to act but**

---

[167] William Cunningham, *Historical Theology*, vol. 2 (Carlisle, Pa.: Banner of Truth Trust, 1862), p. 572.

[168] A. A. Hodge, *Hodge's Outlines of Theology*, ed. W. H. Goold (Edinburgh and New York: T. Nelson and Sons, 1863), p. 271.

[169] Ibid., p. 271.

only in harmony with the character of his heart. So, while it is true that unsaved man has the liberty to will, he can only will as his evil heart pleases. He is free to will but not free in willing. This means when it comes to making spiritual choices, the unsaved person has the liberty to choose what he truly wants, but he does not have the ability to choose what he ought. Apart from God's grace, unsaved man will not choose to receive or act on spiritual truths from God's Spirit (1 Cor. 2:14). They are foolishness to him. Cunningham wrote, nevertheless, unsaved "man is responsible for not willing and doing good, notwithstanding his actual inability to will and to do good, because he is answerable for that inability itself, having, as legally responsible for Adam's sin, [he] inherited the inability, as part of the forfeiture penally due to that first transgression." [170]

John L. Girardeau said this in his book *Calvinism and Evangelical Arminianism:*

> Men's spiritual inability is not original but penal. It is not original, for God conferred upon man at the creation ample ability to comply with all his requirements. There was not inserted into his nature any evil principle from which sin could be developed, nor any weakness or imperfection which, in the absence of determining grace, necessitated a fall. He was, it is true, liable to fall in consequence of mutability of will, but he was at the same time able to stand. When, therefore, he sinned, the fault was altogether his own. He could not lay the blame upon his natural constitution, and so, by implication, upon its divine author. He unnecessarily and inexcusably revolted against the paternal and beneficent rule of God, and consequently subjected himself to the just sentence of a violated law.

---

[170] Cunningham, *Historical Theology*, p. 610.

When he sinned, he wantonly, deliberately, willfully threw away that spiritual ability with which he had been richly endowed. He disabled himself by his own act. His subsequent inability to love God and obey his law was a necessary part of his punishment.[171]

Unsaved man has the liberty to choose between right and wrong. But because he is unsaved, he is unable to choose that which goes against the existing desires and preferences of his sinful human nature. An unsaved person's will does *not function as it ought* because it is spiritually dead; it is in bondage to sin. Therefore, **"free- will" is a myth** if you are referring to an unsaved person's will. It is a fabrication of his imagination.

The unsaved sinner imagines he still has the ability to choose to do good as Adam did before his fall into sin. He thinks he can freely will to do that which is spiritually good and acceptable to God. Moreover, he sees himself as the master of both his mind and will and able of his own power to turn himself toward either good or evil. He fails to see that his moral choices in life flow from his heart's sinful disposition.[172] Since his heart's disposition is sinful, the choices and actions that proceed from it will be sinful also.[173]

Man's will was created as only one part of his soul or human nature. In the N.T. the spiritual entity of the soul (*psyche*) or his human nature is described as made up of three parts: his mind, affections, and will. His will works in conjunction with and is directed by his mind and affections. His will functions as a servant to his mind (understanding and judgment) and as a servant to his

---

[171] John L. Girardeau, *Calvinism and Evangelical Arminianism* (Harrisonburg, Va.: Sprinkle Publications, 1890, 1984), p. 212.
[172] Prov. 4:23.
[173] Matt. 7:16–20.

affections (feelings and desires).[174] His mind and affections provide the subjective motives behind his will, causing it to act. To disassociate his will from his mind and affections is to make it have no rational or moral character. So man's will is neither indifferent nor free to act at random or by itself. Therefore, since God designed man's will to be subordinated to his mind and affections, it cannot act contrary to them.

Let us take this thought one step farther. Just as man's will is subordinate to his mind and affections and cannot act contrary to them, likewise unsaved man's human nature is subordinate to his heart's fallen, sinful disposition and cannot act contrary to it. This evil disposition corrupts man's human nature so that it is only free to act in agreement with the constant inclination of his sinful disposition. This sinful disposition rules his nature by dictating each moral choice of his reason and affections and consequently every action of his will.[175] The apostle Paul said, "For we have already charged both Jews and Greeks that they are all under sin's power" (Rom. 3:9 NEW BERKELEY). Paul also said, "Those controlled by the sinful nature cannot please God" (Rom. 8:8 NIV).

Free-will then in my overly simplistic opinion is the *liberty* to make a choice that does not force you to go against your own will. And, if God has regenerated your will, your will is freed for the first time from sin's domination so that you are made able and willing to choose what you would not normally be able to choose (Psalm 110:3). So, if you did choose Christ as your Savior, you would not be forced to do it against your will. You would do it gladly and willingly.

Since Adam's fall, the definition of "Free-will" would then have to include the *ability* to make choices without the coercion from the *internal force* of indwelling sin, as well as, external forces.

---

[174] Gen. 3:6; James 1:13–14; 1 John 2:15–17; 2 Pet. 1:3–4.
[175] Jer. 17:9; Rom. 8:7; 1 Cor. 1:21; 2:14; James 1:14–15.

However, until the unsaved person's will has been liberated from sin's dominant rule by regeneration, his ability to make a free-will choice about his salvation does not exist. His will is and continues to be a slave to his sinful human nature.

Therefore, Christians who give their wills any credit for their decision to receive Jesus as their Savior have adopted the false belief that while their wills were still in a fallen state, their wills were still freely able to act to determine their salvation. It never occurred to them that their wills needed to be liberated by God's regenerating power so that they could make the choice to receive Jesus. However, they continue even today to advocate for what they call a person's "right" to accept or reject Jesus. They say that their decision to accept Christ must be made without God's influence (i.e., God's regenerating grace). They believe that unless man makes this decision to receive Christ entirely on his own, they could **not** regard his decision to be a legitimately "free" decision. They are so afraid that God will not respect what they call the free-will "rights" of the unsaved sinner. They are so afraid that God will cross their invisible boundary line by intervening into the unsaved sinner's life to rescue him. God's intervention would, in their opinion, take away the unsaved sinner's free-will and make his response like that of a robot. So, while they are proudly defending what they believe to be man's badge of honor (his freedom of choice), they deny the biblical doctrine of regeneration.

The Protestant Reformer Martin Luther wrote:

> "If any man doth ascribe of salvation, even the very least, to the free will of man, he knoweth nothing of grace, and he hath not learnt Jesus Christ aright."

Luther also wrote:

"I frankly confess that, for myself, even if it could be, I should not want "free-will" to be given me, nor anything to be left in my own hands to enable me to endeavor after salvation; not merely because in the face of so many dangers, and adversities, and assaults of devils, I could not stand my ground and hold fast my "free-will" (for one devil is stronger than all men, and on these terms no man could be saved); but because, even were there no dangers, adversities, or devils, I should still be forced to labor with no guarantee of success, and to beat my fists at the air. If I lived and worked to all eternity, my conscience would never reach comfortable certainty as to how much it must do to satisfy God. Whatever work I had done, there would still be a nagging doubt as to whether it pleased God, or whether He required something more. The experience of all who seek righteousness by works proves that; and I learned it well enough myself over a period of many years, to my own great hurt. **But now that God has taken my salvation out of the control of my own will, and put it under the control of His**, and promised to save me, not according to my working or running, but according to His own grace and mercy, I have the comfortable certainty that He is faithful and will not lie to me, and that He is also great and powerful, so that no devils or opposition can break Him or pluck me from Him. "No one," He says, "shall pluck them out of my hand, because my Father which gave them to me is greater than all" (John 10:28–29). **Thus it is that, if not all, yet some, indeed many, are saved; whereas, by the power of**

"free-will" none at all could be saved, but every one of us would perish."[176]

---

[176] Martin Luther, *The Bondage of the Will*, trans. J. I. Packer and O. R. Johnston (Grand Rapids: Fleming H. Revell, 1957), pp. 313–314.

CHAPTER 8

GOD'S SOVEREIGN GRACE

You might ask, "Don't verses in the Bible which use phrases like *whosoever believes shall be saved*, and *come to me* prove that the sinner's natural will is not inhibited by sin? Don't these verses imply that the sinner's unregenerate will is able to act immediately upon hearing God's gospel offer? Why else would God ask us to believe, repent, and come to Him unless we had the natural will power to do it? Besides, how can God hold us accountable for failing to repent and believe if we are unable to do it? Is God insincere about His gospel offer? Is He mocking our inability?

We reply, When a gospel offer or an invitation to come to Christ is made, this does not necessarily imply that we have the ability to respond to it. Nor does our obligation to the duty (command) to repent and believe necessarily imply we have the ability in and of ourselves to do it.

In answering Erasmus' diatribe, Martin Luther wrote,

A command does not always imply ability to fulfill it. Here . . . [Erasmus'] Diatribe will retort: "Ecclesiasticus, by saying 'if thou art willing to keep,' indicates that there is a will in man to keep or not to keep; otherwise, what is the sense of saying to him who has no will, 'if thou wilt'? Is it not ridiculous to say to a blind man: 'if thou art willing to see, thou wilt find a treasure'? or to a deaf man: 'if thou art willing to hear, I will tell thee a good story'? That would be mocking their misery."

I reply: These are arguments of human reason, which is wont to pour out wisdom of this sort. Wherefore, I now have to dispute, not with Ecclesiasticus, but with human reason, concerning an inference; for reason, by her inferences and syllogisms, explains and pulls the Scriptures of God whichever way she likes. I shall enter this dispute readily and with confidence, for I know that all her gabblings are stupid and absurd, and especially so when she begins to make a show of her wisdom in holy things.

First then: if I ask how it is proved that the existence of "free-will" in man is indicated and implied wherever the phrases "if thou are willing," "if thou shalt do," "if thou shalt hear," are used, she will say, "Because the nature of words and use of language among men seem to require it." Therefore, she bases her judgment of things and words that are of God upon the customs and concerns of men; and what is more perverse than that, when the former are heavenly and the latter earthly? Thus in her stupidity she betrays herself as thinking of God only as of man.

But what if I prove that the nature of words and use of language, even among men, is not always such as to make it an act of mockery to say to the impotent, "if thou art willing," "if thou shalt do," "if thou shalt hear"? How often do parents thus play with their children, bidding them come to them, or do this or that, only in order that it may appear how impotent they are, and that they may be compelled to call for the help of the parent's hand? How often does a faithful physician tell an obstinate patient to do or stop doing things that are impossible or injurious to him, so as to bring him by experience of himself to a knowledge of his disease or weakness, to which he cannot lead him by any other course? And what is more common and widespread than to use insulting and provoking language when we would show our enemies or friends what they can and cannot do? I merely mention these things to show reason how stupid she is to tack her inferences on to the Scriptures, and how blind she is not to see that they do not always hold good even in respect of the words and dealings of men. Let her see a thing occur once, and she jumps precipitately to the conclusion that it occurs as a general rule in all the statements of both God and men—generalizing from a particular case, which is the way of her wisdom.

If, now, God, as a Father, deals with us as with His sons, with a view to showing us the impotence of which we are ignorant; or as a faithful physician, with a view to making known to us our disease; or if, to taunt His enemies, who proudly resist His counsel and the laws He has set forth (by which He achieves this end most effectively), He should say: "do," "hear," "keep," or: "if thou shalt hear," "if thou art willing," "if thou shalt do"; can it be fairly concluded from this that therefore we can do these things freely, or else God is mocking us? Why should not this conclusion follow rather: therefore, God is trying us, that by His law He may bring us to a knowledge of our impotence, if we are His friends? or else, He is really and deservedly taunting and mocking us, if we are his proud enemies? For this, as Paul teaches, is the intent of divine legislation (cf. Rom.3:20; 5:20; Gal. 3:19, 24). Human nature is blind, so that it does not know its own strength—or, rather, sickness; moreover, being proud, it thinks it knows and can do everything. God can cure this pride and ignorance by no readier remedy than the publication of His law. We shall say more of this in its proper place. Let it suffice here to have touched upon it so as to refute this inference of a carnal and stupid wisdom: " 'if thou art willing'; therefore, thou canst will freely." The Diatribe dreams that man is whole and sound (as to human view, in his own sphere, he is); hence it argues from the phrases: "if thou art willing," "if thou shalt do," "if thou shalt hear," that man is being mocked, unless his will is free. But Scripture describes man as corrupted and led captive, and furthermore, as proudly disdaining to notice, and failing to recognize, his own corruption and captivity; therefore, it uses these phrases to goad and rouse him, that he may know by sure experience how unable he is to do any of these things.[177]

Obligation does not imply ability....Here is the matter in a nutshell: As I said, by statements of this sort, man is shown, not what he can do, but what he ought to do....It is well known that the Hebrews often use the future indicative for the imperative, as in Exod. 20: "Thou shalt have none other gods but me," "Thou shalt not kill," "Thou shalt not commit adultery" (vv. 3, 13–14); and there are countless such cases. If these words were taken indicatively, as they stand, they would be promises of God; and, since He cannot lie, the result would be that no man would sin; and then it would be needless to give men commandments![178]

Furthermore, God's will according to his precepts is revealed in His written commands, but His preceptive will is sometimes different from what He decrees. His command is sometimes different from His secret purpose. So just because He commands something to be done doesn't mean He decrees it shall be done. He commands all men everywhere to repent and believe. But is this

---

[177] Martin Luther, *The Bondage of the Will*, trans. J. I. Packer and O.R. Johnston (Grand Rapids: Fleming H. Revell, 1957), pp. 151–153.
[178] Ibid., p. 157.

what God has decreed or secretly purposed all men will do? No, for if God had decreed that all men should repent and believe, they would. God has commanded the church to preach the gospel to everyone, but has everyone down through history heard the gospel? We are still coming across individuals, tribes and nations of people today who have never heard the gospel. Did God command Pharaoh through Moses to let His people go? Yes. Did He decree that Pharaoh would consent to do so? No. Pharaoh temporarily consented, but ultimately, he refused to release them. He tried to either bring the Israelites back or destroy them, and he was destroyed instead. Abraham was commanded to sacrifice Isaac. But was it God's decree that Abraham should go through with it? No, it was not. God commanded the Jews to believe and receive their Messiah through the testimony of John the Baptist. However, God decreed that only some of them would immediately receive their Messiah, and the remainder should instead be jealous because the publicans, the common low-life, the common people of Jewish society and even the Gentiles received Him.[179] Another example of God's preceptive will and His decree is that found in His command against murder. God's preceptive will, found in His command, says, "Thou shalt not murder". Yet, He decreed that men, controlled by their own evil motives, would murder His Son.[180]

John Calvin said: "Though I affirm that He ordained it so, I do not allow that He is properly the author of sin....In sinning, they did what God did not will in order that God through their evil will might do what He willed."[181] Yes, in the crucifixion of Christ, we have a perfect example of how man's wrath against God is

---

[179] John 1:12–13; 12:37–40; Rom. 10:19–21; 11:1-11; Luke 14:15–24.

[180] Acts 2:23; 4:27.

[181] John Calvin, *Concerning the Eternal Predestination of God,* trans. J.K.S. Reid (London: James Clarke & Co., 1961), p. 123.

sovereignly turned around and is made to praise God instead (Ps. 76:10). The Westminster Confession of Faith states the doctrine of God's Eternal Decree thus: "God from all eternity did, by the most wise and holy counsel of his own will, freely and unchangeably ordain whatsoever comes to pass: yet so, as thereby neither is God the author of sin, nor is violence offered to the will of the creatures, nor is the liberty or contingency of second causes taken away, but rather established."[182]

So just because God commands you to repent and believe or just because Jesus asks you to come to Him does not mean you have the spiritual ability to perform these spiritual duties. On the contrary, even though God's preceptive will requires you to repent and believe, you lost the ability to do it by your sin. "To us [our very] nature is made a punishment, and what was just punishment of the first man is nature [natural] to us."[183] Therefore, unless God has decreed from eternity past that you would repent and come to Christ, you cannot.

Before the world was made, God exercised His decretive will to determine to whom He would give the grace or ability needed to be saved by Jesus' work of salvation. His decree determined whether or not to grant you His gracious gift of supernatural rebirth so that you would be able to repent and come to Jesus by faith. Therefore, you cannot come to Jesus unless God has already decreed before the world began that you would come to Him. Someone has rightly said, "No one can come to Jesus unless God

---

[182] "Of God's Eternal Decree," chap. 3, art. 1, in *The Westminster Confession of Faith* (Iverness, Scotland: Free Presbyterian Publications, 1976), p. 28.

[183] Augustine, *De Servit. Et Liberat. Hum. Arbitrii,* Opp. Ed. Amstel., vol. 8, in John L. Girardeau, *Calvinism and Evangelical Arminianism* (Harrisonburg, Va.: Sprinkle Publications, 1890, 1984), p. 372.

draws him to Jesus. And no one is ever kept from coming to Jesus who wants to come to Him."[184] The Bible says: "No one can come to me unless the Father who sent me draws him" (John 6:44 NIV). "Yea, I have loved thee with an everlasting [eternity past] love: therefore with lovingkindness have I drawn thee" (Jer. 31:3). "We love him, because he first loved us" (1 John 4:19). "Therefore, I have said to you that no one can come to Me unless it has been granted to him by My Father" (John 6: 65 NKJV). "All that my Father gives to me will come to me, and I will never, no, never reject anyone who comes to me" (John 6:37 WILLIAMS).

You may ask about the scripture verses that seem to say anyone by his free-will can choose eternal life. For example, what about Revelation 22:17, "Whosoever will, let him take the water of life freely"? We answer, "whosoever will" and "whosoever believes" are expressions that describe the free offer of the gospel. They are used to call all the people who come within the range of God's gospel. However, it is up to God to make His gospel call effectual. He must take that general, external call and make it an internal or spiritual call. He gives the grace needed to the hearts of His elect people so they will hear God's gospel call. That is, He must cause them to be willing to receive it and by faith rest on it when they hear it. The Bible says: "Thy people shall be willing in the day of thy power" (Ps. 110:3). "A certain woman named Lydia...heard us: whose heart the Lord opened to give heed unto the things which were spoken by Paul" (Acts 16:14 ASV). And again, "For it is God who works in you both to will and to do for His good pleasure" (Phil. 2:13 NKJV).

Someone said: "Those who are called by the good news about Jesus into God's kingdom will read the words WHOSOEVER WILL written on a sign over its gate. But when they pass through the gate, they look back, and on the other side of the same sign it will read,

---

[184] Author unknown.

CHOSEN FROM THE FOUNDATION OF THE WORLD."[185] Those who have been drawn to God and called internally by the Holy Spirit understand they have been chosen by God. Jesus said, "For many are called, but few chosen" (Matt. 22:14 ASV).

What about the difficulty raised by our doctrinal opponents that our teaching implies that God's offer of salvation is insincere? We represent God as insincere, they claim, because we say that God freely extends His offer of salvation to all, but apart from His grace, no one can receive it. Those who bring up this difficulty fail to consider that God's gospel offer of salvation is genuine despite the fact that man has forfeited the ability to receive it by his sin. So the sincerity of God's offer of salvation depends on the Giver, not the receiver. It is all of God's grace. His salvation is there for all who want to receive it through belief in Christ. So when we preach the gospel offer, we are not offering what cannot be given.

On the other hand, our opponents claim that God has given all people the free-will ability to receive the offer of salvation found in the gospel. And for this reason they have greater difficulty than we do explaining the sincerity of the gospel offer. Why? Because God did not make known the gospel offer to countless millions of people from the beginning of time. Those people died and never heard the gospel. The implication is that God was insincere about His offer because He gave them all the ability to receive salvation, but He never got around to making the gospel offer to them. God failed to make sure that those people would be providentially reached with His message. Now, who really represents God as being insincere?

We preach the gospel indiscriminately to everyone because God commands us to do this, and we do not know the elect from the reprobate. We preach the gospel because we are bound to seek the good of all men. But we are assured that God will reach every elect person with the gospel wherever he is. When he hears the

---

[185] Author unknown.

gospel, God will regenerate him to give him the ability to receive Christ by faith for salvation. This is determining grace. Determining grace is God using His special providence to bring the gospel and regeneration to His elect people.[186] John L. Girardeau wrote: "To deny determining grace is to deny determining providence. To admit determining providence is to admit determining grace."[187] Arthur W. Pink adds, "Let it not be forgotten that God's providences are but the manifestations of His decrees: what God does in time is only what He purposed [to do] in eternity [before time]—His own will being the alone cause of all His acts and works."[188]

The teaching of "free-will" is opposed to the teaching of God's determining grace. Those who believe in free-will insist that God must meet them on their terms. They say, to be fair, God can assist them with His grace, but He must not determine their wills with His grace because this would be invading the sovereignty of man's so-called free-will. However, if God treated them precisely as they demanded He should, who would be saved? Nobody!

---

[186] Isa. 55:11; Acts 16:6–10; 18:1–11; 19:1–10.
[187] Girardeau, *Calvinism and Evangelical Arminianism*, p. 409.
[188] Arthur W. Pink, *The Sovereignty of God* (Grand Rapids: Baker, 1976), p. 84.

CHAPTER 9

SOVEREIGN GRACE: GOD'S CHOICE OF THE SINNER OR THE SINNER'S CHOICE OF GOD?

God's grace is sovereign grace. As our Creator and Redeemer, God has the sovereign right to choose who will receive His saving grace. His purpose to give these chosen individuals His grace is to save them. Some refuse to believe this. Instead, they think that God's grace does not actually save any particular individual; it only makes salvation possible for all. Thus, they say it is not grace that saves the sinner. Instead, the sinner is saved by his choice to make use of God's offer of grace.

Those who believe this way think it is the sinner himself who must determine whether or not he will be saved. How? He must by using his unregenerate will choose to believe in Jesus. They mistakenly view the sinner's decision to believe as the condition he must perform to obtain regeneration. They do not view belief as being the first gracious effect of regeneration. Those who think this way cannot avoid the logical conclusion that the sinner is the one who ultimately saves himself by conjuring up belief in Jesus on their own.

However, a person's regeneration does not depend on his decision to believe. Regeneration is entirely contingent upon God's decision to regenerate someone. Regeneration is just the first part of God's gift package of redemption. This gift is given at Jesus Christ's expense. He paid for it by satisfying all the covenant conditions for man. Jesus Christ's accomplished work of redemption is then applied by God's Holy Spirit to the heart of his elect. The Holy Spirit regenerates us by powerfully working saving faith in our hearts to convert us.

This follows the chronological order of salvation found in Reformation teaching of the Ordo Salutis. Thus, regeneration must immediately accompany faith for our conversion. Those that object to this order would say Regeneration does not precede or accompany faith but instead it follows it.

They base their objection on Ephesians 1:13-14. But let's back up to verse 11.

" In him we have obtained an inheritance, having been predestined according to the purpose of him who works all things according to the counsel of his will, so that we who were the first to hope in Christ might be to the praise of his glory. In Him you also, *when you heard the word of truth, the gospel of your salvation, and believed in him, were sealed with the promised Holy Spirit*, [it's translated "were sealed with the Holy Spirit of Promise" in the Geneva Bible and KJV], who is the guarantee of our inheritance until we acquire possession, to the praise of his glory." (English Standard Version)

They say this passage proves, that hearing the Gospel comes first comes, then comes faith, then comes regeneration by the Holy Spirit." However, the key to their error is their interpretation of the phrase "sealed by the Holy Spirit". They interpret "Sealed by the Holy Spirit" to mean "regenerated".

However, this scripture passage is not saying "the sealing of the Holy Spirit" is the same thing as the Holy Spirit's work of regeneration. This "sealing", rather, is describing the "Holy Spirit's work of conveying to believers an authentic, lasting impression on their hearts of their identity as God's possession. And as God's possession they are sealed with the Holy Spirit's guarantee or down payment to protect and preserve them until they reach their inheritance in glory.[189]

The Reformation view of the Ordo Salutis (the order of salvation) is quite different from those who would say that Christians receive regeneration after they believe and because they have believed.

But what does the Bible have to say about the order of salvation in Ephesians 1:4-6 and Romans 8:29-30?

"For those whom he **foreknows** [first, the elect are chosen before the world began] he also **predestinated** to be conformed to the image of his Son . . . And those whom he predestinated he also called [then, comes effectual calling or regeneration], and those whom he called he also justified [then, comes justification by faith], and those whom he justified he also **glorified** [and finally, comes glorification].

Nevertheless, some think that all a sinner must do is simply decide on his own, without God's help, to be saved. He exercises his will in a democratic fashion to save himself. God casts His vote for the sinner; Satan casts his vote against him, but the sinner must cast the deciding vote. So when the sinner finally casts his vote, it is not grace that determines his will. Rather, it is his will "improves" grace. Between the balance of grace and the sinner's will, the added influence needed to tip the scales in favor of deciding "to accept Jesus" comes not from grace but from the sinner's will.

John Owen wrote this about free-willers:

---

[189] Eph. 4:30; 2 Cor. 1:22; 1 Pet. 1:5; Rev. 7:2-3; 1 Thess. 1:5; Rom. 15:13.

Having thus extenuated the grace of God, they affirm, "that in operation the efficacy thereof dependeth on free-will": so the Remonstrants in their Apology. "And to speak confidently," saith Grevinchovius, "I say that the effect of grace, in an ordinary course, dependeth on some act of our free-will." Suppose, then, that of two men made partakers of the same grace,—that is, [who] have the gospel preached unto them by the same means,—one is converted and the other is not, what may be the cause of this so great a difference? Was there any intention or purpose in God that one should be changed rather than the other? "No; he equally desireth and intendeth the conversion of all and every one." Did, then, God work more powerfully in the heart of the one by his Holy Spirit than of the other? "No; the same operation of the Spirit always accompanieth the same preaching of the word." But was not one, by some almighty action, made partaker of real infused grace, which the other attained not unto? "No; for that would destroy the liberty of his will, and deprive him of all the praise of believing." How, then, came this extreme difference of effects? who made the one differ from the other? or what hath he that he did not receive? "Why, all this proceedeth merely from the strength of his own free-will yielding obedience to God's gracious invitation, which, like the other, he might have rejected: this is the immediate cause of his conversion, to which all the praise thereof is due." And here [Owen says,] the old idol [free will] may glory to all the world, that if he can but get his worshippers to prevail in this, he hath quite excluded the grace of Christ, and made it "nomen inane," a mere title, whereas there is no such thing in the world.[190]

Thus, if you believe Grevinchovius, man's natural will determines his salvation, not grace. Grevinchovius idolizes the teaching of "free-will" because it takes away God's sovereign right to choose or elect certain individuals to salvation by grace and replaces it with man's right to choose or reject God.

According to the teaching of free-will, God must not infringe upon the sovereign decision-making rights of the sinner's free-will. This means that man must take the initiative to save himself. God must not take the initiative to save man.[191] God must not have any influence over the sinner's decision to receive Jesus. Those who believe this say that God's hands are tied when it comes to a person making a decision to receive Jesus. God is seen as helpless for He must wait for the sinner to make a decision.[192] The Lord must be patient and wait until the sinner's fallen, hostile will is ready to cooperate with Him. Until the sinner's will is ready to cooperate with God, God cannot save him. All God is really able to do is bite His fingernails and hope for the best. Why? Because this view only makes God's will sovereign when it comes to providing salvation, but not in applying salvation. According to them God's will is conditioned by the acts of man's will. In this regard, J. I. Packer wrote,

This view in effect denies our dependence on God when it comes to making vital decisions, takes us out of His hand,

---

[190] John Owen, "A Display of Arminianism," in *The Works of John Owen*, vol. 10 (Carlisle, Pa.: Banner of Truth Trust, 1967), p. 132.

[191] Note, this is totally contradictory to Phil. 1:6.

[192] Note, this is totally contradictory to John 1:13.

tells us that we are, after all, what sin taught us to think we were—masters of our fate, captains of our souls—and so undermines the very foundation of man's relationship with his Maker....[This view] compels itself to cheapen grace and the Cross by denying that the Father and the Son are sovereign in salvation; for it assures us that, after God and Christ have done all they can, or will, it depends finally on each man's own choice whether God's purpose to save him is realized or not....[This view] compels us to misunderstand the significance of the gracious invitations of Christ in the gospel of which we have been speaking; for we now have to read them, not as expressions of the tender [freely offered] patience of a mighty sovereign, but as the pathetic pleadings of impotent desire; and so the enthroned Lord is suddenly metamorphosed into a weak, futile figure tapping forlornly at the door of the human heart, which He is powerless to open. This is a shameful dishonor to the Christ of the New Testament.[193]

The Protestant Arminian's view of salvation stands in stark contrast to the Biblical view of salvation because he blatantly denies God's sovereignty in man's salvation. In the last analysis, then, as Dr. Miner Raymond [an Arminian], Professor in Garrett Biblical Institute, Illinois, coolly but candidly puts it, "man determines the question of his salvation;" and if so, it is but right and just that God should acknowledge the fact. God appoints the

---

[193] J. I. Packer, "Introductory Essay," in *An Introduction to John Owen's The Death of Death in the Death of Christ* (Venice, Fla.: Chapel Library, 2000), pp. 26–27.

condition: believe and persevere; but he cannot make the sinner believe and persevere.[194]

This false Arminian view also suggests that sinners have the ability to accept or refuse God's grace when He effectually calls them.

> "Our human system," says Dr. Whedon, "is a system of free agents upon whose will and determination it depends whether they will attain eternal bliss or eternal woe....In the sinner's act of acceptance of God's saving grace we promptly deny any 'will-making' on the part of God which excludes man's power of not-willing or refusing. God demands a free acceptance. He does not make a farce of our probation by first requiring our free-willing, and then imposing upon us a 'make-willing.' The free-willing and the 'make-willing' are incompatible."[195]

Dr. Whedon's statement proves that those who hold this unscriptural view believe that the final determination of man's salvation is regarded as being in the power of his will. According to this view, it is man's will that really assists God's grace to save him. The synergistic principle upon which this salvation is based is less on that of grace and more on human willing. Also, Dr. Whedon's unscriptural view completely overlooks the fact that after Adam, no sinner was ever put on probation when he entered this world. Man's probation ended when Adam, man's federal head and legal representative, sinned. If one believes he is on probation, he would be admitting that he is trying to gain salvation by his works.

---

[194] John L. Girardeau, *"Calvinism and Evangelical Arminianism"*, p.70
[195] Ibid., p. 70.

To reinforce the false Arminian teaching of the "rights" of man's free-will, some say, "God will not save the sinner against the sinner's will." This statement is true to a certain extent because God recognizes that the unsaved sinner's will is naturally hostile toward God's will when it goes against his own. So, God must persuade the sinner by His love and grace to save him. And in order to do this God uses the ordinary means given to man. God uses the ordinary means of our minds, our affections and our wills. God does not bypass them as if we did not have them. God does not work directly through us. He does not believe for us, repent for us, or choose to receive Christ for us. No, God applies His grace to our minds, and affections them to convince them of the truth of His word which in turn changes their wills. *God's enabling grace is always efficacious because it is determining grace,*

God's enabling grace does not force us to become Christians. Instead, God woos us by making His intentions of His love for us known to us and He wins us by His love. His careful courtship of us through His love letters from the Bible speaks to our minds, affections, and wills. Martin Chemnitz said: "For it is certain that the Holy Spirit does not in conversion abolish, destroy, or extinguish the elements of the soul, but He does that in such a way that He mortifies and takes away the corruption that clings to them [the mind, affections and will], so that, when these organs have been renewed and prepared, He can use them for the impulses and actions of the new man." God's Holy Spirit works in us and upon us; yet He preserves our wills and voluntary obedience. He works by changing or renewing our minds, affections, and wills. He works in us and not against us or without us.

God uses ordinary means to supernaturally convert us. As Augustine said: "The grace of God through our Lord Jesus Christ is not bestowed on stones, or on wood, or on cattle; for they lack the necessary endowments, namely, mind and will, in which God is accustomed to work in His usual way, through the Word and sacraments, and in which conversion must take place." The Holy Spirit liberates our minds, affections, and wills so that we will be affectionately drawn by and rationally persuaded of God's love for us as was shown to us through Christ Jesus. The Holy Spirit spiritually illuminates our understanding by using the ordinary path of reason, which in turn influences and frees the regular motion of our wills to humbly and to joyfully submit to God's will for our salvation.

As Stephen Charnock said in his book, *The Doctrine of Regeneration,* "The understanding going before with light, the will following after with love....No man can be forced to believe against his reason, or love against his will, or desire against his inclinations."[196] So, in this sense the saying, "God will not save the sinner against the sinner's will" is true because God changes or renews the sinner's will so that he willingly desires to be saved. "Thy people shall be willing in the day of thy power." (Psalm 110:3).

Martin Luther said: "When the blessed fathers defend free-will, they praise its capacity for freedom, namely, that it can be turned to good by the grace of God and become free indeed, for which it was created." Therefore, through this means of supernatural regeneration a person's will is spiritually set free or enabled to freely will, for the first time, to do anything spiritually good.[197]

So, God's choice to distribute His grace to some sinners and not to other sinners is neither dependent upon nor determined by their wills. We must remind you, if it were left up to the sinner's natural will, he would never choose God or His salvation offered through Jesus. It is the sinner's hands that are spiritually tied, not God's.

---

[196] Stephen Charnock, *The Doctrine of Regeneration* (Grand Rapids: Baker, 1840), p. 269.
[197] Jer. 13:23; Matt. 7:18; Rom. 3:9–12; Acts 18:27; 11:18; Phil. 2:13.

Therefore, the sinner's salvation is dependent upon God's decree made before the foundation of the world either to give His irresistible grace to the sinner or to withhold it from him. God's choice determines whether or not the sinner will receive Jesus. God refuses to share the merit of His grace with anyone else. As the apostle Paul said, "So one's destiny does not depend on his own willing or strenuous actions but on God's having mercy on him" (Rom. 9:16 WILLIAMS). "For it is by His unmerited favor [grace] through faith that you have been saved; it is not by anything you have done, it is the gift of God. It is not the result of what anyone can do, so that no one can boast of it" (Eph. 2:8–9 WILLIAMS).

Those who claim they were saved by exercising their free-will to accept Jesus do not have a biblical understanding either of their own total depravity, or the irresistible grace offered in the Holy Spirit's work of regeneration. They believe all men were born with a God-given free-will that could choose either to accept or reject Jesus. They do not believe their will was ever in bondage to sin, so they never really needed God's gracious, liberating work of regeneration to receive Jesus by faith. These people credit the human will for nothing less than a "savior" or "co-redeemer" type of virtue.

God's sovereign grace is selective. He chose some to be saved and left others in their sins. He alone determines who will be saved.

The apostle Paul said, "What then shall we say? Is God unjust? Not at all! For he says to Moses, "I will have mercy on whom I will have mercy, and I will have compassion on whom I will have compassion....Therefore God has mercy on whom he wants to have mercy, and he hardens whom he wants to harden. (Rom. 9:14, 18 NIV; see also 11:1–8).

Some refuse to believe this because it seems undemocratic and unjust. They believe man should be able to choose his own destiny. And so do we. But you see, man has already chosen his destiny in the Garden of Eden. Adam and all mankind in Adam chose death and hell for their eternal destinies.

Some think that for God to be fair He must choose everyone or none at all or He must give everyone an equal opportunity to believe. To them, God's love must not discriminate between individual sinners. Yet God's love made a discriminatory choice between Jacob and Esau (twins) when they were still in Rebecca's womb. God told Rebecca, "Jacob have I loved, but Esau have I hated."[198] Here we have an example of God's electing love. He chose to love Jacob and to hate Esau.

There are some who contend that this Scripture passage is only meant to announce God's choice or election of Jacob's descendants, the nation of the Israel, from all the nations. They say this Scripture "was only fulfilled in the national subjection of the Edomites, the descendants of Esau, to the Israelites, the descendants of Jacob." It must be "admitted that Jacob and Esau were the respective heads of different nations, and it cannot be denied that they were also individuals [with the same mother and father]. The language of Scripture in regard to them cannot, without violence, be confined to them as national heads. It refers to them chiefly as persons in relations to the divine purpose. Meyer, whose commentaries are held in high repute for critical ability and exegetical fairness and who certainly was not influenced by a partisan zeal for Calvinism, says: Paul, however, has in view, as the entire context, vv. 10, 11, 13 evinces, in the 'the elder and the younger' (the greater and lesser) *Esau and Jacob themselves,* not their *nations.*"[199]

It also cannot be denied that, within the elect nation of Israel, God has chosen or elected individuals. Or else how could Paul say

---

[198] Rom. 9:13

[199] Girardeau, *Calvinism and Evangelical Arminianism*, p. 80.

in Romans 9:6, "They are not all Israel, which are of Israel"?[200]
John Girardeau commented,

> Paul in Romans and Galatians explicitly distinguishes
> between those whom, on the one hand, he designates as
> Israel according to the flesh, outward Jews, the natural
> descendants of Abraham, and those whom, on the other, he
> characterizes as Israel according to the Spirit, inward Jews,
> the true, spiritual children of Abraham and heirs of the
> promise. Both these classes had been elected to the
> enjoyment of particular privileges, but it is remarkable that
> he terms the latter "a remnant according to the election of
> grace." Here then is a palpable distinction between a
> national election to privileges and an individual election to
> salvation. Without it the apostle's language is
> unintelligible.[201]

What does the Bible say about God's electing love?

> I will have mercy on whom I will have mercy, and I will
> have compassion on whom I will have compassion. (Rom.
> 9:15 ASV)

> Was not Esau Jacob's brother? saith the LORD: yet I loved
> Jacob, and I hated Esau. (Mal. 1:2–3)

> The Lord did not set his love upon you, nor choose you,
> because ye were more in number than any people; for ye
> were the fewest of all people: but because the LORD loved
> you. (Deut. 7:7–8)

---

[200] See also Romans 11:5,7
[201] Girardeau, *Calvinism and Evangelical Arminianism* p. 88.

Thus, says the LORD God unto Jerusalem; Thy birth and thy nativity is of the land of Canaan; thy father was an Amorite, and thy mother an Hittite. And as for thy nativity, in the day thou wast born thy naval was not cut, neither wast thou washed in water to supple thee; thou wast not salted at all, not swaddled at all. None eye pitied thee, to do any of these things unto thee, to have compassion upon thee; but thou wast cast out in the open field, to the loathing of thy person, in the day that thou wast born. And when I passed by thee, and saw thee polluted in thine own blood, I said unto thee when thou wast in thy blood, Live....I have caused thee to multiply as the bud of the field, and thou hast increased and waxen great, and thou art come to excellent ornaments: thy breasts are fashioned, and thine hair is grown, whereas thou wast naked and bare. Now when I passed by thee, and looked upon thee, behold, thy time was the time of love; and I spread my skirt over thee, and covered thy nakedness: yea, I sware unto thee, and entered into a covenant with thee, saith the LORD God. (Ezek. 16:3–8)

Because you are precious in My eyes, you are honored, and I love you; therefore, I will give men in your place and nations in exchange for your life. (Isa. 43:4 NEW BERKELEY)

In all their affliction he was afflicted, and the angel of his presence saved them: in his love and in his pity he redeemed them; and he bare them, and carried them all the days of old. (Isa. 63:9 ASV)

Doubtless thou art our father, though Abraham be ignorant of us, and Israel acknowledge us not: thou, O LORD art our father, our redeemer; thy name is from everlasting. (Isa. 63:16)

Can a woman forget her suckling child, that she should not have compassion on the son of her womb? yea, they may forget, yet will I not forget you. (Isa. 49:15)

The LORD hath appeared of old unto me, saying, Yea, I have loved thee with an everlasting love: therefore with lovingkindness have I drawn thee. (Jer. 31:3)

The LORD thy God in the midst of thee is mighty; he will save, he will rejoice over thee with joy; he will rest in his love, he will joy over thee with singing. (Zeph. 3:17)

I in them and You in Me; that they may be made perfect in one, and that the world may know that You have sent Me, and have loved them as You have loved Me....And I have declared to them Your name, and will declare it, that the love with which You loved Me may be in them, and I them. (John 17:23, 26 NKJV)

Behold, what manner of love the Father hath bestowed upon us, that we should be called the sons of God. (1 John 3:1)

In this was manifested the love of God toward us, because that God sent his only begotten Son into the world, that we might live through him. Herein is love, not that we loved God, but that he loved us, and sent his Son to be the propitiation for our sins....We love him, because he first loved us. (1 John 4:9–10, 19)

Now our Lord Jesus Christ himself, and God, even our Father, which hath loved us, and hath given us everlasting consolation and good hope through grace, comfort your hearts, and stablish you in every good word and work. (2 Thess. 2:16–17)

John Girardeau continued,

> To some of these proof texts it is objected, that they have
> exclusive reference to Israel as a community elected to
> national privileges....The passages cannot possibly be
> limited to the outward nation of Israel apart from the true,
> spiritual Israel [the Old Testament Church (Acts 7:38)] who
> are in Scripture emphatically characterized as the seed of
> Abraham and Jacob. Take the powerful passage quoted
> from the thirty-first chapter of Jeremiah, as an example. The
> whole context in which it stands, and especially the great,
> evangelical promise which is connected with it, make it
> apparent that the electing love, which it proclaims,
> terminates not only on Israelitish and Jewish believers, but
> also on all God's true people, and is the fountain of spiritual
> and saving blessings: "Behold, the days come, saith the
> LORD, that I will make a new covenant with the house of
> Israel, and with the house of Judah: not according to the
> covenant that I made with their fathers in the day that I took
> them by the hand to bring them out of the land of Egypt;
> which my covenant they brake, although I was an husband
> unto them, saith the LORD: but this shall be the covenant
> that I will make with the house of Israel; after those days,
> saith the LORD, I will put my law in their inward parts, and
> write it in their hearts; and will be their God, and they shall
> be my people. And they shall teach no more every man his
> neighbor, and every man his brother, saying, Know the
> LORD: for they shall all know me, from the least of them
> unto the greatest of them, saith the LORD: for I will forgive
> their iniquity, and I will remember their sin no more." [202]

---

[202] Ibid., pp. 58–59.

When God makes this New Covenant He makes it with the New Testament Church which includes the house of Israel, the house of Judah, and all the Gentile nations (Gen. 12:1-3; Gal. 3:6-9,26,28-29; Rom. 2:28-29).

Stop and consider this. God would not be unjust if He withheld His love and grace from all. Nor would He be unjust if He withheld His love and grace from some. God did not have to choose any sinners, but it pleased Him to choose many. "Blessed is the man whom thou choosest, and causeth to approach unto thee, that he may dwell in thy courts" (Ps. 65:4). The apostle Paul said, "Even as He [God the Father] chose us in Him [God the Son] before the foundation of the world in love having foreordained us unto adoption as sons through Jesus Christ unto Himself [God the Father]" (Eph. 1:4 ASV).

God is a God of love, justice, and goodness. His justice causes Him to rightfully condemn to hell for their sins those His love has not elected. He has left all fallen angels in their sin, and we believe this is consistent with His goodness. Why then is it inconsistent with His goodness to leave some fallen men in their sin? As John Girardeau said, "If all men are sinners by their own free self-decision and therefore, by their own fault, there would have been no injustice had God withheld his grace from all."[203] For those who still find fault with God about this, the apostle Paul wrote,

> O man! who are you, anyway, to talk back to God? The thing that is being molded does not say to the one who molds it, "Why do you make me this way," does it? Does not the potter have the right with the clay to make from the same lump one utensil for noble use and another for ignoble use? What if God, wanting to show His anger and to evidence His power, with great patience endured the agents

---

[203] Ibid., p. 190.

that deserve wrath and have been prepared for destruction, so that He might make known the wealth of His glory to the recipients of mercy, whom previously He prepared for glory, even us whom He has called not only from among the Jews but also from among the Gentiles? (Rom. 9:20–22 NEW BERKELEY)

CHAPTER 10

GOD'S SOVEREIGN GRACE: HIS LIMITED OR DEFINITE ATONEMENT

Christ's death was unique in that as High Priest, He did not offer up an animal sacrifice. He offered Himself as the innocent sacrifice. Christ voluntarily offered up Himself through His death on the cross as a sacrifice to God for sins. He did not die for His own sins because He was sinless.

Well, then, for whom did Christ die? John Owen asked, Did Christ die for "all of the sins of all men, all of the sins of some men, or some of the sins of all men?"[204] **The answer is Christ died for all of the sins of some men**.

While it is true that Jesus' shed blood is sufficient to pay for the sins of all mankind, it did not pay for the sins of all mankind. Otherwise, all mankind will be saved as some claim. In other words, if Jesus secured the salvation of all men by his death, why does Jesus bother to warn men of eternal torment in a place called Hell?

If Christ died for all the sins of all men, John Owen asks, "Why are not all men free from the punishment due unto their sins? Some answer, Because of unbelief. Is this unbelief a sin, or is it not? If it be, then Christ suffered the punishment due unto it, or He did not. If He did, why must that hinder them more than their other sins for which He died? If He did not, He did not die for all their sins!"[205]

It is only those whom God has chosen before the world existed who are those for whom Christ died. God designed Jesus'

---

[204] John Owen, *For Whom Did Christ Die?* (Venice, Fla.: Chapel Library, n.d.).
[205] John Owen, Tract entitled "For Whom Did Christ Die?", Chapel Library, Venice, FL, 33595

atonement to be limited. It is limited by its purpose. Its intended purpose was to secure salvation only for those sinners whom God has chosen. This design of a definite, limited or particular atonement was made by God's righteous judgment and was carried out by His sovereign will. The Bible says:

Shall not the judge of the earth do right? (Gen. 18:25)

What his soul desireth, even that he doeth. (Job 23:13)

Jehovah of hosts hath sworn, saying, Surely, as I have thought, so shall it come to pass; and as I have purposed, so shall it stand: ...For Jehovah of hosts hath purposed, and who shall annul it? and his arm is stretched out, and who shall turn it back? (Isa. 14:24, 27 ASV)

And all the inhabitants of the earth are reputed as nothing: and he doeth according to his will in the army of heaven, and among the inhabitants of the earth: and none can stay his hand, or say unto him, What doest thou? (Dan. 4:35 ASV)

O the depth of the riches both of the wisdom and knowledge of God! how unsearchable are his judgments, and his ways past finding out! For who hath known the mind of the LORD? or who been his counsellor? or who hath first given to him, and it shall be recompensed unto him again? For of him, and through him, and to him, are all things: to whom be glory forever. Amen. (Rom. 11:33–36)

Matthew 20:28 describes Jesus' blood atonement as a ransom for many, not for all.[206] We are aware that 1 Timothy 2:6 says that Jesus is given as a ransom for all. But we believe that the word *all*

---

[206] Matt. 20:28.

used in this verse means that Christ's ransom is freely offered to all people regardless of their nationalities because the Bible says that His blood does "ransom men for God from every tribe and tongue and people and nation."[207] However, this does not mean He died for every person who ever lived, lives now, or will live. If it did, why does the Bible say Jesus ransomed men from every tribe, tongue, people, and nation if it really meant to say Jesus ransomed every tribe, tongue, people, and nation? At the establishment of the sacrament of the Lord's Supper, Jesus said, "This is my blood of the new testament, which is shed for many [notice He did not say all] for the remission of sins."[208]

You may ask, What about the Bible verses—John 1:29; 3:16; 2 Corinthians 5:19; 1 John 2:2; 4:14—that speak about Jesus dying for "the world" and "all men"? We answer that these expressions are intended to show Jesus died for all men without distinction. For example, Jesus died for the whole world, that is, He died not only for Jews but also for Gentiles.[209] His atonement is international in its scope. Furthermore, He not only died for kings but also for janitors.[210] He not only died for males but also for females.[211] Jesus' atoning death is offered to sinners regardless of their races, classes, or genders.

However, Jesus did not die for all people without exception. This means He did not die for all Jews and all Gentiles. He died for many from both of these categories of the human race. The object and range of Jesus' atonement was limited by God's intention to save only the particular individuals He chose to give to Jesus.[212] He

---

[207] Isa. 53:11–12; Rev. 5:9; Gen. 12:3; Gal. 3:16.

[208] Matt. 26:28.

[209] Gen. 12:3; Isa. 9:1–2; 49:5–6; Acts 26:23.

[210] Ps. 72:8–11; Isa. 49:23; Matt. 2:1–2.

[211] Gal. 3:28.

[212] Isa. 53:10; John 6:37; 17:9; Heb. 2:13.

laid His life down for particular individuals called His sheep or His elect people.[213] Arthur Pink explained, "The objects of God's love in John 3:16 are precisely the same as the objects of Christ's love in John 13:1: 'Now before the Feast of the Passover, when Jesus knew that His time was come that He should depart out of this world unto the Father, having loved His own which were in the world, He loved them unto the end.' "[214] Jesus loved His own, His elect sheep. He neither loved the goats (the non-elect), nor did He die for them.[215]

Arthur Pink commented in his book, *The Sovereignty of God:*

In Scripture the word "all" (as applied to humankind) is used in two senses—absolutely and relatively. In some passages it means *all without exception*; in others it signifies *all without distinction*. As to which of these meanings it bears in any particular passage, must be determined by the context and decided by a comparison of parallel scriptures. That the word "all" *is* used in a *relative* and *restricted* sense, and in such case means all without distinction and *not* all without exception, is clear from a number of scriptures, from which we select two or three as examples. "And there went out unto him *all* the land of Judea, and they of Jerusalem, and were *all* baptized of him in the river Jordan, confessing their sins" (Mark 1:5). Does this mean that *every man, woman, and child* from "*all* the land of Judea and they of Jerusalem" were baptized of John in Jordan? Surely not. Luke 7:30 distinctly says, "But the Pharisees and lawyers rejected the counsel of God against

---

[213] John 10:11; Eph. 5:25.
[214] Arthur W. Pink, *The Sovereignty of God* (Grand Rapids: Baker, 1976), pp. 204–205 (emphasis in original).
[215] Matt. 25:31–46; John 10:26.

themselves, *being not baptized of him.*" Then what does "all baptized of him" mean? We answer it *does not mean* all without exception, *but* all without distinction, that is, all classes and conditions of men. The same explanation applies to Luke 3:21. Again, we read, "And early in the morning He came again into the Temple, and *all the people* came unto Him; and He sat down and taught them" (John 8:2); are we to understand this expression absolutely or relatively? Does "all the people" mean all without exception or all without distinction, that is, all classes and conditions of people? Manifestly the latter; for the Temple was not able to accommodate *everybody* that was in Jerusalem at this time, namely, the Feast of Tabernacles. Again, we read in Acts 22:15, "For thou (Paul) shalt be His witness *unto all men* of what thou hast seen and heard." Surely "all men" here does not mean every member of the human race. Now we submit that the words "who gave Himself a ransom *for all*" in 1 Timothy 2:6 mean all without distinction, and *not* all without exception. He gave Himself a ransom for men of all nationalities, of all generations, of all classes; in a word, for all the elect, as we read in Rev. 5:9, "For Thou wast slain, and hast redeemed us to God by Thy blood *out of every* kindred, and tongue, and people, and nation." That this is not an *arbitrary* definition of the "all" in our passage is clear from Matt. 20:28 where we read, 'The Son of Man came not to be ministered unto, but to minister, and to give His life *a ransom for many*," which limitation would be quite meaningless if He gave Himself a ransom for all without exception. Furthermore, the qualifying words here, "to be testified in due time," must be taken into consideration. If Christ gave Himself a ransom for the whole human race, in what sense will this be "*testified* in due time"? seeing that multitudes of men will certainly be eternally lost. But, if our text means that Christ gave Himself a ransom for God's elect, for all without distinction, without distinction of nationality, social prestige, moral character, age or sex, then the meaning of these qualifying words is quite intelligible, for in "due time" this *will* be "testified" in the actual and accomplished salvation of *every one of them.*[216]

Nevertheless, we will examine a few passages to satisfy any objections our readers may still have. Authur W. Pink again wrote:

There is one passage more than any other which is appealed to by those who believe in universal redemption, and which at first sight appears to teach that Christ died for the whole human race. We have therefore decided to give it a detailed examination and exposition. "And He is the propitiation for our sins: and not for ours only, but also for the sins of the whole world" (1 John 2:2). This is the passage which, apparently, most favors the Arminian view of the Atonement, yet if it be considered attentively it will be seen that it does so *only* in appearance, and not in reality. Below we offer a number of conclusive proofs to show that this verse *does not* teach that Christ has propitiated God on behalf of all the sins of all men.

In the first place, the fact that this verse opens with "and" necessarily links it with what has gone before. We, therefore, give a literal word for word translation of 1 John 2:1 from Bagster's Interlinear: "Little children my, these things I write to you, that ye may not sin; and if any one

---

[216] Pink, *The Sovereignty of God,* pp. 68–70 (emphasis in original).

should sin, a Paraclete we have with the Father, Jesus Christ (the) righteous." It will thus be seen that the apostle John is here writing *to* and *about* the *saints* of God. His immediate purpose was two-fold: first, to communicate a message that would keep God's children from sinning; second, to supply comfort and assurance to those who might sin, and, in consequence, be cast down and fearful that the issue would prove fatal. He, therefore, makes known to them the provision which God has made for just such an emergency. This we find at the end of v.1 and throughout v.2. The ground of comfort is two-fold: let the downcast and repentant believer (1 John 1:9) be assured that, first, he has an "Advocate with the Father"; second, that this Advocate is "the propitiation for our sins." Now *believers only* may take comfort *from this,* for they alone have an "Advocate," for them alone is Christ the propitiation, as is proven by *linking* the Propitiation ("and") with "the Advocate"!

In the second place, if other passages in the New Testament which speak of "propitiation" be compared with 1 John 2:2, it will be found that it is *strictly limited* in its scope. For example, in Romans 3:25 we read that God set forth Christ "a propitiation *through faith* in His blood." If Christ is a propitiation "through faith," then He *is not* a propitiation to those who have no faith!...

In the third place, *who* are meant when John says, "He is the propitiation for *our* sins"? We answer, *Jewish believers.* And a part of the proof on which we base this assertion we now submit to the careful attention of the reader.

In Gal. 2:9 we are told that *John*, together with James and Cephas, were apostles "unto the circumcision" (i.e., *Israel*). In keeping with this, the Epistle of James is addressed to "the twelve tribes, which are scattered abroad" (1:1). So, the first Epistle of Peter is addressed to "the elect who are sojourners of the Dispersion" (1 Peter 1:1 RV). And John also is writing *to* saved Israelites, but *for* saved Jews *and* saved Gentiles.

Some of the evidences that John *is* writing *to* saved Jews are as follows. (a) In the opening verse he says of Christ, "Which *we* have seen with *our* eyes…and *our* hands have handled." How impossible it would have been for the Apostle Paul to have commenced any of *his* epistles to *Gentile* saints with such language!

(b) "Brethren, I write no new commandment unto you, but an old commandment which *ye* had *from the beginning*" (1 John 2:7). The "beginning" here referred to is the beginning of the public manifestation of Christ—in proof compare 1:1; 2:13, etc. Now these believers the Apostle tells us, *had* the "old commandment" *from the beginning.* This was true of *Jewish* believers, but it was not true of *Gentile* believers.

(c) "I write unto you, fathers, because *ye have known* Him from the beginning" (2:13). Here again, it is evident that it is *Jewish* believers that are in view.

(d) "Little children, it is the last time: and as ye *have heard* that Antichrist shall come, even now are there many antichrists; whereby we know that it is the last time. *They* went out from *us,* but they were not of us" (2:18, 19). These brethren to whom John wrote *had* "heard" from Christ Himself that Antichrist should come (see Matt. 24). The "many antichrists" whom John declares "went out *from us*" were all *Jews,* for during the first century none but a *Jew* posed as the Messiah. Therefore, when John says, "He is the propitiation for *our* sins," he can only mean for the sins of *Jewish believers*.[217]

In the fourth place, when John added, "And not for ours only, but also for *the whole world*," he signified that Christ was the propitiation for the sins of *Gentile* believers *too,* for, as previously shown, "the world" is a term *contrasted* from Israel. This interpretation is unequivocally established by a careful comparison of 1 John 2:2 with John 11:51, 52, which is a strictly parallel passage: "And this spake he not of himself: but being high priest that year, he prophesied that Jesus should die for that nation; And not for that nation only, but that also He should gather together in one the children of God that were scattered abroad." Here Caiaphas, under inspiration, made known *for whom* Jesus should "die." Notice now the corespondency of his prophecy with this declaration of John's: "He is the propitiation for our (believing Israelites) sins." "He prophesied that Jesus should die for that nation." "And not ours only." "And not for that nation only." "But also for the whole world." That is, Gentile believers scattered throughout the earth. "He should gather together in one the children of God that were scattered abroad."

In the fifth place, the above interpretation is confirmed by the fact that no other is consistent or intelligible. If the

---

[217] Ibid., pp. 257-259, footnote, p. 259: "It is true that many things in John's Epistle apply equally to believing Jews *and* believing Gentiles. Christ is the Advocate of the one, as much as the other. The same may be said of many things in the Epistle of James which is also a *catholic*, or *general* epistle, though expressly addressed to the twelve tribes scattered abroad."

"whole world" signifies the whole human race, then the first clause and the "also" in the second clause are absolutely meaningless. If Christ is the propitiation for *everybody*, it would be idle tautology to say, first, "He is the propitiation for *our* sins and *also* for everybody." There could be no "also" if He is the propitiation for the entire human family. Had the apostle meant to affirm that Christ *is* a universal propitiation he had omitted the first clause of v. 2, and simply said, "He is the propitiation for the sins of the world." Confirmatory of "not for ours (Jewish believers) only, but also for the whole world"—Gentile believers, too; compare John 10:16; 17:20.

In the sixth place, our definition of "the whole world" is in perfect accord with other passages in the New Testament. For example: "Whereof ye heard before in the word of the truth of the Gospel; which is come unto you, as it is in *all the world*" (Col. 1:5, 6). Does "all the world" here mean, absolutely and unqualifiedly, all mankind? Had all the human family heard the Gospel? No; the apostle's obvious meaning is that, the Gospel, instead of being confined to the land of Judea, had gone abroad, without restraint, *into Gentile lands*. So in Romans 1:8: "First, I thank my God through Jesus Christ for you all, that your faith is spoken of throughout *the whole world.*" The apostle is here referring to the faith of these Roman saints being spoken of in a way of *commendation*. But certainly all mankind did not so speak of their faith! It was the whole world *of believers* that he was referring to! In Revelation 12:9 we read of Satan "which deceiveth *the whole world.*" But again this expression cannot be understood as a universal one, for Matthew 24:24 tells us that Satan does not and cannot "deceive" God's elect. Here it is "the whole world" *of unbelievers*.

In the seventh place, to insist that "the whole world" in 1 John 2:2 signifies the entire human race is to undermine the very foundations of our faith. If Christ is the propitiation for those that are lost equally as much as for those that are saved, then what assurance have we that believers too may not be lost? If Christ is the propitiation for those now in hell, what guarantee have I that I may not end in hell? The blood-shedding of the incarnate Son of God is the *only* thing which can keep any one out of hell, and *if* many for whom that precious blood made propitiation are now in the awful place of the damned, then may not that blood prove inefficacious for me! Away with such a God-dishonoring thought.

However men may quibble and wrest the Scriptures, one thing is certain: The Atonement is no failure. God will not allow that precious and costly sacrifice to fail in accomplishing, completely, that which it was designed to effect. Not a drop of that holy blood was shed in vain. In the Last Great Day there shall stand forth no disappointed and defeated Saviour, but One who "*shall* see of the travail of His soul and *be satisfied*" (Isaiah 53:11). These are not our words, but the infallible assertion of Him who declares, "My counsel shall stand, and I will do *all* My pleasure" (Isa. 46:10). Upon this impregnable rock we take our stand. Let others rest on the sands of human speculation and twentieth-century theorizing if they wish. That is their business. But to God they will yet have to render an account. For our part we had rather be railed at as a narrow-minded, out-of-date, hyper-Calvinist, than be found repudiating God's truth by reducing the Divinely-efficacious atonement to a mere fiction.[218]

The most common response that people give you when you tell them that *world* in John 3:16 does not include every last individual on the planet and that *world* does not always mean *world* is, "Yes, it does. *World* means *world.*" According to Mr. Pink, the word *world* or *kosmos* in the Greek language can be used several different ways, depending on the context in which it is used.

Below we will refer to a few passages where the term occurs, suggesting a tentative definition in each case:

1. "Kosmos" is used of the Universe as a whole: Acts 17:24-"God made *the world* and all things therein, seeing that He is Lord of *heaven and earth.*"
2. "Kosmos" is used of the earth: John 13:1; Eph. 1:4, etc., "When Jesus knew that His hour was come that He should depart *out of the world* unto the Father, having loved His own which were *in the world,* He loved them unto the end." "Depart out of this world" signifies, leave this earth. "According as He hath chosen us in Him before *the foundation of the world.*" This expression signifies, before the earth was founded—compare Job 38:4, etc.
3. "Kosmos" is used of the world-system: John 12:31, etc. "Now is *the judgment* of this *world*: now shall *the Prince of this world* be cast out."—compare Matt.4:8 and 1 John 5:19., R.V.
4. "Kosmos" is used of the whole human race: Rom. 3:19, etc.—"Now we know that what things soever the law saith, it saith to them who are under the law: that *every* mouth may

---

[218] Ibid., pp. 257–261 (emphasis in original).

be stopped, and *all the world* may become guilty before God."

5. "Kosmos" is used of humanity minus believers: John 15:18; Rom. 3:6—"If *the world hate* you, ye know that it hated Me before it hated you." Believers do not "hate" Christ, so that "the world" here *must* signify the world of *un*-believers in contrast from believers who love Christ. "God forbid: for then how shall God *judge the world?*" Here is another passage where "the world" *cannot* mean "you, me, and everybody," for *believers will not* be judged by God, see John 5:24. So that here, too, it must be the world of *un*-believers which is in view.

6. "Kosmos" is used of Gentiles in contrast from Jews: Rom. 11:12, etc. "Now if the fall of them (Israel) be *the riches of the world*, and the diminishing of them (Israel) *the riches of the Gentiles*; how much more their (Israel's) fulness."....Here, again, "the world" *cannot* signify all humanity for it *excludes* Israel!

7. "Kosmos" is used of believers only: John 1:29; 3:16, 17; 6:33; 12:47; 1 Cor.4:9; 2 Cor. 5:19. We leave our readers to turn to these passages, asking them to note, carefully, exactly *what is said and predicted of* "the world" in each place.[219]

In 2 Cor. 5:19 we read, "To wit, that God was in Christ, reconciling *the world* unto Himself." What is meant by this is clearly defined in the words immediately following, "not imputing their trespasses unto them." Here again, "the world" *cannot* mean "the world of the ungodly," for *their* "trespasses" *are* "imputed" to them, as the judgment of the Great White Throne will yet show. But 2 Cor. 5:19 plainly

---

[219] Ibid., pp. 253–54 (emphasis in original).

teaches there *is* a "world" which *are* "reconciled," reconciled unto God, because their trespasses are *not* [imputed] reckoned to their account, having been borne by their Substitute. Who then are they? Only one answer is fairly possible—the world of God's people.[220]

In 2 Cor. 5:14 we read, "One died *for all*." But that is not all this scripture affirms. If the entire verse and passage from which these words are quoted be carefully examined, it will be found that instead of teaching an unlimited atonement, it emphatically argues a limited design in the death of Christ. The whole verse reads, "For the love of Christ constraineth us; because we thus judge, that if One died for all, then were all dead." It should be pointed out that in the Greek there is the definite article before the last "all," and that the verb here is in the aorist tense, and therefore, should read, "We thus judge: that if one died for all, then they all died." The apostle is here drawing a conclusion as is clear from the words "we thus judge, that if...then were." His meaning is, that those for whom the One died are regarded, judicially, as having died too. The next verse goes on to say, "And He died for all, *that* they which live should not henceforth live unto themselves, but unto Him which died *for them*, and rose again." The One not only died, but "rose again," and so, too, did the "all" for whom He died, for it is here said they "live." Those for whom a substitute acts are legally regarded as having acted themselves. In the sight of the law the substitute and those whom he represents are one. So it is in the sight of God. Christ was identified with His people and His people were identified with Him, hence when He died they died (judicially) and when He rose they rose also.

---

[220] Ibid., p. 204 (emphasis in original).

But further we are told in this passage (v. 17), that if any man be in Christ he is a new creation; he has received a new life in fact as well as in the sight of the law, hence the "all" for whom Christ died are here bidden to live henceforth no more unto themselves, "but unto Him which died for them, and rose again." In other words, those who belonged to this "all" for whom Christ died, are here exhorted to manifest practically in their daily lives what is true of them judicially: they are to "live unto Christ who died for them." Thus the "One died for all" is defined for us. The "all" for which Christ died are they which "live," and which are here bidden to live "unto Him." This passage then teaches three important truths, and the better to show its scope we mention them in their inverse order: certain ones are here bidden to live no more unto themselves but unto Christ; the ones thus admonished are "they which live," that is live spiritually, hence, the children of God, for they alone of mankind possess spiritual life, all others being dead in trespasses and sins; those who do thus live are the ones, the "all," the "them" for whom Christ died and rose again. This passage therefore teaches that Christ died for *all His people*, the elect, those given to Him by the Father; that as the result of His death (and rising again *"for them")* they "live"—and the elect are the *only* ones who *do* thus "live"; and this life which is theirs through Christ must be lived "unto Him," Christ's *love* must now "constrain" them.[221]

"But we see Jesus, who was made a little lower than the angels for the suffering of death, crowned with glory and honor; that He by the grace of God should *taste death for every man"* (Heb. 2:9). This passage need not detain us

---

[221] Ibid., pp. 67–68 (emphasis in original).

long. A false doctrine has been erected here on a false translation. There is no word whatever in the Greek corresponding to "man" in our English version. In the Greek it is left in the abstract—"He tasted death for every." The Revised Version has correctly omitted "man" from the text, but has wrongly inserted it in italics. Others suppose the word "thing" should be supplied—"He tasted death for every thing"— but this, too, we deem a mistake. It seems to us that the words which immediately follow explain our text: "*For* it became Him, for whom are all things, and by whom are all things, in bringing many sons unto glory, to make the captain of their salvation perfect through sufferings." It is of "sons" the apostle is here writing, and we suggest an *ellipsis* of "son"—thus: "He tasted death for every"—and supply *son* in italics. Thus instead of teaching the unlimited design of Christ's death, Hebrews 2: 9,10 is in perfect accord with the other scriptures we have quoted which set forth the *restricted* purpose in the Atonement: it was for the "sons" and not the human race our Lord "tasted death."[222]

The Puritan, John Owen, said this: "The present description of the [every man or] all for whom Christ tasted death by the grace of God will not suit to all and every one, or any but only the elect of God. For, verse 10, they are called, 'many sons to be brought to glory;' verse 11, those that are 'sanctified,' his 'brethren;' verse 13, 'the children that God gave him;' verse 15, those that are 'delivered from the bondage of death;'— none of which can be affirmed of them who are born, live, and die the 'children of the wicked one.'"....For these and like reasons we cannot be induced to hearken to our adversaries' petition, being fully

---

[222] Ibid., p. 70 (emphasis in original).

persuaded that by every one here is meant all and only God's elect, in whose stead Christ, by the grace of God, tasted death.[223]

There are people who say that 1 Timothy 2:4 tells us that God loves everyone and therefore, it is God's desire that "all men" be saved. From this passage they mistakenly try to interpret God's desire to save "all men" to mean God's has decreed to save "all men". Well, if that is true, God's decree is impotent because it has failed. We know that there are people who die every day who have not received Jesus Christ as their Savior. What then does 1 Timothy 2:4 say? It says, "who desires all men to be saved and to come to the knowledge of the truth." What is the context here? Paul is talking about prayer being made on behalf of all men, especially men in authority, even those who oppose us. It would be normal not to pray for those who oppose us, but God does not see things as we see them. He sees our prayers for those who oppose us as something admirable. When men of authority come to the knowledge of the truth and are saved they bring tranquility and calm to those under their authority. The conditions of tranquility and calm promote the spread of the gospel. So, the expression "all men" here in verse 4 must refer back to verses 1 and 2. "In this sense, [and in this sense only,] salvation is universal. It is not restricted to any group of men. So the church must not think that prayers must be made for subjects, not for rulers; for Jews, not for Gentiles. No, it is the intention of God our Savior that "all men without distinction of rank, race, or nationality" be saved."[224]

---

[223] John Owen, "The Death of Death," in *The Works of John Owen,* vol. 4 (Carlisle, Pa.: Banner of Truth Trust, 1967), p. 350.
[224] William Henriksen, The New Testament Commentary, Baker Book House, Grand Rapids, MI, 1957, p.95.

People use 1 Timothy 4:10 to say that it speaks of Christ as the Savior of all mankind. This verse says, " . . . that we have put our hope in the living God, who is the Savior of all men, and especially of those who believe" (NIV). But this verse is not speaking of Christ Jesus as the Savior of every individual on the planet. Rather, it is speaking of God the Father and His protecting providence towards all (both man and beast,[225] and especially towards His church.[226] And why would Paul make this distinction between the Savior of "all man" and "those who believe", unless there was a distinction? It is because Paul is saying God the Father shows His protecting providence to all men but especially to believers.

But what about 2 Peter 3:9 which seems to indicate that it is God's will that all should be saved and that none will perish? This chapter is addressed to believers (see verses 1 and 8). Starting with verse 8, Peter tells believers not to be anxious about the promise of Christ's coming. Some believers were probably anxious about the fact that Christ the Lord had not returned in judgment as He had promised He would, and they began to doubt His coming. Others believed His coming was imminent and were probably concerned about their unsaved relatives and friends. Peter tells believers to be patient with the timing of Christ's coming because God is being patient for the elects' sake. Peter is telling them that the Lord will not return before or until every elect person is saved. Notice that Peter says the Lord is "longsuffering to us-ward, not willing any should perish, but that all should come to repentance." According to Turretin, "The will of God here spoken of 'should not be extended further than to the elect and believers, for whose sake God puts off the consummation of the ages, until their number shall be completed.' This is evident from 'the pronoun *us* [in the word *usward*] which precedes, with sufficient clearness designating the

---

[225] Psa. 36:6
[226] 2 Cor. 1: 9–10

elect and believers, as elsewhere more than once, and to explain which he adds, not willing that any, that is, of us, should perish."[227] Peter's language here and elsewhere is similar to that of Paul's when Paul says that Christ will not return until the fullness of the elect Gentiles has come in.[228]

Yet even after reading this, some will continue to say, "Jesus died for all men." They will not be convinced of anything different. They cannot see the difference between God's special, electing love for His elect people and His general, benevolent love or preserving mercy for all.[229] God's benevolent love is an ambiance of many undeserved blessings that serve to support the main idea or picture of His special, undeserved, electing love. These blessings of His benevolent, undeserved love are the blessings of gifts and talents He distributes freely to all to help them earn their living and promote development in all fields of knowledge. Other blessings are good health, food, clothing, faithful spouses, responsible parents, and obedient children. Another blessing is God's sovereign, direct, providential intervention in all people's lives to curb their sins or to protect them from being harmed by someone else's sin.[230] This is God's restraining grace. When God restrains evil by His grace, He maintains moral order in the universe.

Nevertheless, those who do not distinguish between God's sovereign, special, electing love and His general, benevolent love tend to interpret both of them as being one and the same for everyone. After all, God makes His sun to rise on the good and the evil, and He sends the rain on the just and the unjust. Therefore, for

---

[227] David Engelsma, *Hyper-Calvinism and The Call of the Gospel* (Grand Rapids: Reformed Free Publishing, 1980), p. 96.
[228] Acts 15:14; Rom. 11:25.
[229] 1 Tim. 4:10; Luke 6:35; Ps. 145.
[230] Gen. 12:9–20; 20:1–18; 50:15–20; 2 Sam. 15:31; Ps. 76:10; 146:9; Prov. 16:7; 21:1; Acts 3:26.

them, it does not seem to be a big jump in their thinking from God's universal benevolence to a universal atonement as well.

Keep in mind those who think that God, out of His benevolent love, sent Christ to die for all are saying that Christ paid the ransom price to save everyone. On the other hand, they say that Jesus' death only made everybody "saveable." This means His death did not actually ransom anyone. Instead sinners must make free-will decisions to accept Jesus as their Savior before Christ's ransom can secure their salvation. What we have here is Jesus' atoning death which serves as a general ransom payment for all, but which secures salvation for none and was wasted on those who reject it.

We believe, however, that God, out of His sovereign, electing love, sent Christ to die for elect sinners only. Christ's death did not make every sinner "saveable." Instead, man's sin did that for him. Man's helpless condition through his bondage to sin required that someone else must save him by paying a ransom for him to release him from his bondage.[231] He could not rescue himself from his bondage or why use word "ransom"? Christ's ransom payment actually secured salvation for many. However, history and reality show that Christ did not make a ransom payment for all because not everyone gets released from their bondage to sin. This release is only realized by those elect sinners whom God has chosen to ransom.

Based on what has been said thus far, we have questions for those who disagree with us. Our first question is: If sinners' wills are in bondage to sin from birth (and they are), how can they make free-will decisions to accept Christ unless He first releases their wills from bondage? If their reply is that people are born with free-wills, we must ask another question: If men are born with free-wills, why then was it necessary for Christ to make a ransom payment? Our answer is that Christ died for elect sinners to secure the release

---

[231] Romans 5:6

of their wills from the slavery to sin by regeneration and hearing the gospel. Here you have God's method of applying His grace to elect sinners which insures they will hear God calling them to receive Christ by faith, thus, securing their salvation.

The next question is: Since Christ paid the ransom to regenerate men, and our opponents say He paid this for all, why are not all men regenerated? They reply: Because they do not believe on Christ. We ask: How can spiritually dead persons believe on Christ? They must first be regenerated before they can believe. We do not think our free-will opponents want to try to untie this knot by replying that all men are born regenerated.

Finally, we ask: If Christ died for all men and if His death is the ransom payment needed to set sinners free to believe on Him, why do many die still held in their bondage to unbelief? Why are not all men saved? The answer is: Christ *did not* die for all men. He paid the ransom price to save only His elect people.

We will now turn our attention to a rather strange comment made on an obscure passage found in 2 Peter 2:1. Charles R. Smith, Professor of Theology, New Testament, and Greek at Grace Theological Seminary, said in his book, *Did Christ Die Only for the Elect?*

It is true that the word *redemption* is sometimes used as a synonym for salvation. But several of the Greek words used for expressing the idea of redemption refer only to the concept of "paying a price" (the normal words for purchasing or buying). At least two biblical passages speak of Christ "paying a price" for *more* than just the elect. [According to Dr. Smith, the first passage is 1 Timothy 2:6, and we have already covered that.] Second Peter 2:1 speaks of false teachers who deny the Master "who bought them." [According to Dr. Smith,] He [Jesus] "paid the price" for even these false teachers who were definitely lost and bound for hell (vv. 20–23).[232]

Commenting on the clause "who bought them," Henry Alford confidently states: "No assertion of universal redemption can be plainer than this." So Dr. Smith and Dr. Alford are saying that Jesus Christ shed His blood for the redemption and salvation of all the unbelieving and unrepentant false teachers who have died and passed out of this world.

In reply to Dr. Smith and Dr. Alford, we will quote and summarize some of John Owen's comments on 2 Peter 2:1:

The next place is much insisted on—namely, 2 Peter 2:1, "There shall be false teachers among you, denying the Lord that bought them, and bringing upon themselves swift destruction." All things here, as to any proof of the business in hand, are exceedingly dark, uncertain, and doubtful. *Uncertain*, . . . whether the purchase or buying of these false teachers refer to the eternal redemption by the blood of Christ, or a deliverance by God's goodness from the defilement of the world in idolatry, or the like, by the knowledge of the truth,—which last the text expressly affirms [the text reads as follows: "For if after they have escaped the pollutions of the world through the knowledge of the Lord and Saviour Jesus Christ, they are again entangled therein, and overcome, the latter end is worse with them than the beginning. For it had been better for them not to have known the way of righteousness, than, after they have known it, to turn from the holy commandment delivered unto them. But it is happened unto

---

[232] Charles R. Smith, *Did Christ Die Only for the Elect?* (Winona Lake, Ind.: BMH Books, 1975), p. 7.

them according to the true proverb, The dog is turned to his own vomit again; and the sow that was washed to her wallowing in the mire." Verses 20-22]; *uncertain*, whether the apostle speaketh of this purchase according to the reality of the thing, or according to their apprehension and their profession.

On the other side, it is most *certain*—First, That there are no spiritual distinguishing fruits of redemption ascribed to these false teachers, but only common gifts of light and knowledge....Of the former *uncertainties*, whereon our adversaries build their inference of universal redemption (which yet can by no means be wire-drawn thence [proved], were they most certain in their sense), I shall give a brief account, and then speak something as to the proper intendment of the place....

It is most *uncertain* that by buying of these false teachers is meant his purchasing them with the ransom of his blood....Now, the [Greek] word here used, signifieth primarily the buying of things; translatitiously, the redemption of persons;—and the [Hebrew] word in the Old Testament, answering thereunto, signifieth any deliverance, as Deut. 7:8; 15:15; Jer. 15:21, with innumerable other places: and, therefore, some such deliverance is here only intimated. *Secondly*, Because here is no mention of blood, death, price, or offering of Jesus Christ, as in other places, where proper redemption is treated on. The apostle setting forth at large the deliverance they [the false teachers] had had, and the means thereof, verse 20, affirms it to consist in the "escaping of the pollutions of the world," as idolatry, false worship, and the like, "through the knowledge of the Lord and Saviour Jesus Christ"; plainly declaring that their buying was only in respect of this separation from the world, in respect of the enjoyment of the knowledge of the truth; but of the washing in the blood of the Lamb, he is wholly silent. Plainly, there is no purchase mentioned of these false teachers, but a deliverance, by God's dispensations toward them, from the blindness of Judaism or Paganism, by the knowledge of the gospel; whereby the Lord bought them to be servants to him, as their supreme head. So that our adversaries' argument from this place is this:—"God the Lord, by imparting the knowledge of the gospel, and working them to a professed acknowledgment of it and subjection unto it, separated and delivered from the world divers [different people] that were saints in show,— really wolves and hypocrites, of old ordained to condemnation: therefore, Jesus Christ shed his blood for the redemption and salvation of all reprobates and damned persons in the whole world." Who would not admire our adversaries' chemistry?

Neither is it more certain that the apostle speaketh of the purchase of the wolves and hypocrites, in respect of the reality of the purchase, and not rather in respect of that estimation which others had of them,—and, by reason of their outward seeming profession, ought to have had,—and of the profession that [they] themselves made to be purchased by him whom they pretended to preach to others; as the Scripture saith [of Ahaz], "The gods of Damascus smote him," because he himself so imagined and professed, 2 Chron. 28:23. The latter hath this also to render it probable,—namely, that it is the perpetual course of the Scripture, to ascribe all those things to every one that is in the fellowship of the church which are proper to them only who are true spiritual members of the same; as to be *saints, elect, redeemed,* etc. Now, the truth is, from this their profession, that they were bought by Christ, might the apostle justly, and that according to the opinion of our adversaries, press these false teachers, by the way of aggravating their sin. For the thing itself, their being bought, it could be no more urged to them than to heathens and infidels that never heard of the name of the Lord Jesus.[233]

Simon J. Kistemaker, in his *Commentary on Peter and Jude,* wrote,

Were the false teachers former members of the church? The answer to the question must be the affirmative. Peter writes that these teachers are "even denying the sovereign Lord who bought them."...They are "apostate Christians who have disowned their Master." In due time, therefore, Jesus will swiftly destroy them.

The clause *who bought them* presents difficulties for the interpreter. Can those whom Christ has redeemed ever be lost? Did the false teachers lose their salvation? Some commentators assert that "Christ bought them at the tremendous price of his blood to be his forever." But the fact the teachers faced swift destruction contradicts this interpretation. . . . But, if Jesus had given these teachers eternal life, they would have never fallen away. Scripture clearly teaches that those people to whom Jesus has given eternal life "shall never perish" (John 10:28; also see Rom. 8:29–30, 32–35; Eph.1:3–14).

Although Christ's death was sufficient to redeem the whole world, its efficiency comes to light only in God's chosen people. Were the false teachers recipients of God's saving

---

[233] Owen, *The Works of John Owen*, pp. 362–364.

grace? Apparently not, for they repudiated Christ. If we look at the words "denying the Lord who bought them" in the light of the broader context, we discover a clue. They made it known that Jesus had bought them, but they eventually rejected Christ and left the Christian community. As John writes, "They went out from us, but they did not really belong to us" (1 John 2:19 and see Heb. 6:4–6; 10:26–29). Hence, their denial of Christ showed that they were not redeemed.[234]

So the point is, these false teachers were never truly ransomed, bought, or redeemed as they professed to be. It appears they were temporarily separated or delivered from worldly pollutions and idolatry through mere head knowledge (as opposed to heart knowledge) that they had gained from the gospel. These false teachers are like the soil infested with thorns mentioned in the parable of the sower.[235] Like Hymenaeus, Philetus, and Alexander, they gladly received the seed (the gospel) at first, then rejected it; in its stead, they invented heresies for "filthy lucre's" [money] sake.[236] They heard the Word, but the cares of this world and the deceitfulness of riches choked the word, and they were unfruitful.

Jesus said, "Not everyone who says to Me, 'Lord, Lord,' shall enter the kingdom of heaven, but he who does the will of My Father in heaven. Many will say to Me in that day, 'Lord, Lord, have we not prophesied in Your name, cast out demons in Your name, and done many wonders in Your name?' And then I will declare to

---

[234] Simon J. Kistemaker, *New Testament Commentary: James, Epistles of John, Peter, and Jude* (Grand Rapids: Baker, 1987), pp. 281–283.

[235] Matt.13:18-23.

[236] 1 Tim. 1:20; 2 Tim. 2:17; 1 Tim.3:3,8; Titus 1:7, 9–11, 16; 1 Pet. 5:2.

them, 'I never knew you: depart from Me, you who practice lawlessness!' "[237]

It must be understood, explained L. Boettner in *The Reformed Doctrine of Predestination,* that "when the atonement is made universal, its inherent value is destroyed. If it is applied to all men, and if some are lost, the conclusion is that it makes salvation objectively possible for all, but that *it does not actually save anybody.*"[238] In other words, those who say Jesus died for all men actually deny the ransom power of His atonement. If He died for all, this ransom payment must have been exhausted because it failed to secure the intended salvation of all men. It follows from this that "universal atonement" calls into question the sufficiency of the ransom power of Jesus' atonement for any one particular person. If Christ's ransom failed to secure the intended salvation of all men (remember, they say, "Christ died for all men"), how can we be sure it actually secures the salvation of any one particular person? As Charles Spurgeon, that great Baptist minister of old said, "As for a hazy atonement that atones for everybody in general and for nobody in particular—an atonement made equally for Judas and for John—I care nothing for it. But a literal, substitutionary sacrifice—Christ vicariously bearing the wrath of God on my behalf—this calms my conscience with regard to the righteous demands of the law of God and satisfies the instincts of my nature, which declare that, since God is just, He must exact the penalty of my guilt."[239] (See also The Savoy Declaration and the Baptist Confession of 1689, chapter XX entitled, "Of the Gospel and of the extent of the Grace thereof.")

---

[237] Matt. 7:21–23 (NKJV).
[238] Loraine Boettner, *The Reformed Doctrine of Predestination* (Phillipsburg, N. J. : Presbyterian and Reformed Publishing, 1976), pp. 152–153 (emphasis in original).
[239] Charles Spurgeon, *The Fullness of Joy* (New Kensington, Pa.: Whitaker House, 1997), p. 67.

The truth is, as Mr. Boettner points out, Jesus' limited or particular ransom atonement is "like a narrow bridge which goes all the way across the stream." It is planned and constructed to reach its destination on the opposite side. However, those who believe that Jesus died for all men imagine that Jesus' atonement is like a wide bridge. They are so proud of its width that they refuse to consider its length. In their desire to see all men included on their wide bridge, they have forgotten the purpose of the bridge. What good is a wide bridge if its length (its purpose to secure salvation through a ransom) fails to reach its destination on the other side? Their bridge has created its own paradox. Their paradox is that Christ has only made salvation possible for all, and therefore impossible for any. Consequently, if Jesus died to only make salvation possible for all and not to make it actual or certain for anyone, He died in vain.

Jesus died only for His elect people, the church.[240] He died only for those His Father foreknew and predestinated to be His people before time began.

---

[240] Eph. 5:25.

CHAPTER 11
REPROBATION

What is the real underlying objection of the Arminian to the biblical teaching of God's Election, if it is not its complement, the teaching of Reprobation?

The two doctrines [of election and reprobation] stand or fall together. They are opposite sides of the same truth. We have seen that the teaching of Scripture is, that of His mere mercy and according to the good pleasure of His sovereign will, He decreed to save some of the fallen and sinful mass who were thus contemplated as justly condemned. That is Election. The rest consequently, were not elected to be saved, but were passed by and ordained to continue under the just condemnation of Adam's sin and their own sins. That is Reprobation.[241]

The teachings of Election and Reprobation cannot be more clearly taught than in Romans chapter 9.

" . . . for though the twins [Jacob and Esau] were not yet born and had not done anything good or bad, so that God's purpose according to His choice would stand, not because of works but because of Him who calls, it was said to her [Rebekah], 'The older shall serve the younger.' just as it is written, 'Jacob I loved, but Esau I hated.' What shall we say then? There is no injustice with God is there? May it never be! For He says to Moses, 'I will have mercy on whom I will have mercy and I will have compassion on

---

[241] John Girardeau, *Calvinism and Evangelical Arminianism,* pp. 174-176

whom I will have compassion' So then it does not depend
on the man who wills, or the man who runs, but on the
God who has mercy. You will say to me then, 'Why does
He still fault? For who resists His will?' On the contrary,
who are you, 'O man, who answers back to God? The
thing molded will not say to the molder, 'Why did you
make me like this,' will it? Or does not the potter have a
right over the clay, to make from the same lump one
vessel for honorable use and another for common use?
What if God, although willing to demonstrate His wrath
and to make His power known, endured with much
patience vessels of wrath prepared for destruction? And
He did so to make known the riches of His glory upon
vessels of mercy, which He prepared beforehand for
glory, even us whom He also called, not from among Jews
only, but also from among the Gentiles."

"The Westminster Confession of Faith says, 'God from all
eternity did by the most wise and holy counsel of His own will,
freely and unchangeably *fore-ordain whatsoever* comes to pass".
Arthur Pink observes, "If then God *has* fore-ordained whatsoever
comes to pass then He must have decreed that vast numbers of
human beings should pass out of this world unsaved to suffer
eternally in the Lake of Fire."[242]
    The Arminian may object here by reminding us that 1 Timothy
2:4 says: "Who [God] will have all men to be saved, and to come
unto the knowledge of the truth." Again, those who think that this
passage contradicts reprobation argue from the illusion that God
wills that all men without exception be saved. However, the
apostle's meaning here is apparent. Paul is saying that God wills all

---

[242] Arthur Pink, *The Sovereignty of God* (Grand Rapids: Baker,
1976), p. 84.

men without distinction to be saved. This means no nation or rank of society is excluded from salvation, since God wills to offer the gospel to all without distinction.

The Westminster Confession of Faith states:

> In Reprobation God withholds from them or abstains from conferring upon them, those special supernatural, gracious influences, which are necessary to enable them to repent and believe; so that the result is, that they continue in their sin, with the guilt of their transgression upon their head. God also acts positively and judicially by "fore-ordaining to everlasting death" and "ordaining those who have been passed by to dishonor and wrath for their sin." (John 17:9, 12; Romans 9:13, 17–18, 21–23; 11:7–10; 2 Timothy 2:17–20; 1 Thessalonians 5:9; 1 Peter 2:8; 2 Peter 2:3, 12; Jude 4; Revelation 13:8; cf.17:8).

Why is this important to understand? It is important because the Arminian represents the Calvinist as saying something different from this. The Arminian says, "By unconditional election divines of this class [Calvinists] understand an election of persons to eternal life without respect to their faith of obedience, those qualities in them being supposed necessarily to follow as consequences of their election; by unconditional reprobation, the counterpart of the former doctrine, is meant a non-election or rejection of certain persons from eternal salvation; unbelief and disobedience following this rejection as necessary consequences."[243]

___

[243] Richard Watson, *Theological Institutes*, vol. 2, p. 326, in John L. Girardeau, *Calvinism and Evangelical Arminianism*

Concerning reprobation John L. Girardeau argued,
Let these statements be compared. The Calvinist says, God
finds men already disobedient and condemned, and leaves
some of them in the condition of disobedience and
condemnation to which by their own avoidable act they had
reduced themselves. The Arminian represents the Calvinist
as saying, God decrees to reject some of mankind from
eternal salvation, and their disobedience follows as a
necessary consequence. That is to say, if the language
means anything, God's decree of reprobation causes the
disobedience of some men, and then dooms them to eternal
punishment for that disobedience. But who would deny that
to be unjust? That is not what the Calvinistic doctrine
teaches....

This is the first blunder in the Arminian statement of the
Calvinist position. It is represented to be: that God decreed
to cause the first sin of man and then decreed to doom some
of the fallen race to destruction for its commission. The true
statement is: that God decreed to permit sin, and then
decreed to continue some of the race under condemnation
which he foreknew they would, by their own fault, incur.

The second blunder in the Arminian statement of the
Calvinist position is, that the decrees of election and
reprobation are represented as being equally
unconditional....This representation is only partly correct;
and how far it is correct and how far incorrect, it is
important to observe. It is admitted that both the decrees of
election and reprobation are conditioned upon the divine

(Harrisonburg, Va.: Sprinkle Publications, 1890, 1984), pp. 185–
186.

foreknowledge of the Fall; that is to say, the foreknowledge of the Fall is, in the order of thought, pre-supposed by each of these decrees. This is the doctrine of Calvinistic Confessions, and even of Calvin himself [commentaries on Romans 9:11; 1 Peter 1:20]. But the question before us is, whether the divine foreknowledge of the special acts of men, done after the Fall, conditioned these decrees. It has already been shown that in this regard the decree of election is unconditional. It is not conditioned by the divine foreknowledge of the faith, good works and perseverance therein of the individuals whom God wills to save. The question being, whether the decree of reprobation is also unconditional, here a distinction must be taken. The preterition—the passing by—of some of the fallen mass, and leaving them in their sin and ruin, is unconditional. It is not conditioned by the divine foreknowledge of their special sins, rendering them more ill-deserving than those whom God is pleased to elect. So far reprobation is unconditional. In this regard, it is, like election, grounded in the good pleasure of God's sovereign will. But the judicial condemnation—the continuing under the sentence of the broken law—of the non-elect, is conditional. It is conditioned by the divine foreknowledge of the first sin and of all actual transgressions, the special sins which spring from the principle of original corruption. In this respect, and to this extent, the decrees of election and reprobation are different, the one being unconditional, and the other conditional. To say, then, that they are entirely alike in being both unconditional is to misrepresent the Calvinistic position.[244] This exposition is supported by the following

[244] John L. Girardeau, *Calvinism and Evangelical Arminiansm* (Harrisonburg, Va.: Sprinkle Publications, 1984), pp. 185–189.

statement of Principal [William] Cunningham: "God ordains none to wrath or punishment, except on account of their sin, and makes no decree to subject them to punishment which is not founded on, and has reference to, their sin, as a thing certain and contemplated. But the first, or negative, act of preterition, or passing by, is not founded upon their sin, and perseverance in it, as foreseen."[245]

"The third blunder in the Arminian statement of the Calvinistic position is, that the decrees of election and reprobation are alike in being causes from which human acts proceed as effects; the former being the cause of holy acts in those who are to be saved, the latter, of sinful acts in those who are to be lost. After what has already been said there is little need to dwell upon the defectiveness of this statement. A sinner is destitute of any principle of holiness from which holy acts could spring. The efficiency of grace is a necessity to the production of holiness in his case. But the principle of depravity in a sinner's nature is itself a cause of sinful acts. Unless, therefore, the Calvinistic doctrine could be fairly charged with teaching that God causes the sinful principle, it cannot be held to teach that he causes the sinful acts which it naturally produces. On the contrary, it maintains that the principle of sin in the nature of man is self-originated. Its consequences are obviously referred to the same origin: all sin, original and actual is affirmed to be caused by man himself. God, in reprobating the sinner for his sins, cannot be said to cause his sins....Our Standards...afford no sort of shelter to the Hopkinsian error,

---

[245] William Cunningham, Historical Theology, Banner of Truth Trust, Vol. 2 pp. 429-430.

that [God] divine agency…is as positively employed in men's bad volitions and actions as in their good." [246]

Arthur W. Pink adds, "**First**, the doctrine of Reprobation does not mean that God purposed to take innocent creatures, make them wicked, and then damn them. Scripture says,

"God hath made man upright, but they have sought out many inventions."[247]

"God has not created sinful creatures in order to destroy them, for God is not to be charged with the sin of His creatures. That responsibility and criminality is man's. God's decree of Reprobation contemplated Adam's race fallen, sinful, corrupt and guilty. From it God purposed to save a few as monuments of His sovereign grace; the others He determined to destroy as the exemplification of His justice and severity. In determining to destroy these others, God did them no wrong They had already fallen in Adam, their legal representative; they are therefore born with a sinful nature, and in their sins He leaves them. Nor can they complain. This is as they wish; they have no desire for holiness; they love darkness rather than light. Where then, is there any injustice if God "gives them up to their own hearts' lusts".[248]

"**Second,** the decree of Reprobation does not mean that God refuses to save those who earnestly seek salvation. The fact is that the reprobate have no longing *for* the Savior: they see in Him no beauty that they should desire Him. They will not come to Christ-why then should God force them to? He turns *none* away who do

---

[246] Girardeau, Calvinism and Evangelical Arminianism, pp. 189–190.
[247] Ecclesiastes 7:29
[248] Psalm 81:12; Romans 1:18-32

come-then is there injustice of God fore-determining their just doom [it is in this method or sense they are fitted for destruction]? None will be punished but for their iniquities; where then, is the supposed tyrannical cruelty of the Divine procedure? Remember that God is Creator of the wicked, not their wickedness; He is the Author of their being, but not the Infuser of their sin.

"God does not (as we have been slanderously reported to affirm) compel the wicked to sin, as the rider spurs on an unwilling horse. God only says in effect that awful word, 'Let them alone.'[249] He needs only slacken the reins of providential restraint, and withhold the influence of saving grace, and apostate man will only too soon and too surely, of his own accord, fall by his iniquities. Thus, the decree of reprobation neither interferes with the bent of man's own fallen nature, nor serves to render him the less inexcusable." [250]

"**Third,** the decree of Reprobation in no wise conflicts with God's goodness. Though the non-elect are not the objects of His goodness in the same way or the same extent as the elect are, yet they are not wholly excluded from a participation of it. They enjoy the good things of Providence (temporal blessings) in common with God's own children, and very often to a higher degree. But how do they improve them? Does the (temporal) goodness of God lead them to repent? Nay, verily, they do but

> "despise His goodness, and forebearance, and
> longsuffering, and after their hardness impenitency of
> of heart treasure up unto themselves wrath against the
> day of wrath."[251]

---

[249] Matt.15:14

[250] Pink, *The Sovereignty of God,* p. 101.

[251] Matthew 5:45; Romans 2:4-5; Matthew 6:19; Luke 12:14-21

"On what righteous ground, then, can they murmur against not being the objects of His benevolence in the endless ages to come? Moreover, if it did not clash with God's mercy and kindness to leave the entire body of the fallen angels [252] under the guilt of their apostasy; still less can it clash with the Divine perfections to leave some of fallen mankind in their sins and punish them for them."

John Girardeau continued,

But it will be replied that the difficulty is not entirely removed; for reprobation supposes that God withholds from the sinner the efficiency of grace by which alone he could produce holy acts, and so is represented as causing the absence of those acts and the commission of sinful. The rejoinder is plain: the assertion of a correspondence between the two decrees [election and reprobation] in regard to causal efficiency operating upon the sinner is given up. The only similarity remaining is one between election as directly and positively causing holy acts and reprobation as indirectly and negatively occasioning sinful. [In other words, God's decree of reprobation does not directly or positively cause the reprobate sinner to commit sinful acts; his own sinful nature does that. God, however, leaves the reprobate sinner in his sinful condition to continue in his sin]. This amounts to a relinquishment of the analogy affirmed to obtain between them, and the preferment of a separate charge against the justice of reprobation: namely, that God is unjust in withholding from some sinners the efficient grace which he is said to impart to others. But, if all men are sinners by their own free self-decision, and therefore, by their own fault, there would have

---

[252] 2 Peter 2:4

been no injustice had God withheld his grace from all. Consequently, there could have been no injustice in withholding it from some. What is true of all must be true of some....

..."It is clear, in view of what has been said, that the implication contained in the fore-cited Arminian statement of the Calvinistic doctrine of reprobation is far from correct—namely, that God, by virtue of that decree, causes the sins of the non-elect in the same way as, by the virtue of the decree of election, he causes the faith and good works of the elect....

"It might, with some color of plausibility, be said that God was not good in saving some and leaving others to perish, but how it can be pleaded that he was unjust passes comprehension. [Answering the plausibility of the implied argument that, "God was not good because He saved some and left others," Girardeau later asks.]....If the reprobation of *all* the fallen angels was consistent with goodness, why not the reprobation of *some* fallen men?...God, as the supreme Sovereign, pleases to exercise clemency towards some of them, and, as supreme Judge, continues to exercise justice upon others for the purpose of glorifying both his grace and his justice in the eyes of the universe (Rom.9:22-23). God's execution of justice upon criminals is always dreadful; it can never be unjust.

"Arminians and other anti-Calvinists object to the Calvinist doctrine of reprobation because, as they contend, it involves this monstrous assumption: that God judicially condemns to everlasting punishment those whose sin was unavoidable and was therefore no fault of their own. God is represented as magnifying his justice in the punishment of the innocent.[253]

"To say that they [the reprobates] do not will to be damned, is only to say that they are not willing to experience the retributive results of their own self-elected conduct. No criminal is willing to be hanged. But, if he is hanged, his hanging is of his own getting. God gives no man the will to sin, but he justly inflicts the doom of self-elected sin. Nor can his sentence of reprobation be, in any sense, regarded as the cause of that doom. It inflicts what the sinner has freely chosen. Reprobation did not cause sin; it justly punishes it".[254]

Arthur Pink argued,

[Quoting John Calvin] "Predestination we call the decree of God, by which He has determined in Himself, what He would have become of every individual of mankind. For they are not all created with a similar destiny: but eternal life is foreordained for some, and eternal damnation for others. Every man, therefore, being created for one or the other of these ends, we say, he is predestinated either to life or to death."[255] We ask our readers to mark well the above language. A perusal of it should show that what the present writer has advanced in this chapter *is not* "Hyper-

---

[253] Girardeau, *Calvinism and Evangelical Arminianism*, pp. 189–190, 192, 279.

[254] Ibid., pp. 411–412.

[255] "Institutes of Christian Religion" (1536 A.D.), book 3, chapter 21, entitled, "Eternal Election, or God's Predestination of Some to Salvation and of Others to Destruction.

Calvinism" but *real* Calvinism, pure and simple. Our purpose in making this remark is to show that those who, not acquainted with Calvin's writings, in their *ignorance* condemn as ultra-Calvinism that which is simply a reiteration of what Calvin himself taught—a reiteration because that prince of theologians as well as his humble debtor have both found this doctrine in the Word of God itself.

Martin Luther in his most excellent work, "De Servo Arbitrio" (Free Will a Slave), wrote: "All things whatsoever arise from, and depend upon, the Divine appointments, whereby it was preordained who should receive the Word of Life, and who should disbelieve it, who should be delivered from their sins, and who should be hardened in them, who should be justified and who should be condemned. This is the very truth that razes the doctrine of freewill from its foundations, to wit, that God's eternal love of some men and hatred of others is immutable and cannot be reversed.[256]

---

[256] Pink, *The Sovereignty of God*, pp. 105–106 (emphasis in original).

CHAPTER 12

IS GOD'S GRACE COMPATIBLE WITH GOD'S LAW?

"The Covenant of Redemption may be defined as the agreement between the Father and the Son, the Father giving the Son as Head and Redeemer of the elect, and the Son, voluntarily taking the place of those whom the Father had given Him."[257] It is not as though the Holy Spirit was left out of this agreement. The Holy Spirit is the One who applies the plan of salvation, i.e., Jesus' work and the promises of redemption through Christ to our hearts (1Thess. 1:5; 2 Thess. 2:13; 1 Pet.1:2).

This counsel and covenant agreement of God took place in eternity past. [258] In this covenant agreement Christ was promised things (for example, a kingdom, Luke 22:29, a people, John 17:6,9,24 and future glory, John 17:5; Phil. 2:9-11) before He was born and He later refers to His commission from the Father and the task He entrusted to Him.[259] In this Covenant of Redemption "the Father required of the Son, [260] as the last Adam, that He should do what Adam failed to do by keeping the moral law perfectly and atone for Adam's sin and the sins of those whom the Father had given Him. This Covenant of Redemption is a Covenant of Grace to all His spiritual progeny because it secured eternal life for them.

---

[257] L. Berkhof, Systematic Theology, Wm. B. Eerdmans Publishing Co. Grand Rapids, MI, 1939, p.271.
[258] (Eph. 1:4ff; 3:11; 2 Thess. 2:13; 2 Tim. 1:9; Jas. 2:5; 1 Pet. 1:2, etc).
[259] (John 5:30,43; 6:38-40; 10:18; 17:4-12).
[260] (Rom. 5:12-21; 1 Cor. 15:22)

So, there is a mutual role or integral relationship between the moral law in the Covenant of Works made with Adam (Hos. 6:7) and the same moral law in His Covenant of Redemption made with Christ (Psa. 89:3; Isa. 42:6). Even though these two different covenants were made with two different people, the main requirement and basis of both covenants is perfect obedience to God's moral law. So, when the Holy Spirit taught Paul the meaning of the Gospel, Paul understood its direct connection with the moral Law of God. He understood he could not have received God's grace if Christ Jesus had not obeyed the moral law perfectly for him. Therefore, to teach Grace without teaching its connection with God's moral Law will produce an incomplete gospel.

The Covenant of Works (obeying God's commandments perfectly) made with Adam is still in force for **unbelievers** today and because of Adam's failure to keep it, it can no longer be offered to anyone as a Covenant of Life, it can only offer them condemnation. However, it is no longer in force for **believers** because the Covenant of Works, which was based upon condition of Adam's perfect obedience to God's moral law, was fulfilled by Jesus for them. A. W. Pink quoting from A.A. Hodge effectively sharpens our understanding about the abrogation of the Covenant of Works for believers when he said:

In what sense is the covenant of works abrogated? and in what sense is it still in force? We cannot do better than subjoin the answers on one of the ablest theologians [A.A. Hodge] of last century. "This covenant having been broken by Adam, not one of his natural descendants is ever able to fulfill its conditions, and Christ having fulfilled all of its conditions in behalf of all of His own people, salvation is offered now on the condition of faith in Christ Jesus' perfect obediece. In this sense the Covenant of Works having been fulfilled by the second Adam is henceforth abrogated [for believers] under the Gospel.

"Nevertheless, since it is founded upon the principles of immutable justice, it still binds all men who have not fled to the refuge offered in the righteousness of Christ. It is still true that 'he that doeth these things shall live by them', and 'the soul that sinneth it shall die.' This law in this sense remains, and in consequence of the unrighteousness of men condemns them, and in consequence of their absolute inability to fulfill it, it acts as a schoolmaster to bring them to Christ. For He having fulfilled alike its condition wherein Adam failed, and its penalty which Adam incurred, He has become the end of this covenant for righteousness to everyone that believeth, who in Him [Christ] is regarded and treated as having fulfilled the covenant, and merited its promised reward" (A.A. Hodge).[261]

To be sure, Christians ended their relationship with the moral law *as a Covenant of Works* since Christ satisfied its covenant requirement of perfect obedience for them. Being placed into union with their federal head or covenant representative, Jesus Christ, they are freed from the rigor, condemnation and curse of the moral law as a Covenant of Works. God's moral Law can never again condemn them. They are forever acquitted of Adam's sin and their sins because Jesus placed Himself under the Law's condemnation and its curse of death in their place. God will never put Christians on trial for their offenses against God's Law because they have already been tried and condemned in their substitute, Jesus Christ.[262] God will not put a Christian in double jeopardy by requiring two deaths from the same person. John Girardeau, in his book *Calvinism and Evangelical Arminianism,* explains,

---

[261] A. W. Pink, The Divine Covenants, Baker Book House, Grand Rapids, MI, 1973, pp. 61-62.
[262] Rom. 8:1.

Can justice require two deaths—one of the substitute and another of the principle? Would not that be equivalent to two deaths of the principal? Even human governments do not inflict this injustice. During the Napoleonic wars, a recruiting officer told a certain man that he would enroll [draft] him and send him to the field. The man replied that he was not liable to military duty, as he was dead. "How are you dead," said the officer, "when you are speaking to me?" "I hired a substitute," was the rejoinder; "he was killed in battle and I died in him." "I will report the case to the emperor," exclaimed the sergeant. He did so, and the emperor confirmed the position taken by the man. "Let him alone," said Napoleon, "the man is right." He who does a thing through another does it himself."[263] So, did God appoint Christ as our substitute? Did Christ willingly accept the appointment or task and did He not fully perform what was required of Him as our substitute? Then, it is impossible for those who died a legal death in Christ's death to be required to die a second death for the punishment of their sins. "

For some this example of the emperor acting as a just judge may give an even deeper insight into God's **justice** found in 1 John 1:9, which says, "If we confess our sins, God is faithful and *just* to forgive us our sins and to cleanse us from all unrighteousness." It is because God is **just** and because He has satisfied His justice by condemning our substitute in our place for our sins that He can be trusted to forgive us of our sins and not bring them up again to condemn us. "Shall not the Judge of all the earth do right?"

---

[263] John L. Girardeau, *Calvinism and Evangelical Arminianism* (Harrisonburg, Va.: Sprinkle Publications, 1890, 1984), pp. 483–484.

Therefore, Christians may have an assurance of their salvation while they live, that is, before they die because they know they will never experience God's condemnation after they die.[264]

Now what about the Covenant of Works? Is the Covenant of Works altogether abrogated then? "To what extent, then does the consistent Reformed theologian hold the Covenant of Works to be abrogated? The answer may be given by a series of propositions, which will commend themselves to belief by their mere statement: (1) The Ruler's claims to obedience are not abrogated by the subject's failing by transgression, under penal relations to Him: So, all moralists and jurists hold, of all governments. (2) God's [moral] law being the immutable expression of His own perfections, and the creature's obligation to obey being grounded in his nature and relation to God, it is impossible that any change of the legal status under any covenant imaginable, legal or gracious, should abrogate the authority of the law as a rule of acting for us. (3) It remains true under all dispensations, that "the wages of sin is death". (4) It remains forever true, that a perfect obedience is requisite to purchase eternal life. And such a compliance is rendered to the covenant of works for our justification, namely, by our Surety, Jesus Christ. So, let us be careful how we speak of the Covenant of Works as in every sense abrogated; for it is under that very covenant that the second Adam has acted, in purchasing our redemption. That is the covenant which He actually fulfills, for us. Again, it is that covenant under which the sinner out of Christ now dies, just as the first sinner was condemned under it. The moral law is still in force, then, in three respects: (1) as the dispensation under which our Substitute acts for us: (2) as the rule of our obedience; and (3) as the rule by which transgressors dying out of Christ are condemned. Some, even, of the Reformed, have been incautious as to conclude,

---

[264] Rom. 8:1.

that by the rule that "a compact broken on one side, is broken for both sides," transgression abrogates the legal covenant wholly, as soon as it is committed. One plain question exposes this: By what authority, then, does the Ruler punish the transgressor after the law is broken? If, for instance, a murder abrogated the legal covenant between the murderer and the commonwealth [the state], from the hour it was committed, I presume that he would be exceedingly mystified to know under what law he was going to be hung! The obvious statement is this: The transgression has indeed terminated the sinner's right to the sanction of reward; but it has not terminated his obligation to obey, nor to the penal sanction."

This last statement shows us, "in what sense the covenant of works was abrogated when Adam fell and this is obviously the sense of Paul. The proposal of life by the law is at an end for the fallen [in Adam]; they have forever disabled themselves for acquiring, under that law, the sanction of reward, by their own works. [And although Jesus proposed the promise of eternal life by perfectly keeping the moral law to the rich young ruler and to the lawyer, Jesus made that proposal to reveal to them that they had not kept the moral law perfectly (Luke 10:25-37; 18:18-23). In Romans 10:5 Paul also offers this challenge to all of us who may claim that we personally have kept God's law perfectly. James offers this same challenge to all of us again in James 2:10-11.]."[265] .

But. if the question. "Is perfect obedience to the moral law or the Ten Commandments, given to us by Moses abrogated?" is still left unanswered in our minds, G.I. Williamson answers by saying this, " . . . the grace that is given to the sinner has a legal basis. . . There is no grace without the fulfilling of the law"

---

[265] Robert Lewis Dabney, Lectures in Systematic Theology, Zondervon Publishing House, 1878/1975, pp.636-637.

[266] "No, indeed, the whole course of salvation, including the Mosaic code and Christ's redemptive work, unfolds in positive relationship to the moral law. The covenant of grace, accordingly, cannot be hostile to the law, but encompasses it as a condition. [It is the condition of perfect obedience kept by Christ for us, for our justification]. "In the everlasting covenant, God promised a certain reward upon His fulfilling certain conditions – executing the appointed work. The inseparable principles of law and gospel, grace and reward, faith and works were expressly conjoined in that compact which God entered into with the Mediator before the foundation of the world. Therein we may behold the "manifold wisdom of God" in combining such apparent opposites; and instead of carping at their seeming hostility, we should admire the omniscience which has made the handmaid of the other. Only then are we prepared to discern and recognize the exercise of this duel principle in each of the subordinate covenants" (Pink, The Divine Covenants, p. 105).

Thus, the Puritan, John Norton observed that until the completion of Christ's satisfaction, the Mosaic covenant was administered, though imperfectly through the Mosaic law [e.g., grace by faith in the atonement through the sacrifice of animals and ceremonies that showed the grace of God's forgiveness through the shed blood of the coming Christ.]"

Accordingly, John Norton noted, *the moral law republished through Moses may be understood in three senses:*

---

[266] G,I.Williamson, The Westminster Confession of Faith for Study Classes, The Presbyterian and Reformed Publishing Co., 1964, p.145

[1] either as a law of works obliging man unto pure legal obedience, and accordingly to expect life or death:

[2] or as a rule of universal and absolute obedience, obliging man not only to what was commanded at present, but also unto whatsoever should afterwards be required.

[3] or as the covenant of grace itself, though dispensed after a legal manner, comprehending the law as a perpetual rule of righteousness, yet, freed from its pure legal nature of co-action, malediction and justification by works.

The first sense includes all who have not heard the call of the gospel. [Samuel Bolton, (1606 1654) author of *The True Bounds of Christian Freedom* adds this to this first sense. It is used to a political end: The Punishment and Restraint of Criminals (Leviticus 18:5; Deuteronomy 27:26; Exodus 19:8; 1 Tim. 1:9).]

The second sense applies to those who have heard the call and therefore stand obliged to believe in Christ. [Samuel Bolton adds this, to the second sense, its Theological Ends: to reveal sin and to humble Sinners and drive them to Christ's righteousness alone].

The third sense, which presupposes faith in the heart, is realized in the lives of the regenerate". [Bolton adds this, "To teach believers their duties, To reflect, and reprove their defects to keep them humble and dependent on Christ. To spur believers forward in obedience]" [267]

The Puritan Colquhoun put it another way: "The Law of God strictly taken, in the aspects which it bears on mankind, is to be considered in a *threefold p*oint of view : First, as *written on the heart* of man in his creation; Secondly, as given under the form of

---

[267] Wm. K. B. Stover, *A Faire and Easie Way To Heaven,* Wesleyan University Press, 1978, p. 91

a *covenant of works* to him; and Lastly, *as a rule of life,* in the hand of Christ the Mediator, to all true believers."[268]

As to the importance of our basic understanding of the relationship of Law to the Gospel of grace, Colquhoun had this to say, "If then a man cannot distinguish aright, between the law and the gospel; he cannot rightly understand so much as a single article of Divine truth. If he have not spiritual and just apprehensions of the holy law, he cannot have spiritual and transforming discoveries of the glorious gospel : and on the other hand, if his views of the gospel, be erroneous or wrong his notions of the law, cannot be right."[269]

It should be noted here that the Westminster Assembly claimed three senses or uses of the moral law. ***The moral law used in the Covenant of Works*** promised life upon fulfilling it and death upon the breach of it. After Adam's fall the moral law is used ***to restrain evil*** (1 Tim. 1:9-10; Janes 2:11; Rom. 13:1-14). It is used ***as an evangelical means to drive souls to Christ for salvation*** and it is also used ***as the rule of righteousness for believers*** as a means of their sanctification (John 17:19; Eph. 5:26. 1 Cor, 6:11).

These different uses of the moral law may help us clarify the Puritan's thinking about its use when it was dispensed on Mt. Sinai. The Puritan, Edward Fisher said God's purpose for this vigorous republishing of the moral law on Mount Sinai at this point in time in Israel's history was to enact the Covenant of Works the second time. He said that the moral law given on Mt. Sinai was republished to renew the Covenant of Works that was made with Adam.

Fisher continues by saying that the Covenant of Works was "added by way subserveincy and attendance, the better to advance and make the Covenant of Grace:" It certainly did that by defining

---

[268] Colquhoun, John. A Treatise on the Law and the Gospel, Wiley & Long Publisher, 161 Broadway, 1835, p.7
[269] Ibid, p.2

sin, revealing what is right or wrong, and by revealing the nature of human sin. And by this method of instruction and revelation God used His holy moral law to help His people to see the hopelessness of trying to keep it perfectly and the need for His grace when they transgressed it.

However, it is interesting that Fisher quickly qualified or clarified his statement about it being the Covenant of Works. Previously, he had said the moral law given on Mt. Sinai in the Covenant of Works was the *renewal* of same covenant as the Covenant of Works given to Adam. Then he changed it slightly when he said that the Covenant of Works given on Mt. Sinai **was not exactly the same as that made with Adam** because it was not given for the same purpose for which it was given to Adam. Fisher said this:

". . . although the same covenant that was made with Adam was renewed on Mt. Sinai, yet I say still, it was not for the same purpose. For this was it that God aimed at, in making the covenant of works with man in innocency, to have that which was his due from man: but God made it with the Israelites for no other end, than that man, being thereby convinced of his weakness, might flee to Christ."

It was not exactly the same because it introduced grace into the equation. Thomas Boston agreed with Fisher's statement in his footnote below Fisher's srarement. Boston said if God's end or purpose for making the Covenant of Works was to have that was His due from man, this was not the purpose of repeating it on Sinai.

Fisher then elaborates further on the renewal of the Covenant of Works. He said, "that it was renewed only to help forward and introduce another and better covenant; and so to be a manuduction unto Christ, viz: to discover sin, to waken the conscience, and to convince them of their own impotency, and so drive them out of themselves to Christ. "Know it then, I beseech you, that all this while there was no other way of life given, either in whole, or in part, than the covenant of grace. All this while God did but pursue the design of his own grace; and, therefore, was there no inconsistency either in God's will or acts; only such was his mercy, that he subordinated the covenant of works, and made it subservient to the covenant of grace, and so tend to evangelical purposes".

Fisher goes on to say, ". . . But God knew well enough that the Israelites were never able to yield such an obedience : and yet he saw it meet to propound eternal life to them upon these terms; that so he might speak to them in their humour, as indeed it was meet: for they swelled with mad assurance in themselves, saying, 'All that the Lord commandeth we will do,' and be obedient, Exod. xix. 8. Well, said the Lord, if you will needs be doing, why here is a law to be kept; and if you can fully observe the righteousness of it, you shall be saved: sending them of purpose to the law, to awaken and convince them, to sentence and humble them, and to make them see their own folly in seeking for life that way; in short, to make them see the terms under which they stood, that so they might be brought out of themselves, and expect nothing from the law, in relation to life [justification], but all from Christ."[270]

> G. I, Archer said, "The earliest phase of the covenant (that entered into at Sinai) is shown to have been *temporary and provisional* because of the flagrant violation of it by the Israelite nation as a whole, and because of their failure to know or

---

[270] Fisher, Edward, The Marrow of Modern Divinity, Reiner Publications, Swengel, PA, 1978, p. 63-64

acknowledge God as their Lord and Saviour."[271] (see Hebrews 8:8-9) The Scripture says that the law was added to the Mosaic covenant because of transgressions. The Israelites seemed to be ignorant of God's moral law coming right out of the gate of Egypt's bondage. They persuaded Aaron to make them an image to worship. Herman Witsius informs us "The time of the publication of the law is supposed to be the fiftieth day from the departure of the people out of Egypt, and from the celebration of the Passover. How to find out this number of days, see Rivet on Exod, 19:1. And thus the Israelites were taught, that they were not then to be at their own disposal, when they were delivered from Egyptian bondage by a bountiful hand, so as for the future to live at their own discretion; but to enter into the service of God, and to apply themselves to it with the greater earnestness, the more they were set at liberty from the bondage of others: as Zachariah also prophesies, Luke 1:74,75 "That being delivered out of the hands of our enemies, we might serve him without fear, in holiness and righteousness before him, all the days of our life . . . When Moses came down from the mount, with the tables written by God, in his hand, and, on his approach to the camp of the Israelites, observed the calf which Aaron had cast or founded at their command, he was moved with a holy indignation, and threw the tables out of his hand and broke them Exod, 32:19, Deut, 9:16,17. We are by all means to conclude, that Moses, fired with a zeal for

---

[271] Archer, G.I., *Baker's Dictionary of Theology*. Baker Book House, Grand Rapids, Michigan, 1960, p,143.

God, broke these tables consistently with his duty. For this conduct tended 1st, To strike the Israelites with shame and terror, since, by *this alarming* action, he much more effectually convinced them of their breach of covenant, than he could possibly have done by any vehemence or warmth of words; by depriving them of that inestimable treasure, whereby they had otherwise excelled all other nations of the world. 2dly. To demonstrate, that by their breach of the most solemn covenant, they made themselves unworthy of the symbol of divine presence : For, the words of the covenant were written on the tables, in order to their being placed in the ark, and that God might dwell upon the ark in the tabernacle. Therefore, by this indignation of Moses, God so ordering it, it came to pass, that there was nothing which could be deposited in the ark; and so the tabernacle could neither be erected, nor the propitiatory or mercy-seat be in the midst of Israel." (The Economy of the Covenants Between God and Man, pp, 167-168, 172-173)

The terms "temporary" and "provisional" used by Archer, we believe, meant that the temporary and provisional nature of the Sinai covenant made with the nation of Israel ended with the end of the "old earth and the old heavens" or the whole Old Testament dispensation. It ended with Christ's first coming when He established the new heavens and the new earth (the Newer Administration of the Covenant of Grace or the New Testament dispensation), Jer. 31:31-33; Heb. 8:9-13.

However, the moral law of God did not end with the establishment of the new heavens and new earth or the Newer Administration of the Covenant of Grace. The moral law was neither temporary nor provisional. It was perpetual. David Chilton has given us some interesting insights into the perpetuity of the Decalogue from his exposition of the book of Revelation.[272] He points out the Covenant with the Israelites was given in the form of two stone tables (or the Decalogue) which were placed in the Temple of the Tabernacle. The Tabernacle, in which the Testimony was placed, was called the **Tabernacle of the Testimony** (Ex.38:21; Num. 1:50, 53; 9:15; 10:11; Acts 7:44). The Tabernacle consisted the **Sanctuary,** or Holy Place and the **Inner Sanctuary** (Holy of Holies). In Revelation 15 St. John's vision opens up with what is called the Temple of the Tabernacle of the Testimony in heaven. Matthew Henry describes John's vision of this "as an illusion to the holiest of all the tabernacle [the Holy of Holies], where was the mercy-seat, covering of *the ark of the testimony*; where the high priest made intercession, and God communed with His people, and heard prayers."[273] Chilton reminds us that the Tabernacle built by Moses was just a divine pattern, a shadow or copy of the true Tabernacle in heaven (Heb, 8:2). Thus, both Tabernacles, earthly and heavenly, were called the **Tabernacle of the Testimony**. Chilton states, "The basic . . . document of the Covenant was the Decalogue; this was often called **the Testimony,** emphasizing the legal character as the record of the Covenant oath [made by the church in the wilderness] (Ex. 16:34; 25:16, 21-22; 31:18; 32:15; cf. Ps. 19:7; Isa. 8:16, 20).

---

[272] Chilton, David, *The Days of Vengeance,* Dominion Press, Ft. Worth, Texas, 1987, p.150.

[273] Henry, Matthew, Commentary on the book of Revelation, Vol. 6, Hendrickson Publishers, 2014, page 940.

"A major aspect of St. John's message in *Revelation* is the coming of the New Covenant. In his theology (as the rest of the New Testament) the Church is the *naos,* the Temple. The writer to the Hebrews shows that the O.T. Mosaic Tabernacle was a copy of the heavenly Original which foreshadowed the Church in the New Covenant age (Heb. 8:5; 10:1); St. John draws the conclusion, showing that these two, the heavenly Pattern and the final form, coalesce in the New Covenant age. " [274] In the N.T. age the church has become God's rebuilt spiritual Temple in which He dwells by His Holy Spirit (Heb. 3:3-4; 1 Cor. .6:19; 2 Cor. 6:16; 1 Peter 2:4-5; Acts 15: 12-18; Eph. 2:19-22), and the Testimony (the Decalogue or moral law) has also been placed within its innermost part (into the ark of the Holy of Holies) or into the innermost part of the Christian's being – their hearts.

Incidentally, If God has already rebuilt His Temple and is still rebuilding it today, why is there any reason for some to look for His temple to be rebuilt in the future in Jerusalem?

The stone tablets of Ten Commandments placed within the ark of the covenant in the earthly Temple served as a picture of the very same ten commandments which God placed into the ark of the heavenly Temple (the Church in heaven), that is, they are now seen as being placed spiritually by God into the ark of the hearts of New Testament believers (Jer. 31:33). *So, the point is,* the moral law of love (the Ten Commandments) proves itself to be perpetual because it is established as a part of the New Covenant age (Rom. 3:31).

"Although in the NT this covenant is described as *new,* such passages as Rom. 4 and Gal. 3 show it is essentially one with

---

[274] Chilton, David, *The Days of Vengeance,* Dominion Press, Ft. Worth, Texas. 1987, pp. 388-389,

the covenant under which believers lived in OT times. Salvation was shown to be of grace and not of merit, for the OT sacrifices were prefigurative of the atoning death of Christ [Luke 22:20]. But the same O.T. covenant [of grace], is described as the *better* covenant under the NT dispensation, because it is now administered not by Moses, a servant, but by Christ the Son (Heb. 3:5, 6)."[275] It was now better because it was superior and it superseded it.

"Concerning the Hebrew nation at Sinai, who had stoutly affirmed 'All the Lord hath said, we will do,' God declared, 'Oh, that there were such a heart in them, that they would fear me, and keep all my commandments always, (Deut.5:29). Ah, that explains their wilderness perverseness, and the whole of their subsequent history: they had *no heart* to serve God, their affections were divorced from Him. And it is just at this point that the new covenant differs so radically from the old. God has given no new law, but He has bestowed upon His people – a heart in harmony with its holiness and righteous requirements. This enables them to render unto Him that obedience, which, through the mediation of Christ, is accepted by Him. Each of them can say with the apostle, 'I delight in the law of God after the inward man' (Rom. 7:22).[276]

Returning now to Norton's argument for the republishing of the Covenant of Works. He said, "The Mosaic moral law, of course, contains the substance of *as the Covenant of Works*: the Decalogue in essence and is the same law Adam received in

---

[275] Harrison, Everett F., Baker's Dictionary of Theology, Baker Book House, Grand Rapids, Michigan, 1960, p.144.
[276] Pink, Arthur, *the Divine Covenants,* Baker Book House, Grand Rapids, Michigan, 1973, p. 280

integrity as the rule of universal and absolute obedience and as the condition of the first covenant."[277]

Thomas Boston explains Norton's statement this way by saying, "And while Adam failed to keep the condition of the Covenant of Works (when he ate the forbidden fruit), the real breach of the Covenant of Works occurred when he broke the moral basis of the Covenant of Works (the Ten Commandments), being the natural moral law, which was written on Adam's heart upon his creation before the condition of the Covenant of Works had been made with him (Rom. 2:12-15; 5:14). So, when Adam and Eve took the forbidden fruit, they not only went against their conscience and their nature, they transgressed in one way or another, every one of those Ten Commandments written on their hearts.

"(1) They chose new gods. They made their belly their god by their sensuality; self their God, by their ambition: yea and the devil their God, believing him and disbelieving their Maker.

(2) Though they received, yet they observed not that ordinance of God, about the forbidden fruit. They contemned that ordinance so plainly enjoined them, and would carve out to themselves, how to serve the Lord.

(3) They took the name of the Lord their God in vain; despising his attributes, his justice, truth, power, etc. They grossly profaned that sacramental tree; abused his word, by not giving credit to it; abused that creature of his which they should not have touched, and violently misconstrued his providence, as if God, by forbidding them that tree, had been standing in the way of their happiness: and therefore, he suffered them not to escape his righteous judgment.

---

[277] Stover, Wm K. B. Stover, *A Faire and Easie Way to Heaven, Covenant Theology and Antinomianism In Early Massachusetts,* Wesleyan University Press, Middletown, Conn.1978, p. 91

(4) They remembered not the Sabbath to keep it holy, but put themselves out of a condition to serve God aright on his own day. Neither kept they that state of holy rest wherein God had put them.

(5) They cast off their relative duties: Eve forgets herself, and acts without advice of her husband to the ruin of both. Adam, instead of admonishing her to repent, yields to the temptation, and confirms her in her wickedness. They forgot all duty to their posterity. They honored not their Father in heaven; and therefore, their days were not long in the land which the Lord their God gave them.

(6) They ruined themselves and all their posterity.

(7) They gave themselves up to luxury and sensuality.

(8) They took away what was not their own, against the express will of the great Owner.

(9) They bore false witness, and lied against the Lord, before angels and devils, and one another; in effect giving out that they were hardly dealt by, and that heaven grudged their happiness.

(10) They were discontented with their lot, and coveted an evil covetousness to their house; which ruined both them and theirs. Thus, was the image of God on man defaced all at once"[278]

Norton notes that "the decalogue. . . *included* those who, by faith in the promise, were under the Covenant of Grace." But, by saying this, was Norton superimposing the Covenant of Works over the Covenant of Grace and thereby confounding them and thereby annulling the Covenant of Grace or promise given to Abraham 430 years before?

---

[278] Boston, Thomas, The Beauties of Thomas Boston, Christian Focus Publications, 1831/1979, pp. 388-389.

According to Norton, there was no doubt that there were two covenants - a Covenant of Works and a Covenant of Grace. One covenant was a covenant of promise or of grace and the other of works of the law, one to be believed, the other to be done (Gal. 3:12). This kind of seemingly duel covenant relationship was different than ever before. It seems that *in Norton's view*, two separate covenants were renewed, at the same time and they stood side by side in stark contrast to or in conflict with each other (Deut. 5: 1-3; Deut. 4:13; 9:9,11; Gal. 4:24).The clue to solve this puzzle is not to confuse the the use of the moral law used in the Covenant of Works with its use with the Covenant of Grace.

However, Matthew Henry and others did not adopt Norton's renewal of two covenants idea., Matthew Henry threw light on this puzzle by using Jesus' words in Matthew 5:21-30 as an interpretation of the allegory of the two covenants found in Galatians 4:24. Henry says the two women in this allegory did not typify two covenants but the two women in this allegory typified two dispensations of the Covenant of Grace. Henry says, "These things says he [Jesus], are an allegory: wherein, besides the literal and historical sense of the words, the Spirit of God might design to signify something further to us. That these two Agar and Sarah, are two covenants, or were intended to *typify* and prefigure the two different dispensations of the [same] covenant. [In other words this was not two separate or external covenants but two dispensations or two administrations of the same covenant of Grace – the O.T or the older administration. of the Covenant of Grace and the N.T.

or the newer administration of the Covenant of Grace]. The former Agar, represented that which was given from Mt. Sinai, and which gendereth to bondage, which though **it was a dispensation of grace,** yet, in comparison of the gospel state, was a dispensation of bondage [because some O.T. and N.T. Hebrews who misunderstood this renewal of the covenant of Grace tried to enter this covenant like it was a covenant of Works], and became more so to the Jews,through their mistake of the design of it [that is, the mistake of their understanding of the use of the moral law and the ceremonial law (blood sacrifices and circumcision) as a Covenant of Works], and expecting to be justified by the works of it. . . . But the other, Sarah, was intended to prefigure Jerusalem which is above, or the state of Christians under the new and better dispensation of the covenant, which is free from the bondage of the ceremonial law , and is the mother of us all – a state into which all, both Jews and Gentiles, are admitted, upon their believing in Christ." (Matthew Henry, Commentary on Galations, p.539.Vol. 6, Hendrickson Publisher, 1991.)

William Hendricksen's explanation of the allegory in Galatians 4:24 may give us further insight into this puzzle. According to Hendriksen the allegory in Galatians 4:24 about the two women (Hagar and Sarah) has been interpreted by some as a comparison between the Covenant of Works and the Covenant of Grace. But Hendiicksen says something significant here about the moral law.He says, " God gave his law to Israel **in the context of grace**, but that law was unable to save anyone." This might imply that this is not a comparison between the covenants of works and grace but rather a difference in the way the moral law was misunderstood and used by the Jews in these covenants.

Edward Fisher also intimated that the moral law was given on Mt. Sinai in the context of the Covenant of Grace. Fisher stated the moral law was given on Mt, Sinau with a different intended purpose, that is, it was given to be subservient to the covenant of grace and therefore its use or function changed for believers. It was not given to oppose the Covenant of Grace.

If we are not aware of the different uses of the moral law, it could prejudice our thinking, as Christians, against continuing to obey God's commandments. For example, in the allegory found in Galatians 4:24. and in his letter to the Corinthians Paul speaks negatively about the moral law where he describes it as "the letter killeth" and "a ministration of condemnation"? He does this because some of the Jews of the New Testament times were copying what some of their legalistic forefathers attempted to do during Moses' time — that is, they understood it as a covenant of works and made the moral law into a covenant of works for their justification.[279] They were actively trying to persuade Christians to apostasize by joining them in their incorrect thinking about justification by keeping the moral law . Paul, himself confessed that before he became a Christian, he, too, thought that trying to obey God's moral law was the way to earn eternal life.[280] To this day trying to keep the moral law as a Covenant of Works veils the Jews' eyes from seeing that the perfect obedience of their Messiah is their only means of salvation.

The correct and incorrect uses of the moral law in both of these senses is excellently described, in the allegory of Hagar

---

[279] Deut. 27:26
[280] Rom. 7:10.

and Sarah, the figures of the two Covenants, Hagar in her first and proper station, was but a serviceable hand-maid to Sarah, as the Law is used as schoolmaster to Christ. But, when Hagar the hand-maid is taken into Sarah's bed (their justification by theirr obedience to the moral law), it brings forth children out of wedlock, children that aspire to the inheritance, then saith the Scripture, Cast out the bond-woman, with her son. So it is in this allegory; take the Moral Law in both of its primary uses here, as God designed it, as a Schoolmaster, and or a Hand-maid to Christ in its relationship to the promise, so it is consistent with the promise, and excellently subservient to it; but if we marry this hand-maid, and espouse it as a Covenant of Works, then we are bound to it for life, and must have nothing to do with Christ . . . This fatal mistake of the use and intent of the Law is the ground of those seeming contradictions in Paul's Epistles. Sometimes he magnifies the Law, when he speaks of it according to God's end and purpose in its promulgation, Rom. 7:12, 14, 16, but as it was fatally mistaken by the Jews, and as it was set in opposition to Christ; so he thunders against it, calls it a ministration of Death and Condemnation and by this distinction, whatsoever seems repugnant or dangerous [about the Law] in Paul's Epistles, may be sweetly reconciled; and 'tis a distinction of his own making, 1 Tim. 1: 8. Paul says, we know that the Law is good, if we use it lawfully. There is a good and evil use of the Law.

> Witsius (Vol. 2, p. 185) speaking about Gal. 4:24-25 said this: "To the same purpose it is, that, Gal. 4:24-25, he compares to the Ishmaelites the Israelites, while they tarried in the deserts of Arabia, which was the country of the former, who are born to bondage of their mother Hagar, or the covenant of mount Sinai, and being destitute of true righteousness, shall, with Ishmael, be

at length turned out of the house of their heavenly Father. For, in that place, Paul does not consider the covenant of mount Sinai as in itself, and in the intention of God, offered to the elect, but as abused by carnal and hypocritical men. Let Calvin again speak: The apostle declares, that, by the children of Sinai, he meant hypocrites, persons who are at length cast out of the church of God, and disinherited. What therefore is that generation unto bondage, which he there speaks of? It is doubtless those, who basely abuse the law, and conceive nothing concerning it but what is servile. The pious fathers who lived under the Old Testament did not so. For, the servile generation of the law did not hinder them from having the spiritual Jerusalem for their mother. But they, who stick to the bare, supplementary, moral law and did not acknowledge its pedagogy, by which they are brought to Christ, but rather make it an obstacle to their coming to him, these are Ishmaelites [born of Hagar] (for thus, and I think rightly, Morlorat reads) born into bondage." The design of the apostle therefore, in that place, is not to teach us, that the covenant of mount Sinai was nothing but a covenant of works, altogether opposite to the gospel-covenant; but only that the gross Israelites misunderstood the mind of God, and basely abused his covenant; as all such do, who seek for righteousness by the law. See again Calvin on Rom. 10:4."

So, are the Abrahamic and Sinai Covenants two separate, and different covenants competing against each other or are they both covenants of grace with a more emphasiseed role or function of the moral law added to the Sinai Covenant? I will now quote extensively from Louis Berkhof's *Systematic Theology* to answer this question. "The covenant of Sinai was *essentially* the same as that established with Abraham, though the form differed somewhat . . . The reason why it is sometimes regarded as an entirely new covenant is because Paul repeatedly refers to the law and the promise as forming an antithesis, Rom. 4:13 ff.; Gal. 3:17." But it should be noted that the apostle does not contrast the covenant of Abraham with the Sinaitic covenant as a whole, but only the law as it functioned in the Sinaitic covenant, and this function was misunderstood by the Jews. The only apparent exception to that rule is Gal. 4:21 ff., where two covenants are indeed compared.

"There are clear indications in Scripture that the covenant with Abraham was not supplanted by the Sinaitic covenant, but it remained in force. Even at Horeb the Lord reminded the people of the covenant with Abraham, Duet. 1:8; and when the Lord threatened to destroy the people after they had made the golden calf, Moses based his plea for them on that covenant, Ex. 32:13. He also assured them repeatedly that, whenever they repented of their sins and returned unto Him, He would be mindful of His covenant with Abraham, Lev. 26:42; Deut. 4:31. The two covenants [the Sinaitic and Abrahamic] are clearly represented in their unity in Ps. 105:8-10: 'He hath remembered His covenant forever, the word which He commanded to a thousand generations, the covenant which He made with Abraham, and His oath to Isaac, and confirmed the same unto Jacob for a statute, *to Israel for an everlasting covenant.* This unity also follows from the argument of Paul in Gal. 3, where He stresses the fact that an unchangeable God does not arbitrarily alter the essential nature of a covenant once confirmed; and that the law was not intended to supplant, but to serve the gracious ends of the promise, Gal. 3:15-22. If the Sinaitic covenant was indeed a covenant of works, in which legal obedience was the way of salvation, then it certainly was a curse for Israel. For it was imposed on a people that could not possibly obtain salvation by works . . . It is Un-scriptural to assume that more than one covenant was established at Sinai, though it was a covenant with various aspects ... [Then as Berkerf continues he says something significant about *the many different views* about how many covenants were presented on Mt. Sinai. He says,] They are contrary to Scripture in their multiplication of the covenants. *It is un-Scriptual to assume that more than one covenant was sestablished at Sinai, it was a covenant with various aspects. "*[281]

But, how is the moral law presented on Mt, Sinai given in the context of the Covenant of Grace? When the moral law is presented within the context of the Covenant of Grace it could be used to specifically to teach the doctrines of Justification and Sanctification which are set side by side on Mt. Sinai. It is not until later that God brings this Old Testament teaching to its full maturation in the New Testament (Luke 1:74; Titus 2:11-12; 2 Tim. 1:9; 1 Thess. 4:4-8; 2 Thess. 1:11; 2 Pet. 1:10; Heb. 3:1). First, God calls the nation Israel to Justification through the Abrahamic Covenant and He then provides the moral law in written form as a means to help them make their calling and election sure. God affirms His Covenant of Grace by first, justifying the ungodly (the promised seed of Abraham) through a regenerating faith in God's promise of Christ and His perfect obedience to the moral law for them and His atoning death for them. And secondly, at the same time, He brings regenerating sanctification into their lives by which He produces a willingly desire in them to submit and obey God's moral law (Gal.3:19,24; Rom. 8:7; Phil. 2:13)..

But you might ask why did the Apostle Paul write the allegory found in Galatians? The main purpose of this allegory seems to be a comparison of the Covenant of Works and the Covenant of Grace. But,

---

[281] Berkhof, L., Systematic Theology, Wm. B. Eerdmans Publishing Co., Grand Rapids, Michigan, 1939, pp, 297,299.

as it turns out, it is a finer comparison of the difference between the understanding of the believing Jews and the understanding of the unbelieving Jews about the moral law's *function* as it was used in the Covenant of Works and its use in the Covenant of Grace.

On the one hand the moral law's function was seen and understood **by the unbelieving Jews** as a Covenant of Works and therefore, the means of their Justification. But, on the other hand the moral law's *function* was seen and understood differently **by Jewish believers.** The believing Jews understood the use of the moral law as God intended them to understand it was an appendage added to the Promise.- as their duty or reasonable aervice to God and a means of their Sanctification. ". . . Paul begins in his allegory with the former [i.e., the function of the moral law as was seen, understood and adopted by the *unbelieving* Jews was a Covenant of Works]: one from Mount Sinai bearing children [born of the flesh, who were not children of the promise, they were the Ishmaelites] destined for slavery [i.e., slavery to the moral law as a Covenant of Works. So, in the allegory of Galatians 4:24, the apparent, striking, contrast between these covenants is how the function of the moral law was understood and used.] "Though, as was shown earlier . . . God gave His law to Israel in a context of grace, that law was unable to save anyone. Besides, when it is, nevertheless, viewed as a force by means of which a person achieves deliverance and salvation, as the Jews and

Judaizers actually viewed it, then it enslaves."[282] Calvin said, "He [Paul] next concludes that we become the sons of God by promise, after the pattern of Isaac, and that we obtain this honour in no other way. To readers little skilled or practiced in Scripture, this conclusion may seem weak, because they do not hold the principle which is most sure, that all the promises, being grounded in the Messiah, are free [however, they are not free to those who are slaves to their misrakrn idea that the function of the morsl law given on Mt, Sinai was a covenant of works]. It was because the apostle took this for granted that he so fearlessly compared the Abrahamic promise to the Jew's mistaken function of the moral law as a Covenant of Works in this allegory."[283]

Norton, however, was clear that he believed that the two covenants were the renewal of the Covenant of Works made with Adam and the other was the Covenant of Grace made with Abraham (Gen. 12:1-3). In fact, as A.W. Pink has pointed out, Thomas Bell (1814) in his heavy work on *The Covenants* insists that "the covenant of works was delivered from Sinai, yet as subservient to the Covenant of Grace." Such an accurate thinker was bound to feel the presence of those difficulties which such a postulate involves, yet he took a strange way of getting out of it. Appealing to Deuteronomy 29:1, Bell argued that God made "two distinct covenants with Israel," and that "the one

---

[282] Hendriksen, William, . Sinai.T. Comme tary on Galatians, Baker Book House, Grand Rapids, Michigan, 1968, p.182.
[283] Calvin's N. T. Commentaries, Galatians 4, Wm. B. Eerdmans Publishing Co., Grand Rapids, Michigan, 1965, pp.88-89.

made in Moab was the Covenant of Grace," and that "the two covenants mentioned in Deut, 29:1 are as opposite as the righteousness of the law and the righteousness of faith." . . . [To] attempt to show the unsatisfactoriness and untenability of such an inference; suffice it to say there is less warrant for it than to conclude that God made two totally distinct covenants with Abraham (in Genesis 15 and 17): the covenant at Moab was a renewal of the Sinaitic, as the ones made with Isaac and Jacob were the original one with Abraham. (p.143 The Divine Covenants).

The obvious objection to what Norton has said above lies here, namely, the same persons believers and non-believers of the nation of Israel, were under both covenants (Grace and Works) at the same time, which is absurd. Here is Norton's answer to this objection. "The *unbelieving Israelites* were under the covenant of grace made with their father Abraham externally and by profession, in respect of their visible church state; but under the covenant of works made with Adam internally and really, in respect of the state of their souls before the Lord. Herein [says Norton] there is no absurdity; for to this day many in the visible church are thus, in these different respects, under both covenants. [Remember, not all of the physical descendants of Abraham are of the true (spiritual seed of Israel) i.e., the spiritual, descendants of Abraham through Isaac.This way of thinking could be the key puzzle piece to the puzzle about whether or not the Covenant of Works was really replublished on Sinai. This is because the unbelieving, unregenerate, Israelites that were internally in Adam easily misunderstood the giving of the 10 commandments on Sinai as the republishing of the Covenant of Works which was actually still in force for them as well as all unbelievers in every generation and they therefore, misunderstood it **as the means**

of Justification and not as those who were regenerate Israelites who were true, spiritual, Israelites and who were internally in Christ and who would not understand the giving of the 10 commandments as the Covenant of Works but rather as an annexation to the Abrahamic Covenant of Grace **as the means of Sanctification.**]

John Colquhoun says something similar but not exactly the same as Norton. Colquhoun said, " . . . as to believers among them, they were internally and really, as well as externally, under the covenant of grace; and only externally under the covenant of works, and that, not as a covenant co-ordinate with, but subordinate and subservient unto covenant of grace: and in this there is no more inconsistency than in the former . . . Wherefore I [Colquhoun] conceive the covenants to have been both delivered on Mount Sinai to the Israelites. *First,* the covenant of grace made with Abraham (Ex. 20:2; Gen. 17:1,7; 15:14), [and through Abraham, a remnant according to the election of grace] contained in the preface, repeated and promulgated there unto Israel, to be believed and embraced by faith, that they might be saved; to which were annexed the ten commandments, given by the Mediator Christ [Acts 7:37,38; Heb. 12:25,26], the head of the covenant, *as a rule of life* to his covenant people. *Secondly,* the covenant of works made with Adam, (Hos. 6:7) contained in it the same ten commands, delivered with thunders and lightnings the meaning of which was afterwards cleared by Moses, describing the righteousness of the law and sanction thereof, repeated and promulgated to the Israelites there, as the original perfect rule of righteousness to be obeyed; and yet were they no more bound hereby to seek righteousness by the law than the young man was by our Saviour's saying to him, Matt. xix. 17,18, 'If thou wilt enter into life, keep the commandments – Thou shall do no murder,' etc.

". . . It will be proper here to observe that, although believing and unbelieving Israelites, in the Sinai transaction, were under the covenant of grace; yet they could not both be under it, in the *same respects*. The *believers among* them, were *internally* and *really* under it, [as it contained] the moral law as a rule of life, as all true believers in every age are; (Rom. 7:22, 23; 1 Cor. 9:21) but the unbelievers, were only *externally,* in respect of their visible church-state, under it (Rom.9:4) "[284]

Colquhoun understood the different uses of the moral law used on Sinai that day. He says with the givng of the moral law it is prefaced with grace He said, " The covenant of grace, both in itself, and in the intention of God, was therefore published first; as appears from these words, in the preface, standing before the commandments, "I am the Lord *thy God."* These gracious words, in which, Jehovah exhibited himself to the Israelites as their God, were spoken to them, as his peculiar people, the natural seed of Abraham, and as typical of all his spiritual seed (Gal. 3 16-17). To this gracious offer or grant, which Jehovah made of himself to them, as their God and Redeemer, the ten commandments **were annexed, as a rule of duty** [as a means of their sanctification] to them as his professed people, and especially, to true believers among them as his spiritual seed. In virtue of his having engaged to answer for them [through Christ] , all the demands of the law as a covenant of works, he repeats and promulgates it to them, as a rule of life in the covenant of grace. Instead of saying to them, Keep my commandments, that I may become your God; he on the contrary, said to each of them, "I am the Lord thy God,"

---

[284] Colquhoun, John, A Treatise on the Law and the Gospel, Wiley and Long Pubkisher, 1835 p. 62

therefore keep my commandments. This is not the form of the law as it is the covenant of works, but the form of it only as the law of Christ, and as standing in the covenant of grace."[285]

Boston adds, "To it [to the covenant of grace] then was the subservient covenant, according to the apostle, added, put, or set to, as the word properly signifies. So, it was a separate covenant from and was no part of the covenant of [justifying] grace, the which (the covenant of grace) was entire to the fathers before the time that was set to it; . . . for says the apostle, 'It was added [as a schoolmaster] till the seed should come.' Hence it appears that the covenant of grace was, both in itself, in God's intention, the principle part of the Sinai transaction: nevertheless, . . . [the moral law was misunderstood by other Jews as their means of justification] and was the most conspicuous part of it [the event] and lay most open to the view of the people." [286]

"It [the moral law] was not set up by itself as an
entire rule of righteousness, to which alone they were to
look who desired righteousness and salvation, as it was
in the case of upright Adam, 'For no man, since the fall,
can attain to righteousness and life by the moral law,'
Lar. Cat. Quest 94. But it was added to the covenant of
grace, that by looking at it men might see what kind of
righteousness it is by which they can be justified in the
sight of God, and that by means thereof, finding
themselves destitute of that righteousness, they might

---

[285] Colquhoun, John, A Treatise on the Law and the Gospel, Wiley and Long Pubkisher, 1835, pp. 54-55
[286] Thomas Boston footnotes in The Marrow of Modern of Modern Divinity, p.54, 56

be moved to embrace the covenant of grace, in which
that righteousness is held forth to be received by faith."

"Thus, there is no confounding of the two covenants of
grace and works; but the latter was added to the former as
subservient unto it, to turn their eyes towards the promise, or
covenant of grace: 'God gave it [the covenant of grace] to
Abraham by promise. Wherefore then serveth the law? It was
added because of transgressions, till the Seed should come'
(Gal. 3: 18, 19; Deut.18:15). So, this particular use of the moral
law for believers was added unto the promise given to
Abraham, so that this subservient covenant is understood as
given in the context of grace): and that promise we have found
in the preface to the ten commands.
Charles Hodge said, "The special covenant which God formed
with Abraham, and which was solemnly renewed at Mount Sinai
was that He would give to the [Abraham's] children the land of
Palestine as their possession and bless them in that inheritance on
condition that they kept the laws delivered to them by His servant
Moses".[287] [See also the promise of our New Testament
inheiritence which comes from the expected consequent actions of
obedience to God's Law by a person who has been justified by his
faith (James 2:14-26; Acts 26:18; Gal. 5:21)]. But not only were
they promised the land of Palestine, but they asked for, and were
promised a mediator of the covenant of grace (John 5:46; Acts
3:21-22; Acts 7:37) "Making a promise of Christ to them, not only
as" the seed of the woman," but as 'the seed of Abraham,' and yet
more particularly, as 'the seed of Israel: the Lord thy God will raise

---

[287] Charles Hodge, Systematic Theology, Wm. B. Eerdmans
Publishing Company, Grand Rapids, Michigan, 1975, Vol.3, Part
3, Chapter 19, p.277 Genesis 12:7; 13:15; 26:1-5; and 21:34 cf.
Hebrews 11:9

up unto thee a prophet, from the midst of THEE, of THY BRETHREN.' (Deut. xviii. 15-19). And here it is to be observed, that this renewing of the promise and covenant of grace with them was immediately upon the back of giving of the law on Mount Sinai, for at that time was their speech which the Lord commended as well spoken: this appears from Exod. 20. 18,19, compared with Deut. 5.23-29, and upon that speech of theirs was that renewal made, which is clear from Deut. 18.17,18. . . . Thus, you see, when the Lord had, by means of the [moral law which was also found in the] covenant of works made with Adam, humbled them, and made them sigh for Christ the promised Seed, he renewed the promise with them yea and the covenant of grace made with Abraham." [288]

Immediately before God gave the Mosaic laws, He reminded the Israelites beforehand that He was their covenant God and they were His covenant people. And because He is their covenant God, He has been faithful to His covenant promise made to Abraham to deliver them out of Egypt in order to get them to the promised land. But the reader should remember that the promise was made to Abraham and to his seed (Christ and the believers who are in Christ) as heirs. They were not just promised a temporal or earthly piece of land (Canaan).[289] Abraham with eyes of faith looked beyond the earthly land of promise called Canaan to the heavenly land of promise or the Spiritual country of Canaan (Heaven).[290] It was also God's intention and promise to get the children of faith safely into heaven. But in order to prosper their journey on their way there it was necessary to give them His written laws. Regretfully, it appears that one purpose that the written moral law was given on Mt. Sinai was because Israel's conscience was being clouded or darkened by

---

[288] Fisher, Edward, and Footnote by Thomas Boston in *Fisher's Marrow of Modern Divinity*, 1978, p.67

[289] Gal. 3:29; Romans 8:17; Gal. 3:16; 1 Pet. 1:4

[290] Heb. 11:9-16; 1 Pet 1:4

her disobedience. One reason for reissuing the law through Moses, Norton correctly observed, was to restrain wickedness and to preserve some semblance of moral order in a world disordered by the fall. Another was to apprise fallen human beings of their sinfulness, which they are characteristically disinclined to admit, to convince them that justification is impossible by works and thereby to prepare them to receive Christ.

Fisher, in his writing, seems to have already addressed any concern about the moral law found in the covenant on Mt. Sinai. Fisher says it was not given as a means of Justification for believers. Fisher said this

" . . . it is generally laid down by our devines, that we by Christ were delivered from the law as it is a covenant [of works] , (Marrow of Modern Divinity , p. 60): He went on to say, ". . . God never made a covenant of works with any man since the fall, either with expectation that he should fulfill it or to give him life by it; for God never appoints any thing to the end, to the which it is utterly unsuitable and improper. Now the law, as it is the covenant of works, is become weak and unprofitable to the purpose of salvation : and, therefore, God never appointed it to man, since the fall, to that end. And besides, it is manifest that the purpose of God, in the covenant made with Abraham, was to give life and salvation by grace and promise; and, therefore, his purpose in renewing the covenant of works, was not, neither could be to give life and salvation by working; for then there would have been contradictions in the covenants and instability in him that made them, Wherefore let no man imagine that God published the covenant of works on Mt. Sinai, as though he had been mutable, and so changed his determination in that covenant made with Abraham; neither yet let any man suppose that God now in process of time had found out a better way for man's salvation than he knew before: for as the covenant of grace made with Abraham had been needless, if the covenant of works made with Adam would have given him and his believing and life; so after the covenant of grace, was once made , it was needless to renew the covenant of works, to the end that righteousness of life should be had by the observation of it." (Fisher, The Marrow of Modern Divinity, p.62-63_)

It should also be noted as a point of interest that Abraham not only had the gospel (Gal. 3:8; Heb. 4:9), but he was not left without God's moral law and that he kept the moral law for we are told Abraham had kept "the way of the Lord"; he "obeyed my voice, and kept my charge, my commandments, my statutes, and my laws" (Gen. 17:1; 18:19; 26: 5). " . . . All orthodox writers agree that there is both law and gospel in the Old znd New Testament Scriptures" [291] Surely, then the New Testament is not therefore a Covenant of Works! The difference between Abraham and some of the unbelieving Israelites was he was not trying to keep the moral law as a Covenant of Works which would have required Abraham's absolute, perfect, obedience. He was keeping the moral law under the Covenant of Grace through Jesus, its Mediator. This meant through Jesus the provision of forgiveness was made for Abraham when he failed to keep the moral law.

So, what really took place on Mt. Sinai? Kenneth Gentry in his book *Navigating The Book of Revelation* views the covenant given on Sinai as a Covenantal Marriage. "We must recall that 'throughout the Bible, God's relationship to his people is pictured as a marriage'. In the Old Testament particularly, 'the relationship between God and Israel was . . . very frequently viewed as analogous to that of husband and

---

[291] Dabney, Robert l., Lectures in Systematic Theology, Zondervan Publishing House,1878, pp. 455, 456, 457.

wife . . . it appears as a dominant metaphor. Ezekiel 'develops the metaphor to the greatest extent' presenting the clearest imagery of God actually marrying Israel (Eze. 16) . . . Rabbinic Judaism picks up on this imagery and speaks of the Mount Sinai covenant as being Israel's "Day of Espousal" with the Shekinah cloud's descent upon the tabernacle portraying the marital consummation. In Jeremiah's new covenant promise, God complains of Israel's unfaithfulness noting that they broke his covenant, though 'I had mastered [ba'l] them as a husband' (Jer. 31:32). This verb derives from a root meaning "to become master". Therefore, it means to marry 'with an emphasis on the rights and authority the husband exercised,' cp. Gen. 20:3; Numbers 5:19-20,29, Deuteronomy 21:13; 22:22, Whereas the word for 'husband' ('hs) is apparently an endearing expression', (ba'l) emphasizes the legal position of the husband as lord and owner of his wife. The legal relation and subsequent obligation are clearly in view."[292]

"God's relationship with Israel was always defined in terms of the Covenant, the marriage bond by which He joined her to Himself as His special people. This Covenant was a legal arrangement, a binding "contract" imposed on Israel by her King, stipulating mutual obligations and promises."[293] However, Israel's marital relationship with God went downhill because of Israel's marital unfaithfulness (harlotry and infidelity with false gods, with the Roman government, and by killing her prophets, and finally by crucifying her King). Jerusalem became known as the great harlot of Babylon,

---

[292] Gentry, Kenneth, Jr., *Navigating The Book of Revelation,* Good Birth Ministries, Fountain Inn, South Carolina 29644, 1999, p50,51,53
[293] Chilton, David, *The Days of Vengeance,* Intro by Gary North, Dominion Press, Ft. Worth, Texas, 1987, p.13

Sodom, and Egypt. She caused God to bring a covenant lawsuit against her and later give her a bill of covenantal divorcement which was finalized in 70 A.D. with the destruction of Jerusalem and her Temple (Jer. 3:8,11; 1 Peter 5:13; Rev. 17:1,5; 11:8; Mark 13:1-30). Then the kingdom of God was taken from the national, apostate, Israel (i.e., Israel according to the flesh – outward Jews were disinherited) and the Kingdom was given to another (i.e., it was given to the true Israel according to the Spirit – which now consists of inward or converted Jews and converted Gentiles) Gen. 12:1-3; Rom. 2:28-29; 9:6-7; Gal. 3:6, 9, 26, 28-29; Eph. 2:11-13). Israel, the national Old Testament Church (Acts 7:38), became the international New Testament Christian Church or the new Israel of God (Matt. 21:43; 1 Peter 2-9-10; Rev. 5:9-10; 21:1-8, 24-26). Chilton added, "That Israel [as a nation] will someday repent and turn to Christ is, indisputable (Rom. 11). That is not at issue here. The point remains, however, that in order to be restored to the Covenant, Jews must join the Church of Jesus Christ with everyone else. Israel will never have a covenantal identity distinct from the Church."[294]

I believe that the moral law given on Mt. Sinai was added because of Israel's transgressions and therefore, was used as a needed pedagogic appendage to the Abrahamic covenant. It was given to believers *as a rule of duty,* to be kept out of reverence and gratitude to God, and it was fit for a national, religious and political institution for a constitution of true believers then – under a theocracy and as well as, the rule of duty for believers today in the Kingdom of God.

It is my belief that this event was a *display* of the moral law and *not a renewal* of the Covenant of Works. However, it was a *renewal*

---

[294] Chilton, David, *The Days of Vengeance,* Dominion Press, Ft. Worth Texas,1987, fotenote 22 on page 269

of the Covenant of Grace with His covenant people at Mt. Sinai. "It was powerfully confirmed by the fact, that Moses, in confirming the Sinai-Covenant with Israel, tells them more than once, that they enter it as Abraham's seed. (Deut 7:8,9,12; Exod. 3:6,7. Compare Psalm 105:6; Isaiah 41:8). This shows that whatever the covenant with Abraham was, that with Israel was a renewal of it.

So, I believe, the covenant of works was not renewed on Sinai; it was only [the moral law] repeated and displayed. "It was not proposed to them, in order that they might consent, by their own works, to fulfil the condition of it; but it was displayed before them, in subservience to the covenant of grace, that they might see how impossible it was for them as condemned sinners, to perform that perfect obedience, which is the immutable condition of life in it."[295] John Owen said, "In short, the Mosaic covenant is not a revival of the covenant of works strictly, but rather, the moral law is renewed *declaratively* and not *covenantly,* Owen writes 'God did never formally and absolutely renew or give again this law as a covenant [of works] a second time. Nor was there any need that so he should do, unless it were declaratively only, for so it was renewed at Sinai for the whole of it being *an emanation of eternal right and truth,* it abides, and must abide, in full force forever.'[296]

I do not think that the moral law given on Mt. Sinai was an altogether new covenant made at Sanai as some have thought. Rather, the moral law given on Mt. Sinai was used to inform and remind believers about their responsibility of holiness ("Be ye holy as I am holy") which responsibility at once follows their

---

[295] Colquhoun, John, A Treatise on the Law and the Gospel, Wiley and Long Pubkisher, p.63
[296] Beeke, Joel R., and Jones, Mark, *A Puritan Theology, Doctrine for Life,* Reformation Heritage Books, Grand Rapids, Michigan, 2012, pp. 296-297.

Justification. God justified them and then set them apart from an ordinary use to an extraordinary use . He set them apart from all of the other nations to be a holy nation unto Him. After God justified believers in Israel by faith in the Promised Seed of the Abrahamic covenant that was to come in their future, He gave them the moral law as a personal rule of holiness to live by.

The understanding of their Justification (a legal act of divine grace carrued out by Christ that affected the judicial status of the justifed sinner) serves as the only, true, moral incentive to pursue holiness. Justifucation is the basis for the believers' sanctification (a moral, recreative work which is carried out by the Holy Spirit who in co-operation with the believer, progressively changes and inclines the believer's inner, human nature to holiness).

So, I thonk it might have been clearer if we said the renewal of Abrahamic covenant of grace was given with added instructions for national and individual piety. The moral law given on Mt, Sinai for believers was given for the purpose of their Sanctification or spiritual growth. The moral law or rule of life given to Abraham was given to Abraham without the great emphasis it was given on Mt. Sinai. And what rule was Abraham's rule of life? "Walk before Me, and be thou perfect" (Gen. 17:1). The renewal of the Abrahamic Covenant and the moral law given together on Mt. Sinai should be seen like the doctrines of Justification and Sanctification which stand side by side. They are like the two separate and distinct essences of Justification and Sanctification which have a close relationship but are not be confused. This is how W. A. Brrakel describes this close relationship between Justification and Sanctification:

> "First justification is executed by God as righteous Judge;sanctification is executed by God the Holy Spirit as re-creator. Secondly, justification is executed by God toward man as the object; sanctification trsnspires within

man as being the subject. Thirdly, justification removes guilt and punishment, and establishes man in a state of felicity; sanctification removes pollution and restores the image of God. Foirthly, justification is executed perfectly each time; sanctification always remains imperfect as long as man iis upon earth. Fifthly, in natural order justification comes first, and sanctification follows as proceeding from justification. [297] Sanctification is the expected result that follows Justification (James 2:8-26). Because where you have the one (Justification) you will find the other (Sanctification). You cannot have the one without the other. Justification through faith in Christ's perfect obedience to the moral law offers the assurance of salvation to the believer because they place their faith in Christ's perfect obedience to the law accomplished on their behalf and they do not place their faith in their own imperfect obedience gained by their sanctification. This assurance relieves them of their fear of the law's promised curse (eternal death upon disobedience) for Jesus took that curse of disobedience upon Himself on the cross and paid the price of eternal death for the believer. The moral law's function now serves, by God's grace, as the believers' moral compass and by the power of God's Holy Spirit a sanctifying instrument in their spiritual lives.

Witsius clarified his thinking about the giving of the moral law as a Covenant of Works on Mt. Sinai when he said, "We are not, to imagine, that the covenant of works was repeated, in order to set up again such a covenant with the Israelites, in which they were to seek for

---

[297] The Christian's Reasonable Service, Wilhelmus A. Brakel, Reformation Heritage Books, ol. 3, pp, 3-4.

righteousness and salvation. For, we have already proved, Book 1, chapter 9 sec. 20, that this could not possibly be renewed in that manner with a sinner, on account of the justice and truth of God, and the nature of the covenant of works, which admits of no pardon of sin . . . Besides, if the Israelites were taught to seek salvation by the works of the law, then the law had been contrary to the promise, made to the fathers many ages before (Gal. 3:17). The Israelites were, therefore, put in mind of the covenant of works, in order to convince them of their sin and misery, to drive rhem out of themselves, to shew them the necessity of a satisfaction [for their sins], and to compel them to seek Christ. And so, their being thus brought to a remembrance of the covenant of works tended to promote the covenant of grace . . . There likewise accompanied this giving of the law the repetition of some things belonging to the covenant of grace, For, that God should propose a covenant of friendship to sinful man, call himself his God (at least in the sense it was said to the elect in Israel) take to ?himself any people , separated from others, for his peculiar treasure, assign to them the land of Canaan as a pledge of heaven, promise his grace to those that love him and keep his commandments, and circumscribe the vengeance denounced against despisers within certain bounds, and the like ; these things manifestly discover a covenant of grace: and without supposing the suretyship of the Messiah, it could not, consistently with the divine justice and truth, be proposed to man a [unrepentant] sinner.

Judiciously says Calvin on Exod, 19:17 , "by these words we are taught that these prodigies or signs [on Sinai] were not given, to drive the people from the presence of God; nor were they struck with any terror, to exasperate their minds with a hatred of instruction : but that the covenant of God was no less lovely than awful. For, they are commanded to go and meet God, to present themselves with a ready affection of soul to obey him. Which could not be unless they had heard something in the law besides precepts and threatenings. . . Having premised these observations, I answer to the question. The covenant made with Israel at Mt. Sanai as not formally the covenant of works, 1st. Because that cannot be renewed with the sinner, in such a sense as to say. if, for the future, thou shalt perfectly perform every instance of obedience, thou shalt be justified by that, according to the covenant of works. For, by this, the pardon of former sins would be presupposed, which the covenant of works excludes, 2dly, Because God did not require perfect obedience from Israel, as a condition of this covenant, as a cause of claiming the reward ; but [incentive to] sincere obedience, as an evidence of reverence and gratitude. 3rdly, Because it did not conclude Israel under the curse, in the sense peculiar to the covenant of works, where all hope of pardon was cut off, if they sinned but in the least instance . . . However the carnal Israelites not adverting to God's purpose or intention, as they ought, mistook the true meaning of that covenant, embraced it as a covenant of works, and by it sought for righteousness." (See Witsius, Herman, *The Economy of the Covenants Between God and Man*, The den Dulk Christian Foundation, Distributed by Presbyterian and Reformed Publishing Company, Phillipsburg, New Jersey, Reprinted 1990, Vol. 2, pp.183-185)

So, based on what has been said so far, I must remind you once again that your sanctification (that which the Holy Spirit within you empowers you to do), such as keeping God's law, can never replace the perfect obedience of Christ to the moral law on your behalf as the cause of your justification. But I suggest or submit to you, that the moral law given on Mt. Sinai was given as a rule of life for your sanctification or holiness (1 Chron. 16:29; Psa. 29:2; Heb. 2:10, KJV; 13:12; Jude 1, KJV; Eph. 1:4; 1 Thess.4:1-8; 2 Tim. 2:21; Titus 2:11-12, 14; 1 Pet. 1:22, KJV; 3:15, KJV; 1 John 3:3). Israel was a chosen nation. Why was she chosen? She was chosen to be holy as were the chosen Gentiles later in the N.T. – "For He chose us in Him (Christ), before the foundation of the world, *to be holy and blameless* in His sight (Eph, 1:4; Phil. 2:14-15). Therefore, the moral law was **not** used exactly as it was before when it was used with Adam's original covenant of works, (i.e., as the cause for one's Justification). But the moral law now stands with, yet distinct from, supplementary to but neither the equivalent to, nor contradictory to the Covenant of Grace, as it is offered through Christ, the Seed of Abraham as the only cause or source of one's Justification. The giving of the moral law on Mt. Sinai was meant for Israel's sanctification (as well as it was for Abraham's sanctification (Gen. 17:9; Gen. 18:19). It was given for Israel's spiritual growth and God's glorification, "The keeping of the moral law was required of Abraham [and later of Israel] as a duty, test, and demonstration of their sincerity . . . [It was required even though God wills their sanctification and even though it is accomplished by the Holy Spirit and even though they are complete in Christ and because God promises He will complete the good work He has begun in His children, yet God still requires them to produce this kind of imperfect, experimental evidence in themselves of partially cooperating with the

Holy Spirit as part of God's work of Sanctification in their lives (Ex. 31:13; 1 Thess. 4:3-4; 1 Pet. 1:2; Phil. 2:13; 1:6] – both upon entering into, as well as living in the covenant of grace. I realize that I must be careful and jealously guard my words here but there is an inseparable connection between Justification and holinwss. Believers of the New Testament are given commandments of holiness to keep. For example, Whatsoever ye do, do all to the glory of God. However, these commandments are not conditions for salvation. Once a believer has been placed into union with Christ .by faith he or she is free from keeping them as the condition of the Covenant of Works. But in order to make his or her election to holiness sure they must look for holiness in their lives.

" . . . that personal holiness, and justification, being inseparable in the believer, we are unwilling, so much . . . to suppose their separation. Personal holiness we reckon so necessary to the possession of glory, or to a state of perfect holiness and happiness, as is the morning light to the noon-day warmth and brightness – as is a reasonable soul to a wise, healthy, strong, and full grown man – as an antecedent is to its consequent – as a part is to the whole; for the difference betwixt a state of grace and of glory, we take to be gradual only, according to the usual saying 'Grace is glory begun, and glory grace in perfection,' So necessary , again, as motion is to evidence life, or in order to walking, not only habitual, but actual holiness and progress in holy obedience, one continuing in life, we are clear, so necessary, that without the same none can see the Lord. And as it is not only the believer's interest, but his necessary and indispensable duty, to be still going on 'from strength to strength, until he appear before the Lord in Zion:' so the righteous, we believe, 'will hold on his way, and he who is of clean hands will grow stronger and stronger:' for though the believer's progress in holy obedience, by reason of many stops, intterruptions, and assaults he frequently meets with from Satan, the world, and in-dwelling corruption, is far from being alike at all times, yet 'the path of the just,' though he frequently fall, will be 'as the shining light, that shineth more and more unto the perfect day.' Though he may, at times 'become weary and faint in his mind,' yet shall he, by waiting on the Lord, 'renew his strength, and mount up as with eagles' wings,'etc. But still the believer has all this in and from Christ: for whence can our progress in holiness come, but from the supply of His Spirit? Our walking in holy obedience, and every good motion of ours, must be in him, and from him, who is the Way and the Life, who is our head of influences, and the fountain of our strength, and who 'works in us both to will and to do.' 'Abide in me' says he, 'and I in you. For without me ye can do nothing. If a man abide not in me, he is cast forth as a branch, and is withered,'

"But if the meaning of the [question] be [that] the necessity of holy obedience, in order to the possession of glory, *as imports any kind of causality,* we dare not answer in the affirmative; for we cannot look on personal holiness, or good works, as properly federal and conditional means of obtaining the possession of heaven, though we own they are necessary to make us meet for it." (Marrow of Modern Divinity, Appendix, p. 355).

"Though there is no ground from our representation to add more on this head, yet we may say , that a promise of life made to a precept of *doing*, - that is, in consideration or upon condition of one's doing, be the doing more or less, it is all one, the divine will in the precept being the rule in this case, is a covenant of works. And as to believers in Christ, though in the gospel, largely taken, we own there are promises of life, and threatenings of death, as well as precepts; and that godliness hath the promise, not only of this life, but of that which is to come, annexed to it, in the order of the covenant [of grace]: yet *we are clear no promise of life is made to the [believer's]* performance of precepts, nor eternal death threatened in case of their failings whatsoever in performing, else should their title to life be founded not entirely on Christ and his righteousness imputed to them, but on something in or done by themselves; and their after sins should again actually bring them under vindictive wrath and the curse of the law; which upon their union with Christ who was made a curse for them, to redeem them from under it., they are according to Scripture and our Confession, for ever delivered from. Hence we know of no sanction of law, standing in the covenant of grace hath with respect to believers besides gracious rewards, all of them freely promised on Christ's account for their encouragement in obedience, and fatherly chastisement and displeasure, in case of their not walking in his commandments; which to a believer are no less awful and much more powerful restraints from sin than the prospect of the curse and hell itself would be. The Commission will not, we hope, grudge to hear that eminent divine, Mr. Perkins, in a few words, on this head, who having put the objection, 'In the gospel there are promises of life upon condition of our obedience, Rom. 8:13, 'If ye through the Spirit,' etc,; answers "The promises of the gospel are not made to the *work, but to the worker;* and to the worker, not for his work, but for Christ's sake according to his work : e.g.,

The promise of life is not made to the work of mortification, but to him that mortifies his flesh; and that not for his mortification, but because he is in Christ, and his mortification is token and evidence thereof." (Marrow of Modern Divinity, Appendix, p. 351).

The promise which, to Abraham among others, God makes in the covenant of grace is that He will sanctify them. Thus, no one can enter into this covenant unless he has a desire for holiness, and one can neither assure himself nor pretend to be in the covenant of grace unless he is a partaker of holiness." (Psa. 119:4; Eph. 5:3-5; 1 Pet. 1:15-16; James 2:18; Phil. 2:12-13; 1Thess. 4:1, 3; John 15:16; 2 Tim 1:9; 1 Pet. 2:9) (Brakel, Vol. 3, p,52, The Christian's Reasonable Service).

Thus, the moral law stands with or stands beside or accompanies the Covenant of Grace like Sanctification accompanies Justification. It acts like a guardian reminding the believer about the purpose of grace, which is holiness, without which no person shall see the Lord. It also serves as a path for the believer to follow to help him guard against abusing the saving grace he has been given. "God never shows mercy at the expense of his holiness . . . The grace of God must not be magnified to the beclouding of His righteousness, nor His sovereignty pressed to the exclusion of human accountability. The balance can only be preserved by our faithfully adhering to Scripture. If we single out favorite verses and ignore those which are unpalatable to the flesh, we are guilty of handling the Word of God deceitfully, and fall under the condemnation of "according as ye have not kept my ways, but have been partial in the law: (Mal. 2:9). Christ's obedience has not rendered ours unnecessary: rather it has rendered ours acceptable. In that sentence lies the solution to the difficultly. The law of God will accept nothing short of perfect and perpetual obedience; and such obedience the Surety of God's people rendered, so that He brought in an everlasting righteousness which is reckoned to their account. Yet that is only one half of the truth on this subject. The other half is **not** that Christ's atonement has inaugurated a regime of lawlessness or license [to sin], but rather it has placed its beneficiaries under additional obligations. But more: it had procured the needed grace to enable those beneficiaries to discharge their obligations [God has given believers a new heart and as servants of righteousness before God you render your obedience by the Holy Spirit's power to God's moral law as your worship to Him (Rom. 6:15-18; 13: 8-10; 12: 1-2)] not perfectly, but acceptably to God. And how? By securing that the Holy Spirit should bring them from death unto life, impart to them a nature which delights in the law, and work in them the will to do God's good pleasure. The same as it was for His incarnate Son: to be perfectly conformed to the law in thought and word and deed. [And remember we are being conformed to Christ's holy image.] (Pink, The Divine Covenants, p.106).

The Covenant of Grace was accompanied by the moral law on Mt. Sinai. They are separate and distinct. They reflect the mutual relationship of Justification with Sanctification. Our faith must continually fall back on a proper understanding of our Justification and of our Sanctification. For example, Jesus is our holiness. His perfect holiness justifies us before God, yet at the same time, we are justified so that we may live holy lives. The moral law is our moral guide to living holy lives. Christians will seek to know how to walk in paths of righteousness for His name's sake.

Furthermore, the moral law also keeps us from thinking that now that we have grace we may live as we please. Besides the motive of the gracious, compelling, love of Christ, the moral law is also used to help us to steer clear of sin. It keeps us from taking advantage of God's grace by thinking we can live without regard to holiness (God's and ours) or by thinking we can intentionally sin and escape the adverse consequences that will effect our communion or walk with the Lord, our Master, who bought us with His Son's blood. The covenant of grace and the moral law which were both displayed at Mt. Sinai were no different than the Covenant of Grace shown and given to the individuals like Adam after the fall (Genesis 3:15);, Noah (2 Pet. 2:5), and Abraham (Gal. 3:19); who lived before Mt. Sinai.because they were all built on and carried out by the required righteousness and holiness of Jesus in the Everlasting covenant (Titus 1:2) or the Messianic covenant (Gal. 3:16). So, wherever grace was given holiness was also expected and required. However, when the covenant of grace was renewed at. Sinai, the moral law was *for the first time given as a constitutional law for a nation* along with additional ceremonial laws.

Interestingly enough, although A. W. Pink did not agree with Owen's and Witsius' view that the Ten Words given on Mt. Sinai were merely a declaration of God's moral precepts and not a formal covenant, Pink did agree however, with Witsius' understanding about God's dealings with Israel *as a nation* as being a key clue to the purpose of Mosaic covenant on Mt. Sinai. Pink said, " . . . the corporate character of Israel . . . was a distinct line in typical picture, and a feature in marked advance of anything that had preceded. Under the previous covenants, God treated only with individuals; and throughout the history associated therewith, everything was peculiarly individualistic. But at Sinai the Lord established a formal bond between Himself and the favored nation, which anticipated and prepared the way for the establishing of Christianity. (p.189, The Divine Covenants). , , , Let us notice the special and peculiar relation which Israel sustained to the Lord. They were His chosen people, and He was their God in a way that He was the God of no others. It was as the descendants of Abraham, Isaac, and Jacob, as the children of promise, that God dealt with them from the beginning (see Exod. 2:24,25; 6:5). It was in fulfillment of His holy promise to Abraham that "he brought forth his people with joy, his chosen with gladness" (Ps. 105:42,43) from cruel bondage of the land of Egypt. (p. 185 , The Divine Covenants) . . . Until we had carefully contemplated the Mosaic economy as it related to the nation of Israel, their political and temporal welfare, we were not ready to view it in its wider and ultimate significance. God's first and immediate design in connection with the Sinaitic covenant was to furnish a "letter" fulfillment of the promises made to Abraham: to give him numerous seed, to establish them in the land of Canaan, to preserve pure the stock from which the Messiah was to spring, to continue them there until Christ actually appeared in the flesh. Thus, the Mosaic economy had served its purpose when the Son of God became incarnate." (p. 178, The Divine Covenants).

Thus, "We must always bear in mind that the Abrahamic covenant was in nowise superseded or placed in abeyance by the revelation given through Moses; it was still in unabated force. The law was in reality, an "addition" to it and designed to more effectually secure its objects. It was therefore fitting that the grace and mercy made known to Abraham should receive such enlargement and illustration as might make the law but a hindrance, but the handmaid, to believing reception of its truth. [So, in God's covenants you find the majestic doctrines of law and grace. Here in the Abrahamic and Mosaic covenants you have the redeeming grace of Christ securing the promised land (heaven) for His people through both the redeeming and sanctifying uses of His law.] The grace of the Abrahamic covenant and the law of Moses had an important mutual relation. They threw light on one another, and in combination were designed to secure a common end." (See Deut. 7:7-8) (p. 166, The Divine Covenants, A.W. Pink)

So, where did the Apostle Paul stand in relationship to God's moral law after he was converted? Like Abraham, the Apostle Paul, after his conversion, was not under the moral law as a Covenant of Works. Paul was not under the Mosaic ceremonial law either. But even though Paul didn't continue to practice the ceremonial law after Jesus death, in 1 Corinthians 9:19–21, Paul did speak of his occasional efforts to participate in it to win men to Christ during that overlapping period of time when the church was in transition from Judaism to Christianity.[298] Paul said he became as a Jew to the Jews to win the Jews to Christ. This means that after he was a Christian, he observed the ceremonial laws when he was among Jews so that he might preach the gospel of Jesus Christ found

---

[298] John 10:16; Acts 7:38; Eph. 2:11–22, emphasis on v. 16; Gal. 3:7–8, 26, 28–29; Rom. 4:1–3, 9–18; 2:25–29; Matt. 8:11-12; Romans 11:1–25.

symbolically in the ceremonial law. On the other hand, when Paul was among Gentiles, he neither practiced the ceremonial laws nor tried to place the Gentiles under them when he preached Christ to them.

The question was raised whether or not these ceremonies should be included among the precepts of God any longer since their observance is not demanded now. John Calvin commented,

> The answer is that we must consider the purpose and design of the Lawgiver. As God gave rules for ceremonies on the basis that their outward use should last for a period, but their significance be everlasting, one does not do away with [the significance of these] ceremonies, when their reality is kept [by Christ Jesus], and their shadow omitted.[299]

Roderick Campbell in *Israel and the New Covenant* explained *abrogation of the Mosaic ceremonial law,*

> That word [abrogation] may rightly be used to express the fact that the formal observance of the prescribed rites and ceremonies of the Mosaic system was discontinued when the New Covenant was inaugurated by Christ. The old system, however, and its history, still stands, not as curious relics of an antiquated order and worship (a museum piece) but as a valid, concrete, intelligible and needful revelation of the Divine will. It is in itself a revelation of God's relationship to, and His dealings with, men in judgment and mercy, in law and in grace. It [the ceremonial law] stands as a treasure house and mine from which we may ever draw to

---

[299] John Calvin, *Calvin's New Testament Commentaries: Matthew, Mark, Luke,* vol. 1 (Grand Rapids: Eerdmans, 1972), p. 181.

enrich our knowledge of the Christian faith and to increase our devotion to God.[300]

Since, Abraham was under the Covenant of Grace, he was not under the moral law as a Covenant of Works. Abraham may have understood God's moral law better than the Israelites who had been under the bondage of the Egyptians for centuries and who may have consequently have forgotten it and needed to be reminded of it on Sinai. Instead, Abraham understood God's moral law not as a Covenant of Works, but as a rule of righteous living. So too, after the apostle Paul was converted his relationship to God and to His moral law changed. As a believer he was no longer under the moral law as a covenant of works. Paul describes his new relationship to God as being under Grace and his new relationship to God's moral law as being "under the law to Christ." or under the third use of the moral law [301]. This meant he submitted to God's moral law as a rule of righteous living for guidance in his sanctification.

This is why Paul was quick to point out to the Gentile Corinthians that he **was not altogether without law** in his new relationship to God. As a Christian, under the covenant of grace, Paul said he was now under the moral law to Christ. Consequently, these Gentile Christians would naturally understand Paul meant that they too were under the moral law to Christ. "Thus, it becomes *the law of Christ* to them; of which law also the same ten commandments are likewise the matter. In the threatenings of *this law* there is no revenging wrath; and in the promises of it no proper conditionality of works, but here is the order in the covenant of grace, to which the law of Christ belongs; a beautiful order of grace,

---

[300] Roderick Campbell, *Israel and The New Covenant* (Phillipsburg, N.J.: Presbyterian and Reformed Publishing/Geneva Divinity School Press, 1954), pp. 36–37.
[301] 1 Cor. 9:21; Gal. 6:2.

obedience, particular favors, and chastisements for disobedience..."[302]

It meant Jews and Gentiles after they were saved were still obligated to obey the perpetual moral law of God originally administered by and enforced by the hand of Christ, the reigning King. In James 2:8 we are told we would do well to fulfil the King's Royal law. So, the Christian's faith does not nullify the moral law, it establishes it. It is through faith in Christ that the Holy Spirit writes the moral law on our hearts to establish it permanently in our hearts (Jeremiah 31:33; Ezekiel 37:12; 36:26-27; Romans. 3:31; 1 Corinthians 9:21; Hebrews. 8:10).

So, I repeat, "What does the Bible say about the relationship between the Christian's faith and God's moral law after the Christian has been saved? Does it say God's moral law has been replaced by the Christian's faith? Again, No! Romans 3:31 explains it this way:

Does this mean that we are using faith to undermine law?
By no means: we are placing law itself on a firmer footing.
Rom. 3:31 (The New English Bible)

How then is it firmer? It is by our faith in Christ that we place the moral law on a firmer footing. Christ honored God's moral law by keeping it for us. Every time we tell others that is it by faith in Christ, our Surety, who kept the moral law for us, which was found in the Covenant of Works and written on Adam's heart, we will begin to esteem and confirm, as we should, the moral law in our hearts as God's standard of righteousness. And it is only when we start to esteem and delight in God's Moral Law as partakers of the Covenant of Grace that we will be brought to a point of conscious

---

[302] Boston. Thomas, footnote in The Marrow of Modern Divinity, Reiner Publicatons, 1978, p.26

willingness to submit to it *as a rule of life* in our hearts in spite of Antinomians who teach us the moral law as a rule of life has been replaced by our faith.

So, "Instead of making void the law, then by the habit and exercise of [our] holy faith, [Christians] consult in the most effectual manner, the stability and honour of its precepts and [honor the boundaries that keep us from God's chastisements]. Instead of presuming to put it off , , , with [our] own mean and imperfect performances, [we] by exercise of [our] faith, appropriate and present to it, the infinitely perfect and meritorious righteousness of our Divine Redeemer, as the only ground of [our] security from eternal death, and of [our] title to eternal life. ,... Thus, by the habit and exercise of [our] faith, [we] recognize, and assert the sovereign authority, and high obligation of it as [partakers of the] covenant [of Grace]; and so, [we] establish it [the moral law] and make it honourable in that form [of Sanctification] (Isa.42:21; Phil,. 3:8,9)."[303]

When the sinner becomes a Christian by faith in Christ's love for him he is compelled by that love to freely and cheerfully obey God's commandments through the subduing and enabling power of His indwelling Holy Spirit.[304] Thus, the Christian's willing submission to God's moral law is best described as willingly placing himself "under the law to Christ."

God's moral law becomes permanently established as *a rule of righteousness* in the hearts of the redeemed citizens and servants of His kingdom, whereby they openly acknowledge it, and humbly obey it out of gratitude for the grace given to them for their salvation. It is God's perpetual moral law and it was given to all dispensations, and it is for this reason it will never be abrogated.

---

[303] Colquhoun, John, A Ttreatise on the Law and the Gospel, Wiley and Long Publishers, 1835, p.200-201.
[304] 2 Cor. 5:14-15

This is only saying that through the continuity of the moral law in the Old and New Testaments the eternal principles of love and justice are still in force. In this respect, the moral law is subservient in the covenant of grace as the instrument of God's providential government.

So, just because Paul was **"under grace" did not mean he was altogether "without law to God"**. And just because you have become a Christian does not mean you are automatically and totally "without law to God" in your relationship to God. Jesus did not come to destroy the moral law by fulfilling it for you. Fulfillment, in this case, does not imply abrogation as it did for the O.T. ceremonial law. Instead, it implies confirming it. The context of Matthew 5:17–19 explains that not one letter or one stroke of a pen will disappear from God's moral law as long as heaven and earth exist. When you couple the fact that the church has been experiencing the messianic, millennial kingdom from the time of Christ's first coming and ascension to the throne with the fact that God's moral law will last as long as heaven and earth exist, we believe it should be evident the kind of moral rules Christ Jesus uses to govern His kingdom until the end of the world. As King, He uses the same moral precepts of love (the Ten Commandments) that were used in the Old Testament to govern the Kingdom of God today.[305]

If you doubt that the Ten Commandments are the rule of Christ's kingdom today listen to what the Apostle Paul tells us in Romans 13:8-10:

Owe nothing to anyone except to love one another, for he who loves his neighbor has fulfilled the law. For this, "YOU SHALL NOT COMMIT ADULTERY, YOU SHALL NOT MURDER,

---

[305] Mark 16:19; Dan. 7:13–14; Acts 2:31–36; Eph. 1:19–22; Matt. 28:18; Isa. 9:6–7.

YOU SHALL NOT SHALL NOT STEAL, YOU SHALL NOT COVET," AND IF THERE BE ANY OTHER COMMANDMENT, IT IS SUMMED UP IN THIS SAYING,"YOU SHALL LOVE YOUR NEIGHBOR AS YOURSELF." Love does not do wrong to a neighbor; therefore, love is the fulfillment of the law.

Christ uses the Ten Commandments or His "Law of Love" to govern us.[306] And those who cease to practice the Ten Commandments and teach others to do so will be called the least in the kingdom of heaven, but those who keep the commandments and teach others to do so will be great in the kingdom. Those antinomian evangelicals, who label Christians as "Legalist" because thry love God's law, are so eager to escape the Ten Commandments that they forget what "Legalism" means. It means for a person to be a "Legalist" that person would have to believe he should keep God's commandments perfectly in order to gain his salvation. Yet, Christians understand and believe that Jesus has already secured their eternal salvation for them because He kept God's commandments perfectly for them.

What people think about having to keep God's commandments usually depends on their relationship with the Lawgiver. Consider Donald Grey Barnhouse's illustration of the widower's housekeeper:

A widower is left with two small children so he hires a housekeeper to help him. He gives her instructions as to what she shall cook, how she is to keep the house and how she is to dress and care for the children. He goes about the house from time to time to see that all is in order, and that

---

[306] Gen. 49:10; Isa. 9:6; Dan. 7:9–14; Micah 5:2; Acts 2:33, 35–36; Phil. 2:9–11; Ps. 2; 1 Cor. 15:24-28..

she is properly obeying his rules. He watches her dominion over the children and corrects her in a manner befitting the relationship of master and servant. After a year or so he marries the housekeeper. Their relationship is now entirely changed. He no longer follows her around the house to oversee her work. He no longer tells her what to cook for dinner. Now she is his in a relationship of love. Now she delights to do his will [or commandments]. Now she seeks to find out his desires and to perform them. Now she asks him what he would like to have for dinner and goes to some trouble to prepare it. She is no longer under law [as a covenant of works] but under grace. [307]

At first his housekeeper served her master with servile fear and she was only motivated to keep his commandments for her livelihood. Her relationship to her master and her attitude towards his commandments were like one attempting to serve under the law as a taskmaster. Then she was won by her master's love and she married him. The old *relationship* [of bondage to sin and the Covenant of Works] with her master and his law changrd. She now had a new relationship to her master as his bride. She has a new position and consequently, a new attitude toward his commandments. Under the covenant of grace, the believer's yoke of service to the Law is easy because Christ is her husband.[308] She is now under the law to Christ. Since under grace her position in Chrisi has changrd she has the new and correct motivation for obeying God's commandments which comes from her love for Christ.

---

[307] Donald Grey Barnhouse, *Let Me Illustrate: Stories, Anecdotes, and Illustrations* (Grand Rapids: Fleming H. Revell, 1967), pp. 204–205.
[308] Eph. 5:22–33; Matt. 11:29; 1 John 5:3.

Paraphrasing Samuel Bolton : "This was the great end of our redemption. He redeemed us from bondage of sin and the Covenant of Works and brought us into freedom, from slavery to service. That which Christ has redeemed us *to do*, He cannot be said to redeem *from*: but He has redeemed us to service, and therefore cannot be said to redeem us from service (Rom. 6:5-19; 12:1-2). Indeed, He has freed us the manner of our obedience, but not thr matter of our obedience to His moral law. We now obey, but it is from other principles, by other strength, unto othrer ends, than we did before (Samuel Bolton, The True Bounds of Christian Freedom, 1645, Banner of Truth, p.72)

If you claim to love God and His Christ, please pay close attention to the following statements which link your love for God with your obedience to Him. The Puritan, John Preston, said, "Love, in turn, is to be measured by obedience, 'for indeed love cannot be otherwise judged of than in obeying. . . . Therefore, so much diligence in keeping his commands, so much love.' "[309]

Although Jesus was against the commandments and traditions of men He was not against us having and keeping commandments per say.. Jesus said, "Greater love has no one than this, that one lay down his life for his friends. You are my friends if you do what I command you" (John 15:13-14, NASV). He issued commandmenis Himself.. For example. one commandment He issued in particular was, "A new commandment I give unto you,. Love one another as I have loved you."Jesus said, "If ye love me, keep my commandments," and "whoever has my commands and obeys them, he is the one who loves me." "If ye keep my commandments, ye shall abide in my love; even as I have kept my Father's

---

[309] Ernest F. Kevan, *The Grace of Law: A Study of Puritan Theology* (Grand Rapids: Baker, 1976), p. 239.

commandments, and abide in his love. **These things have I spoken unto you, that my joy might remain in you, and that your joy might be full.**"[310] The apostle John wrote, "For this is the love of God, that we keep his commandments; and his commandments are not burdensome."[311] The Puritan, Colquhoun, had this to say about the false idea that God's commandmentsis are "burdensome" to believers:

> "Accordingly, the apostle Paul says of himself and of the believers in Rome, ***in their unregenerate state,*** "When we were in the flesh, the motives of sins, which were by the law did work in our members to bring forth fruit unto death (Rom. 7:5). And of himself in particular he says, "Sin taking occasion by this commandment, wrought in me all manner of concupiscience (Rom.7:8). This is not to be imputed as a fault to the holy law, but is wholly to be charged to reigning depravity of the sinner's nature. , , , [Now, we N.T. believers, as well as, the O.T believers, who heard and who believed the Gospel (Heb. 4:2), were graciously delivered, from this irritating, burdensome, power of the law as a broken covenant. As a believer you must understand or realize that you are no longer married to the law as a covenant of works. You are now married to Jesus Christ now (Romans 7:1-6). Therefore, you died to the the law as a covenant of works it may but should not irritate, burden or haunt you.]. Trusting in the Lord Jesus for complete salvation, relying on his meritorious righteousness for all your title to life eternal, constrained by his redeeming love, and enabled by his sanctifying Spirit, to mortify your depravity, and to

---

[310] John 14:15, 21; 15:10–11.
[311] 1 John 5:3.

perform spiritual obedience; you "delight in the law" as
a rule of duty, and you serve God in newness of
Spirit."[312]

Well, why do Christians still feel this burdensome, irritating
or depressing power of the law at times? "Romans 8:6 – It is not
here insinuated that believers are, in this world, *perfectly* set free
from the irritating power of the law. As, in their practice, they are
only dying to it as a covenant of works; so in proportion to the
degree of this legal temper that remains in them, they may, on many
occasions, be exposed to its irritating power."[313]

God's commandments are still used as a means to sanctify
Christians. The Holy Spirit uses God's commandments to reveal our
sins to us.[314] As we read God's word to see ourselves correctly He
will point out our sins to us. It is as if we are looking at ourselves
in a mirror so that we can acknowlrdge our sins, confess them to
God and ask for His forgiveness and cleansing in order to continue
close fellowship with Him. The Westminster Confession says:

Although true believers be not under the law as a covenant
of works, to be thereby justified or condemned; yet is it of
great use to them, as well as to others; in that, as a rule of
life, informing them of the will of God and their duty, it
directs and binds them to walk accordingly; discovering
also the sinful pollutions of their nature, hearts, and lives;
so as, examining themselves thereby, they may come to
further conviction of, humiliation for, and hatred against
sin; together with a clearer sight of the need they have of

---

[312] Colquhoun, John, A Treatise of the Law and the Gospel, Wiley
& Long Publisher, 1835, p.234-235
[313] Ibid, p.235
[314] John 17:17; Eph. 5:26

Christ, and the perfection of his obedience. It is likewise of use to the regenerate, to restrain their corruptions, in that it forbids sin; and the threatenings of it serve to shew what even their sins deserve, and what afflictions [our Father's chastisements] in this life they may expect for them, although freed from the curse thereof threatened in the law. The promises of it, in like manner, shew them God's approbation of obedience, and what blessings they may expect upon the performance thereof; although not as due to them by the law as a covenant of works: So as a man's doing good, and refraining from evil, because the law encourageth to the one, and deterreth from the other, is no evidence his being under the law, and not under grace." Neither are the forementioned uses of the law contrary to the grace of the gospel, but do sweetly comply with it; the Spirit of Christ subduing and enabling the will of man to do that freely and cheerfully which the will of God revealed in the law requireth to be done.[315]

Still some Christians today still object by saying, we are no longer obligated to obey the Ten Commandments. According to them the Ten Commandments are obsolete and they cannot be applied to New Testament saints. By contrast, Jesus showed that the Ten Commandments were still relevant and can be applied to Christians today because He continued to teach and explain them. Why else why would He bother to take the time to explain them in detail, if they were already obsolete? By working them out in detail for us He reinforced their importance for Christians. For example, Jesus explained the seventh commandment for our application or use in Matthew 5:27-28. Jesus explained that the sin of adultery

---

[315] *The Westminster Confession of Faith*, chap. 19, sec. 6, pp. 83–84.

begins in our sinful imaginations of our hearts or minds before it is ever committed physically. So, we ask, "Is this explanation helpful to Christians?" Can it be applied to Christians today? Are Christians exempt from the danger of the temptation or the sin of adultery today? Jesus using the example of the rich, young ruler explained and applied the tenth commandment for us. In Luke 18:20-25 Jesus uses the Ten Commandments in His evangelistic outreach to the rich, young ruler. The rich, young ruler asked Jesus what he must do to inherit eternal life. Jesus asked him how he measured up to a number of the Ten Commandments in order to prepare the young man's heart to help him to see his need for God's grace. The young man answered that he had kept them all. Then at the end of Jesus' conversation with the young man, Jesus unveiled the man's sin of Covetousness to him by bringing him to see his heart under the light of the tenth commandment. The result of Jesus' application of the tenth commandment is clearly displayed when the young ruler made it known that his love for his earthly riches was greater than gathering treasure in heaven. So, can the Tenth Commandment be applied today? Can it be applied to Christians as well? Are Christians exempt from the temptation or sin of covetousness today? What about Christians who covet their money and possessions so much that they fail to give a minimum of 10% of their gross income to Jesus whose priesthood is permanent according to the priesthood of Melchizedek to whom Abraham tithed his income? (Malachi 3:8-11; Hebrews 7:1-8,14-24).

The second use of the moral law (the Ten Commandments) is used to evangelize unsaved sinners (e.g., the rich young ruler as was just mentioned above) by showing them their sins and their need for God's grace. Under the Covenant of Grace, the third use of the moral law as a rule of righteous living is not only compatible with grace; they do not work without each other. Someone has said, "Grace without law is licentiousness, and law without grace is legalism" (Jude 4; Gal. 5:13). Here the moral law is used to continually drive Christians to Christ's perfect obedience when they begin to doubt or question their justification (Romans 7:25-8:1-4). Even the Beattitudes drive us to Christ's perfect obedience when we fail to obey them (Matt. 5:3-11).

The Ten Commandments were given to us by Jesus, the preincarnate Son, through Moses, and again after Jesus' ascension by the writers of the New Testament through the Holy Spirit. The Ten Commandments are repeated throughout the New Testament on numerous occasions and with new applications. Edward Fisher, in his *Marrow of Modern Divinity,* shows how the Ten Commandments are repeated in the New Testament and how they still serve as a rule and guide for Christians today:

> I entreat you to consider,—first, whether the true knowledge of God is required in John 3:19; and the want of it condemned, 2 Thess.1:8; and the true love of God required in Matt. 22:37; and the want of it reproved in John 5:42; and true fear of God required, 1 Peter 2:17; Heb. 12:28; and the want of it condemned, Rom. 3:18; and the true trusting in God required, and the trusting in the creature forbidden, 2 Cor.1:9; 1 Tim 6:17; be not the substance of the first commandment.

> And consider, secondly, whether the "hearing and reading of God's word," commanded, John 5:39; Rev.1:3; and "prayer," required, Rom.12:12; 1 Thess.5:17; and "singing of psalms," required, Col. 3:16; James 5:13; and whether "idolatry," forbidden, 1 Cor. 10:14; 1 John 5:21; be not the substance of the second commandment.

> And consider, thirdly, whether "worshipping of God in vain," condemned, Matt.15:9; and "using vain repetitions in

prayer," forbidden, Matt. 6:7; and "hearing of the word only, and not doing," forbidden, James 1:22; whether "worshipping God in spirit and in truth," commanded, John 4:24; and "praying with the spirit and with understanding also;" and "singing with the spirit" and "with understanding also," commended, 1 Cor. 14:15; and "taking heed what we hear," Mark 4:24; be not the substance of the third commandment.

Consider, fourthly, whether Christ's rising from the dead the first day of the week, Mark 16:2, 9; the disciples assembling, and Christ's appearing unto them, two several first days of the week, John 20:19, 26; and the disciples coming together and breaking bread, and preaching afterwards on that day, in Acts 20:7; 1 Cor. 16:2; and John's being in the Spirit on the Lord's day, Rev. 1:10; I say, consider whether these things do not prove, that the first day of the week is to be kept as the Christian Sabbath.

Consider, fifthly, whether the apostle's saying, "Children, obey your parents in the Lord for this is right: honor thy father and thy mother, which is the first commandment with promise," Eph. 6:1, 2, and all these other exhortations, given by him and the apostle Peter, both to inferiors and superiors, to do their duty to each other, Eph. 5:22, 25; 6:4–5, 9; Col. 3:18–22; Titus 3:1; 1 Peter 3:1; 2:18; I say, consider whether all these places do not prove that the duties of the fifth commandment are required in the New Testament.[316] [It should be noted that the 5th commandment of the Old Testament which bids children to obey their

---

[316] Edward Fisher, *Marrow of Modern Divinity*, notes by Thomas Boston (Swengel, Pa.: Reiner Publications, 1978), pp. 179–180.

parents is repeated in the New Testament with a the same promise annexed to it.]

Being "under the law to Christ" means being subject to Christ, the Creator and Redeemer, by obeying His law. The Puritan, Thomas Taylor said, "To say, wee obey God by the spirit without a law or a commandment, is meere non-sence: for is any obedience without a law?....What can bee more ridiculous than for a subject to professe obedience to his Prince, but yet hee will not bee under any law?"[317] Even our thought life is to be governed by His law. The apostle Paul said "For I delight in the law of God after the inward man . . . with the mind I myself serve the law of God". The Law of God serves as an anchor or a permanent backdrop of true moral reality from which we can judge all thoughts, ideas, and philosophies that pass in front of it. And by it we are to bring into captivity every thought to the obedience of Christ.[318]

Furthermore, A. W. Pink said, "Christians are going to be judged by the Law, . . . not of course, in order to determine their eternal destiny, but to settle the apportionment of reward or punishment. . .. this judgment for Christians has nothing whatever to do with their salvation. Instead, it is to determine the measure of reward which they shall enjoy in heaven" (1 Cor. 3:7-15; James 2: 8,12) [319]

When God gave us His Ten Commandments, He gave us a written definition of love. Love is defined by the Ten Commandments as summarized by "love the Lord with all your

---

[317] Ernest F. Kevin, *The Grace of Law*, Baker Book House, 1976, p. 196.
[318] 2 Cor. 10:5.
[319] Pink, A. W., *The Law and the Saint*, Classic Domain Publishing, 2014, p.54

heart, mind, soul and strength"[320] and "love your neighbor as yourself."[321] In the New Testament, love is not only defined by 1 Corinthians 13, but it is also defined by other commandments such as, "Love your enemy,"[322] "love one another as I have loved you,"[323] and "husbands, love your wives as Christ loved the church and gave himself for it."[324] Being "under the law to Christ" means being subject to His commandments of love. John, the apostle of love, said, "And by this we learn that we know Him—if we obey His commands. He who professes to know Him, and does not obey His commands, is a liar, and the truth is not in him. But whoever obeys His word, in him love for God has reached perfection. . . . The man who obeys His commands abides in God, and God in him."[325] The apostle John also said: "The love I mean consists in our living in obedience to His commands. God's command is that you should live in love, as you have been taught from the beginning."[326] Christians must live a life of love. Paul defines what Christian love to your God is in the first four commandments and defines love to your neighbor by quoting the other six of the Ten Commandments in Romans 13:8, 10: "Owe no one anything except to love one another, for he who loves another has fulfilled the law....Love does no harm to a neighbor, therefore love is the fulfillment of the law." Paul said, "Now the end [purpose] of the commandment is charity [love], out of a pure heart, and of a good conscience, and of faith unfeigned [genuine, sincere]."[327] And

---

[320] Deut. 6:5; Matt. 22:37.

[321] Lev. 19:18

[322] Matt. 5:44; Luke 6:27.

[323] John 13:34.

[324] Eph. 5:25.

[325] 1 John 2:3–5; 3:24 (WEYMOUTH).

[326] 2 John 6 (WEYMOUTH); see also Eph. 5:2.

[327] 1 Tim. 1:5.

finally, Paul said, "Bear one another's burdens, and so fulfil the law of Christ." [328] *To be under the law of Christ is to be under the law of love, and this love is defined by His commandments (Col. 3:12-23, esp. v.14).* [329] For example, we are commanded in Ephesians 5:2 to walk in love. What kind of love is it speaking about here? We need a definition of love to help us understand how to walk in it. The definition of love is found in the commandments found in Ephesians 4:31-32. The commandments describe what love is and what love is not. They immediately precede and are connected to this verse by the word "Therefore" in Chapter 5, verse 1. So, the kind of love we are to walk in is described as making a conscious effort to get rid of all bitterness, rage, and anger, brawling and slander, along with every kind of malice toward your Christian brothers and sisters. It is also described as replacing those aforementioned loveless attitudes and actions with a conscious effort to be kind and compassionate to one another, forgiving one another, just as in Christ God forgave you. In this way we become imitators of God, and we walk in love just as Christ loved us and gave Himself up for us as a fragrant offering and sacrifice to God.

But what about the common objection raised from **Romans 6:15**? Here Paul states that Christians are not under law but under grace. **Some Christians believe this verse is clear proof that law and grace are *never* compatible.** Yes, **law and grace are not compatible,** if Christians try to keep the law as a covenant of works (Galatians, chapter 3**).**

Turretine tells us,

It is one thing…to be under the law as a covenant [as in the covenant of works]; another thing, to *be under the law as a*

---

[328] Gal. 6:2.
[329] Col. 3:12–23, especially the command in verse 14.

rule of life. In the former sense, Paul says, "That we are not under the law, but under grace," Rom. 6:14, as to its covenant relation, curse, and rigour; but in the latter sense [as a rule of life] we always remain bound unto it, though for a different end; for in the first covenant man was to do this, to the end that he might live; but in the other, he is bound to perform the same thing, not that he may live, but because he lives.[330]

John Owen maintains that in Romans 6: 14-15 Paul does not dismiss the law from the life of the believer, but grapples with it in its mistaken and perverted use. He understands the expression "under the law" in this passage of Scripture to be indicative of a person "contending against sin...from legal principles and motives," this being the wrong use of the Law. We find that John Flavel holds the same view of the meaning of Paul's apparently derogatory statements about the Law, as John Owen did. Flavel argues that the distinction between God's intention in the Law and man's abuse of the Law must be clearly kept in mind.[331] Christians today who try to keep God's law do not do it to be justified by keeping it. They see the purpose of God's law as being subservient to grace in the Covenant of Grace.

Chapter 19 of the Westminster Confession of Faith entitled "Of the law of God" tells us of the subservient use of God's law for the Christian:

---

[330] Boston footnote in Fisher, *Marrow of Modern Divinity*, pp. 184–185.

[331] Ernest Kevin, *The Grace of Law*, Baker Book House, 1976, p. 133.

1. God gave to Adam a law, as a covenant of works by which He bound him and all his posterity to personal, entire, exact and perpetual obedience; promised life upon the fulfilling, and threatened death upon the breach of it; and endued him with with power and ability to keep it.

2. This law, after his fall, continued to be a perfect rule of righteousness, and, as such was delivered by God upon Mount Sinai in ten commandments written in two tables; the first four commandments containing our duty toward God, and the other six our duty to man.

5. The moral law doth forever bind all, as well justified persons as others, to the obedience thereof; and that not only in regard of the matter contained in it, but also in respect of the authority of God the Creator who gave it. Neither doth Christ in the gospel anyway dissolve, but much strengthen, this obligation.

6. Although true believers be not under the law as a covenant of works, to be thereby justified or condemned, yet it is of great use to them, as well as to others; in that, as a rule of life, informing them of the will of God and their duty, it directs and binds them to walk accordingly; discovering also the sinful pollutions of their nature, hearts, and lives; so as examining themselves thereby, they may come to further conviction of, humiliation for, and hatred

against sin; together with a clearer sight of
the need they have of Christ, and the
perfection of His obedience. It is likewise of
use to the regenerate, to restrain their
corruptions, in that it forbids sin, and the
threatenings of it serve to show what even
their sins deserve, and what afflictions in
this life [our Father's chastisements]
they may expect from them, although freed
from the curse thereof threatened in the law.
The promises of it, in like manner, show them
God's approbation of obedience, and what
blessings they may expect upon the
performance thereof; although not as due to
them by the law as a covenant of works: so as
a man's doing good and refraining from evil,
because the law encourageth to the one, and
deterreth from the other, is no evidence of his
being under the law and not under grace.

7. Neither are the forementioned uses of the
law contrary to the grace of the gospel, but
do sweetly comply with it: the Spirit of
Christ subduing and enabling the will of
man to do that freely and cheerfully; which
the will of God, revealed in the law, requireth
to be done [332]

"Although the law as a rule of duty to believers, requires perfect
obedience from them; yet it admits of God's *accepting* of their
sincere obedience performed in faith; though it be imperfect. It

---

[332] *The Westminster Confession of Faith*, chap. 19, sec. 5
(Iverness, Scotland: Free Presbyterian Publications, 1976), p. 82.

admits of His accepting of this obedience, not, indeed, as any part of their justifying righteousness, not, as the foundation of their acceptance of their persons as righteous; but as the fruit and evidence, their being vitally united to His beloved Son as Jehovah their Righteousness, and of their being *already* accepted in Him (Eph, 1:6; Heb.13:16).".[333]

"It may be justly infered from the preceding doctrine, that the distinction of the Divine law, especially, into the law as a covenant of works, and as a rule of life, is a *very important* distinction . . . **To distinguish truly and clearly, between the law as a covenant, and the law as a rule, is, as one expresses it, the *key,* which opens the hidden treasure of the gospel.** No sooner had the Spirit of Truth, given Luther but a glimpse of that distinction, than he declared that, he seemed to himself to be admitted to Paradise, and that the whole face of the Scripture was changed to him. **Indeed, without a spiritual and true knowledge of that distinction, a man can neither discern, nor love, nor obey acceptably, "the truth as it is in Jesus."** Nay, if the law as a covenant, were not to be distinguished from the law as a rule [of life], in the hand of the Mediator, it would inevitably follow, that believers are still under the law as a covenant of works; that they ought to regard God, not as their gracious God and Father, but as their angry and avenging Judge; and that their sins, are still to be considered as transgressions only of this covenant of works, and as rendering them, notwithstanding their justification, *actually subject* to the curse and revenging wrath of God; - contrary to the Scripture (1) and to our Confession of Faith (2).[334]

---

[333] Colquhoun, John, A treatise on the Law and the Gospel, Wiley & Long Publisher, New York, 1835, p. 39.
[334] Ibid, pp. 47-48

As Colquhoun has said, until the Christian understands that the believer is dead to the law and he dies daily to it as a covenant of works, (Gal. 2:19-20) he does not understand that in order to live unto (or for God) he is under the power of the law as a covenant and under the power of sin; for the law under this form is the strength of sin. It will have dominion over him. The Apostle Paul said," Sin shall not have dominion over you for you are not under the law, but under grace. And "having thus become dead to the law by the body of Christ, the weary are at rest (Matt. 11:28). He attains rest to his conscience, in the righteousness of Christ . . . In proportion as his legal spirit is mortified, he rests from his legal and slavish fear of that wrath threatened in the law (p. 239). The consequence or fruit of being delivered from the law as a covenant of works, is, that believers become capable of "serving God in newness of Spirit, and not in the oldness of the letter [i.e., not with a covenant of works spirit or in a mere outward observance of the law]. [Instead] it is a *spiritual* life, the life of a spiritual man, in conformity to the law as a rule."[335]

Therefore, God's moral law was not abrogated in the New Testament.[336] Your faith in Christ Jesus does not make the Ten Commandments void and obsolete. It does just the opposite. Your faith in Christ and love for Him reinforces God's law. God's grace establishes His law by writing the law on your heart.[337] God's grace reinforced His law because man's sinful nature had weakened it. Edward Fisher wrote,

---

[335] Colquhoun, John. A Treatise on the Law and the Gospel, pp. 253-254.
[336] Romans 7:14, 22
[337] Jer. 31:33; Heb. 10:15–16; Rom. 3:31.

Indeed, Musculus, speaking of the Ten Commandments, says, If they be weak, if they be the letter, if they do work transgression, anger, curse, and death: and if Christ, by the law of the Spirit of life, delivered them that believed in him from the law of the letter, which was weak to justify, and strong to condemn, and from the curse, being made a curse for us, surely, they be abrogated. Now, this is most certain, that the Ten Commandments do no way work transgression, anger, curse, and death, but only as they are the covenant of works. Neither hath Christ delivered believers any otherwise from them, than as they are the covenant of works. And therefore, we may assuredly conclude, that they are no otherwise abrogated, than as they are the covenant of works. Neither did Musculus intend any otherwise; for, says he, in the words following, it must not be understood, that the points of the substance of Moses' covenant are utterly brought to nothing; God forbid. For a Christian man is not at liberty to do those things that are ungodly and wicked; and if the doing of those things the law forbids, do not displease Christ; if they be not much different, yea contrary; if they be not repugnant to the righteousness which we received of him; let it be lawful for a Christian man to do them; or else not. But a Christian man doing against those things which are commanded in the decalogue, doth sin more outrageously than he that should so do, being under the law; so far off is he from being free from those things that be there commanded.[338]

So, while Christians must disregard the moral law as a Covenant of Works or a means of justification; they will **not** be led by the Holy Spirit to disregard the moral law as their rule of

---

[338] Fisher, *Marrow of Modern Divinity*, pp. 183–184.

righteous living. The Christian cannot expect to sin (break God's commandments) with impunity. Rather, the Christian can expect that His Father will discipline him for it.

Contrasting the moral law as a means of justification from a means of sanctification, John Calvin said, "Christians, in the case of justification, must raise themselves above the law." He added, "Neither can any man thereby gather that the law is superfluous to the faithful, whom, not withstanding, it doth not cease to teach, exhort, and prick forward to goodness, although before God's judgment-seat it hath no place in their conscience." So, Christians should understand that God's moral law is still in effect.

God gave the law and the gospel to believers both in the older administration of the Covenant of Grace (the Old Testament) and in the newer administration of the Covenant of Grace (the New Testament). The law drove the sinner to grace for justification, and grace pointed him to the law for sanctification or growth in grace. *The law was given that grace might be sought; grace was given that the law might be fulfilled"* (Augustine).

Under the Covenant of Grace God's Holy Spirit freed your will from the bondage of sin through Christ so it can be free to keep God's law in the newness of spirit and life (Ezekiel 18:31; Romans 7:6; 8:1-8) by the resurrection power of the Holy Spirit (Romans 6:1-14) and the inward motivation of love towards Christ (2 Corinthians 5:14). Christian, when you practice obedience, that is, when you habitually walk within the perimeters of God's love as defined by His law, you will experience the joy and freedom of the new person God re-created you to be.[339] David said, "And I will walk at liberty: for I seek thy precepts."[340] James called God's law

---

[339] 2 Cor. 5:17; Gal. 6:15; Eph. 4:22, 24; 5:1–2.
[340] Ps. 119:45.

the law of liberty.[341] Administered from the hand of Christ, God's law is your rule for a liberated life of love.

Some other objections to Christians obeying God's law are as follows:

1 Timothy 1:9 says, " . . . that law is not made for a righteous person, but for those who are lawless and rebellious . . .". "That is to say the Law as an instrument of terror and condemnation, was not made for the righteous but for the wicked. The Law threatening, compelling, condemning, is not made for a righteous man, because he [the righteous man] is pushed forward to duty of his own accord, and is no more led by the spirit of bondage and fear of punishment" (Turretine).

Romans 10:4 says, "For Christ is the end of the law for righteousness to everyone who believes." Anyone who thinks this is proof that the Law has been abrogated, must compare this verse to the verse preceding it. It says, " For not knowing about God's righteousness and seeking to establish their own, they did not subject themselves to the righteousness of God." For if they had believed that the righteousness of God was already established by Jesus' righteousness, as the very ultimate level of righteousness, they would not have attempted to establish their own self-righteousness. They missed the point that Christ established the Righteousness of God because He totally honored God's Law by completely fulfilling it.

Romans 7:4-6 says that we are delivered from the Law and that we are dead to the Law. This means we died to the power and penalty of the Law as a Covenant of Works. We have freedom from its legal claims on us because we have satisfied its demands of perfect obedience through Christ.

Still, the Book of Galatians is proclaimed by many today to be the Emancipation Proclamation of liberty from God's Law. Those

---

[341] James 1:25; 2:12.

who say this say that the Law in its entirety has been cancelled. There is no part of the Law that has any relationship to believers today. For example, they cite Galatians 3:25 as their proof. They say this proves that Christians are no longer under the law as a schoolmaster. No, it just means Christians are no longer under the observance of the ceremonial law as a schoolmaster. Christians are not obligated to observe or practice the ceremonial law. The ceremonial law was only a shadow of things to come. The ceremonial law was used by God as a means to bring Judaism to the age of maturity at the Christ event. Therefore, since Christians have no need of the ceremonial law as a schoolmaster, they are not bound to keep it any longer and they should not seek to return to it (Galatians 4:3, 9). Those who remained under the yoke of the Mosaic ceremonial law were those Judaising teachers who sought to persuade the Christians to return to it. Because these non-believing, Judaisers failed to recognize and trust Jesus, as the Lamb of God, the sacrificial atonement given for the forgiveness of sins and cleansing, yes, even the very reality of the One who the ceremonial law symbolized was traded for the symbol. The promised reality of the new and better covenant order of things had arrived having been introduced by the Lamb of God, the Messiah.

Finally, Colossians 2:13-14 is interpreted by some to mean the Ten Commandments are canceled. It reads "having canceled out the certificate of debt (or handwriting of ordinances) consisting of decrees against us, which were hostile to us; and He has taken it out of the way, having nailed to the cross." This passage can be explained by comparing it with Ephesians 2:11-15. The handwriting of ordinances that have nailed to the cross are the elementary principles of the Old Testament ceremonial laws which have been cancelled so that the Jews and Gentiles have no barrier between them any longer.

Evangelical Legalists, are those, like John Wesley, who say they **earned** their justification by the obedience of faith which replaced perfect obedience to the moral law required by Covenant of Works and was kept perfectly by Christ for us. Wesley and Antinomians alike claim that since they are under grace they do not have to keep any moral law or commandments. They say, "If we are under law to Jesus, it would make Jesus just another Moses". Yes, and what did God tell Moses? God told Moses that He is sending a Prophet greater than Moses (Deuteronomy 18:15, 17-18). God told Moses to tell the Israelites, "The LORD your God will raise up for you a prophet *like Me* from among you, from your countrymen, **you shall listen to [or obey] him**." This Prophet would be greater than Moses because He is God. Jesus is "the Prophet" that God promised to raise up. One way which God promised to raise up Christ is obvious. God provided us with a prophetic illustration of how Jesus would be raised up. Moses was told by God to make a bronze serpent and to raise it up in the wilderness so the people could look upon it in faith as the remedy for the people's sin (Exodus 21:80). This prophecy was fulfilled later when Jesus Christ, was lifted up on the cross as the remedy for the world's sins[342]. But God was making another important point. He was telling us that Jesus' prophetic ministry would replace Moses' prophetic ministry. And at Jesus' transfiguration God was emphatically clear about this transfer of authority and prophetic ministry to Jesus when He spoke to Peter, James, John and *Moses*. This is what God said to them, "This is My beloved Son, with whom I am well-pleased; **listen to [or obey] Him**!"[343]. And do we listen to what "the Prophet", Jesus, tells us about obeying and disobeying His commandments? Jesus said, "If you love me keep my commandments" and "So why do keep calling Me 'Lord, Lord!' when you don't do what I say?" Are your feet guided by the light of Jesus' commandments, do you walk circumspectly and live

---

[342] John 3:13-14,16; 12:32-34
[343] Matthew 17:1-6; John 12:47-49; Acts 3:20-23; Hebrews 3:4

soberly, righteously, and godly? (Phil. 1:27; Eph. 5:15; Tit. 2: 12, 19) "It is also styled, A living and a walking in the Spirit ; (Gal.5:25) a living in the strength of the Spirit of life; (Rom. 8:2) under the guidance of the Spirit; (Rom. 8:14) in the liberty of the Spirit; (2 Cor. 3:17) in the comforts of the Spirit; (Acts 9:31) and in the fruits of the Spirit; (Gal. 5:22-23). Walking circumspectly includes the love and practice of all these duties of piety toward God, of sobriety with respect to himself, and righteousness toward his neighbour." [344]

Finally, consider what God says about not listening to Jesus. When speaking to Moses God said, "I will raise them up a prophet from among their brethren, like unto thee, and will put my words in his mouth; and he shall speak all that I shall command him. And it shall come to pass, that whosoever will not hearken unto my words, which he shall speak in my name, I will require it of him." (Deut. 18:18-19; Acts 3:20-23; Heb.3:4).

So then, in summary, is the moral law compatible with grace? It is NOT compatible with grace when we try to keep it like a Covenant of Works. It could only bring death, if anyone attempted to keep it to gain eternal life. However, the moral law is compatible to the Covenant of Grace when it is used by God as a means to turn people to Christ for grace and when it is used as a moral guide for the saints for righteous living. See the Westminster Confession of Faith, chapter 19 especially paragraphs 2 and 6; the Heidelberg Catechism, Question 115; and the 1689 London Baptist Confession, Chapter 13 paragraph 3.

---

[344]Colquhoun, John, A Treatise of the Law and the Gospel, Wiley and Long Publisher, 1835, pp. 255-256

CONCLUSION

This book *God's Awesome Grace* rests on the Biblical teachings of the historical Protestant Reformation. These teachings are seen from a Reformed perspective and they are found within a Covenant or Federal Theology framework. They teach that due to Adam's disobedience to the Covenant of Works we became sinners and unable to save ourselves. But God foresaw our dilemma and rescued us in eternity past by His awesome, sovereign grace. How did He do it? He chose us BEFORE TIME BEGAN and PREDESTINED us to be saved and adopted into His family (Eph. 1:4; Rom. 8:29). But His choice of us was not based on anything good foreseen in us or done by us. So, we cannot boast of our faith, repentance, or any act of our obedience (Eph. 2:8-9) Instead, God's gracious choice of us was based on Christ's blood and righteousness (His perfect obedience to the Covenant of Redemption done on our behalf). God chose His elect *in Christ* in eternity past. He saw them blameless then in eternity past through Christ's righteousness. Because Jesus honored and obeyed God's commandments perfectly for them, in God's eyes, it is AS IF they had honored and obeyed them perfectly. God looked at His elect before time began and saw them legally righteous in His Son's moral perfection. God also saw that Jesus would shed His blood in the elect's place to pay their penalty for failing keep His commandments perfectly. So, God planned to save only those that He elected before the foundation of the world. That would make God the first cause of their salvation and prove that their salvation is by God's grace alone. It takes the control of salvation out of the sinner's hands and places it rightfully back into the sovereign control of God's hands.

This means that the current, popular, Arminian belief of an unbeliever's election to salvation is false. The Arminian believes that an unbeliever can determine his own election by making "a decision to receive Jesus into his heart". The Arminian believes that because the unbeliever made this decision based on his faith and repentance, he earned his election to salvation. However, the Bible teaches that God and God alone determined the unbeliever's election before the world was created and that Jesus and Jesus alone earned the unbeliever's salvation for him.

God's relationship with mankind has been established either through the covenant made with Adam or through the covenant made with Jesus Christ. As a result, people are found either under the curse of the Covenant of Works or under the blessings of the Covenant of Grace. When Adam broke the Covenant of Works by his free-will decision to eat the forbidden fruit, he, and consequently, all of us through him, became covenant-breakers. This separated us spiritually from God and placed us under His condemnation and wrath.

So, the moral law should be seen in how it is used in two separate and distinct covenants (the Covenant of Works and the Covenant of Grace). The moral law was used differently in the Covenant of Works than in the Covenant of Grace. When it was used n the Covenant of Works the moral law required perfect obedience and no forgiveness if it was disobeyed, This made it separate and distinct from grace. Jesus Christ, however, met the essential condition of perfect, moral, obedience to the moral law required in the Covenant of Works, and He also took its curse of death upon Himself because of our lack of obedience. By doing this, Jesus satisfied the moral law's demands found in the Covenant of Works, both in precept and penalty. So, while it may be said that Jesus kept the moral requirements of a Covenant of Works, they were kept to fulfill the Covenant of Redemption or Grace for His elect sinners.

So, the moral law served in a different function when it was used with the Covenant of Grace. It had an inseparable. symbiotic, subservient connection with the Covenant of Grace. Brcause the moral law was used in two ways the Covenant of Grace. It is used in a subservient way first, to show need for a substitute to save us and secondly, how we should live as Christians).

God sent Jesus to impute His righteousness to us and to ransom us through His death by shedding His blood on the cross for our sins. This was a liturgical procedure for Jesus. As our Priest, He offered worship to God for the guilty through His sacrifice. John Girardeau explained,

> Jesus offered worship for the guilty through the bloody sacrifice of himself. He was the victim offered, and [at the same time] the officiating Priest. His death, voluntarily undergone, was an act of sublimest worship to God, with which the praises of an innumerable company of angels and of a countless assemblage of worlds could bear no comparison. It was the homage of an Incarnate God to Justice and Law. It needs no words to show that as sincere worship involves the affections of the heart, and as Jesus, the God-man, worshiped God by the sacrifice of himself to justice in the room of the guilty, he rendered in dying a free and affectionate obedience to the precept which requires perfect love to God and man. *Subjection* to the penalty was due from sinners, *obedience* to it on his part was the free suggestion of his love to God and his pity for man.[345]

As the apostle John wrote: "Worthy is the Lamb that was slain to receive power and wealth and wisdom and strength and honor and glory and blessing....To Him who is seated on the throne, and to

---

[345] John L. Girardeau, *Calvinism and Evangelical Arminianism* (Harrisonburg, Va.: Sprinkle Publications, 1984), p. 520 (emphasis in original).

the Lamb be blessing and honor and glory and dominion forever and ever" (Rev. 5:12–13 NEW BERKELEY).

Jesus gained heaven for us and delivered us from hell by His perfect obedience that sent Him to death on the cross. On Judgment Day, we Christians will point to Christ's righteousness when we face the righteous claims of God's law and justice. Through Jesus Christ, we see God's sovereign will and grace put into powerful action to save His elect people. God sent Jesus to save His elect people from slavery to sin in this life and from eternal punishment in hell in the next life.[346] **GOD'S GRACE IS AWESOME!**

If you are not a Christian, but you desire to seek God, read the Bible, pray to Him, and confess your sins in Jesus' name and for His sake. You will find God, and He will not turn you away. If you are not seeking God, consider this: Why should you serve Satan and enjoy the pleasures of sin for a time? The wages paid by sin is eternal death in hell. Instead, why not be reconciled to God through Jesus? Receive Him by faith as your covenant representative, your righteousness, and your substitute in death. Then thank God for the gift of Jesus Christ, who is the source of eternal life. His life will permeate your soul when you are placed into union with Him by the Holy Spirit.[347]

If you profess to be a Christian, I hope the questions, How are we saved? and Did God save us, or did we save ourselves? have been answered for you. More specifically, I hope you understand that the credit for your salvation belongs entirely to the Lord.[348] We have the assurance of salvation based on the certainty that we pleased God by the merits of Christ Jesus' works. This is the reason all of the saints glory in their God.

---

[346] Heb. 7:22; 10:16–17; 12:24; 13:20.

[347] 1 John 5:11–13; John 15:1,4-5.

[348] Ps. 3:8; 37:39; 68:20; Jon. 2:9; Luke 2:26–28, 30; Acts 4:10–12; 1 Cor. 1:26–31, emphasis on v. 30; Titus 2:11.

You should be humbled by these truths of God's grace and be careful to give God the praise and glory due Him for your election to salvation.[349]

> Not unto us, O LORD, not unto us, but unto thy name [we] give glory, for thy mercy, and for thy truth's sake. (Ps. 115:1)

> Thou art worthy, O LORD, to receive glory and honor, and power: for thou hast created all things, and for thy pleasure they are and were created. (Rev. 4:11)

> Amen! Blessing and glory and wisdom, thanksgiving and honor and power and might, be to our God forever and ever, Amen. (Rev. 7:12 NKJV)

---

[349] 1 Thess. 1:4; 2 Pet. 1:10.

Bibliography

Augustine, St. *De Servit et Liberat. Hum. Arbitrii.* Opp. Ed. Amstel., vol. 8. In John L. Giradeau, *Calvinism and Evangelical Arminianism,* Harrisonburg, VA,: Sprinkle Publications, 1890, 1984.

Barnhouse, Donald Grey, *Let Me Illustrate: Stories, Anecdotes, and Illustrations,* Grand Rapids: Fleming H. Revell, 1967.

Beeke, Joel R., Jones, Mark, A Puritan Theology, Doctrine for Life, Reformation Heritage Books, Grand Rapids, Michigan, 2012.

Berkhof, L., *Systematic Theology,* Grand Rapids: Eerdmans, 1939, 1974.

Berkouwer G.C., Devine Election, Wm. B. Eerdmans Publishing Co., Grand Rapids, Michigan, 1960

Boettner, Loraine. *The Reformed Doctrine of Predestination,*Phillipsburg,N.J., Presbyterian and Reformed Publishing, 1976.

Bolton, Samuel, *The true bounds of Christian freedom,* the Banner of Truth Trust, 1928

Boston, Thomas, *The Beauties of Thomas Boston,* Christian Focus Publications, 1979

Brimsmead, R. D. "Pinpointing the Issues in the Conflict with Rome", *Present Truth,* vol. 4, no. 5, Oct. 1975.

Broadway, Bennett, "Can God Accept You?", An evangelistic tract, Pittsburgh, PA: Crown and Covenant Publishers, 1989.

Calvin, John, *Calvin's Commentaries: Genesis,* vol.1, Grand Rapids: Eerdmans, 1948

Calvin, John *Calvin's New Testament Commentaries: Matthew, Mark, Luke,* vol. 1. Grand Rapids: Eerdmans, 1972.

Calvin, John, *Calvin's New Testament Commentaries: Hebrews and 1 and 2 Peter,* vol. 12, Trans. W. B. Johnston, Ed. David W. Torrence and Thomas E. Torrence, Grand Rapids: Eerdmans, 1963.

Calvin, John. *Concerning the Eternal Predestination of God,* Trans. J.K.S. Reid, London: James Clarke & Co., 1961.

Calvin, John. *The Institutes of Christian Religion,* book 3. Ed. John T. McNeill, Louisville: Westminster Press, 1975.

Calvin, John, *Commentary on Isaiah,* Wm. B, Eerdmans Publishing, Grand Rapids, Michigan, 1948

Campbell, Roderick, *Israel and the New Covenant,* Phillipburg, N.J.: Presbyterian and Reformed Publishing/ Geneva Divinity School Press, 1954.

Charnock, Stephen. *The Doctrine of Regeneration,* Grand Rapids: Baker, 1840.

Chemniz, Martin, *Examination of the Council of Trent,* St. Louis: Concordia, 1971.

Chilton, David, *The Days of Vengeance,* Dominion Press, Ft. Worth, Texas, 1987

Colquhoun, John, A Treatise on the Law and the Gospel, Wiley & Long Publisher, 1835, Osburn & Buckingham, Printers, 20 Ann-street, CPSIA information can be obtained at www

ICGtesting.com, Printed in the USA, also Amazon,com

Cox, William E., *Biblical Studies in Final Things,* Phillipsburg, N,J.: Presbyterian and Reformed Publishing, 1966.

Cunningham, William, *Historical Theology, vol. 2.* Carlisle, PA : Banner of Truth Trust, 1862.

Dabney, Robert I., *Lectures in Systematic Theology,* Grand Rapids: Zondervan, 1975.

Edwards, Jonathan, *Apocalyptic Writings,* Yale, 1977

Engelsma, David, *Hyper-Calvinism and the Call of the Gospel,* Grand Rapids: Reformed Free Publishing, 1980.

Ferguson, Sinclair B., *The Whole Christ*, Crossway, Wheaton, Illinois, 2016

Fisher, Edward. *Marrow of Modern Divinity,* Notes by Thomas Boston, Swengel, PA, Reiner Publications, 1978.

Gentry, Jr, Kenneth, Jr., *Navigating The Book Of Revelation,* Fountain Inn, South Carolina, Good Birth Ministries, 1999;

Girardeau, John L., *Calvinism and Evangelical Arminianism,* Harrisonburg, VA, Sprinkle Publications, 1890, 1984.

Hendriksen, William, *Exposition of Galatians*, Grand Rapids, Michigan, 1968.

Henry, Matthew, *Commentary on the book of Revelation*, and *Commentary on Luke* Hendrickson Publishers, 2014,

Hodge, A. A., *Hodge's Outlines of Theology.* Ed. W. H. Goold, Edinburgh and New York: T. Nelson and Sons, 1863.

Hodge, Charles, *A Commentary on Romans,* Carlisle, PA: Banner of Truth Trust, 1835.

Kevan, Ernest F. *The Grace of Law: A Study of Puritan Theology,* Grand Rapids: Baker, 1976.

Kistemaker, Simon J. *New Testament Commentary: James, Epistles of John, Peter, and Jude,* Grand Rapids: Baker, 1987.

Luther, Martin, *The Bondage of the Will,* Trans. J. I. Packer and O. R. Johnston, Grand Rapids: Fleming H. Revell, 1957.

Owen, John, *The Death of Death in the Death of Christ,* Intro. J. I. Packer, Venice, FL: Chapel Library tract, 2000.

Owen, John. *A Display of Arminianism,* In the *Works of John Owen,* vol. 10, Carlisle, PA: Banner of Truth Trust, 1967.

Owen, John. *For Whom Did Christ Die?* Venice, FL: Chapel Library tract, n.d.

Owen, John. *The Works of John Owen,* vol. 10, Carlisle, PA: Banner of Truth Trust, 1967.

Packer, J.I., *Freedom, Free Will,* Baker's Dictionary of Theology, Ed. Everett F. Harrison, Geoffrey W. Bromiley, and Carl F. H. Henry, Grand Rapids: Baker, 1960.

Packer, J.I., *Introductory Essay. An Introduction to John Owen's The Death of Death in the Death of Christ,* Venice, FL, Chapel Library, 2000.

Pink, Arthur W. *The Sovereignty of God,* Grand Rapids: Baker, 1976. *An Exposition Of The Sermon*

On the Mount, 1969, *The Divine Covenants,* Baker Book House, 1973

Pipa, Joseph A., *The Lord's Day,* Christian Focus Publications, 1997

Shedd, William G. T. *History of Christian Doctrine,* vol. 2. New York: Charles Scribner's Sons, 1863.

Smith, Charles R. *Did Christ Die Only for the Elect?* Winona Lake, IN: BMH Books, 1975.

Spring, Gardiner, *The Distinguishing Traits of Christian Character,* Phillipsburg, N.J., Presbyterian and Reformed Publishing, 1976.

Spurgeon, Charles, *The Fullness of Joy,* New Kensington, PA: Whitaker House 1997.

Stoever, William K. B. *Faire and Easie Way to Heaven.* Middletown, Conn: Wesleyan University Press, 1978.

Summers, T. O., ed. *Elements of Divinity,* vo. 2. Nashville, TN. Southern Methodist Publishing House, 1882.

Vos. Geerhardus, *Biblical Theology Old and New Testaments,* Wm. B, Eerdmans Publishing Company, Grand Rapids, Michigan, 1948.

Vos, J. G., *The Covenant of Grace,* Blue Banner Faith and Life, Reprinted by Reformed Presbyterian Church of North America Board of Education and Publication, Pittsburgh, PA 15208.

Watson, Richard. *Theological Institutes,* vol. 2, quoted from John L. Girardeau, Calvinism and Evangelical Arminianism, Harrisburg, VA: Sprinkle Publications, 1890, 1984.

Wesley, John, *The Scripture Doctrine Concerning Predestination, Election and Reprobation,* from *Works,* vol. 9, quoted from

Wesley, John, *Sermon on the Righteousness of Faith,* quoted from John L. Girardeau, *Calvinism and Evangelical Arminianism,* Sprinkle Publications,1890.

Witsius, Herman *The Economy of the Covenants Between God and Man*, Presbyterian and Reformed Publishing Co., Phillipsburg, New Jersey, 1990

Wuest, Kenneth S., *Wuest's Expanded Translation Of The Greek New Testament,* Wm. B. Eerdmans

Publishing Company, Grand Rapids, Michigan, 1956

The Westminster Confession of Faith, Iverness, Scotland: Free Presbyterian Publications, 1976.

Made in the USA
Las Vegas, NV
13 October 2021